OCT 18 1990 DATE DUE			

JUN 23 1987

International Relations

International Relations

British and American Perspectives

EDITED BY STEVE SMITH

Basil Blackwell
in association with
the British International Studies Association

© British International Studies Association 1985

First published 1985

Basil Blackwell Ltd
108 Cowley Road, Oxford OX4 1JF, UK

Basil Blackwell Inc.
432 Park Avenue South, Suite 1505,
New York, NY 10016, USA

British Library Cataloguing in Publication Data

International relations: British and
American perspectives.
1. International relations
I. Smith, Steven M.
327   JX1395

ISBN 0-631-14097-2

Library of Congress Cataloging in Publication Data

Main entry under title:
International relations.
Bibliography   p. 213
Includes index.
Contents: The growth of a discipline/William Olson and Nicholas Onuf — Strategic studies/Lawrence Freedman — Foreign policy analysis/Steve Smith — [etc]
1. International relations—Study and teaching—Great Britain—Addresses, essays, lectures.
2. International relations—Study and teaching—United States—Addresses, essays, lectures. I. Smith. Steve, 1952-
JX1293.G7I57   1985 327·41   84-24280
ISBN 0-631-14097-2

Typeset by Dentset, St. Clements, Oxford
Printed in Great Britain by Billing & Sons Ltd, Worcester

Contents

Contributors

David Armstrong   *Lecturer in International Organization, University of Birmingham.*

Michael Clarke   *Lecturer in International Relations, University of Newcastle.*

Lawrence Freedman   *Professor of War Studies, King's College, University of London.*

Stephen Gill   *Senior Lecturer in Politics, Wolverhampton Polytechnic.*

Christopher Hill   *Lecturer in International Relations, London School of Economics.*

Richard Little   *Senior Lecturer in International Relations, University of Lancaster.*

Michael Nicholson   *Visiting Fellow, University of Manchester.*

William Olson   *Dean and Professor of International Relations, The American University, Washington D.C.*

Nicholas Onuf   *Professor of International Relations, The American University, Washington D.C.*

Steve Smith   *Lecturer in International Relations, University of East Anglia.*

Trevor Taylor   *Principal Lecturer in International Relations, North Staffordshire Polytechnic.*

Roger Tooze   *Lecturer in International Relations, North Staffordshire Polytechnic.*

Preface

The origins of this volume date back to a panel at the United States International Studies Association (ISA) Convention in Cincinnati in March 1982. At that panel Roger Tooze and myself gave papers on the theme of this volume with Mike Nicholson acting as a discussant. Later in 1982, the British International Studies Association (BISA) set up a sub-committee (consisting of Adeed Dawisha, Frances Pinter, Barbara Roberson and Trevor Taylor) to investigate the possibility of BISA sponsoring the publication of books. The theme of this volume seemed an ideal starting-point for such a venture, since there have been strong contacts between members of BISA and the US International Studies Association over recent years. Furthermore, the notion of a distinctive 'British' perspective to the study of international relations seemed to crop up often at conferences. With these ideas in mind I approached prospective authors, with the added incentive that all royalties on the book would go to BISA funds! I am pleased to say that no one declined the invitation to contribute on these terms. A draft of the introduction was then sent to each contributor in order to try to ensure that each chapter, while naturally having a specific focus, was written with a notion of the kinds of issues that seemed to be raised by the theme of the volume.

I would, of course, like to thank the contributors for meeting their deadlines with only the occasional nudge. I would also like to thank Trevor Taylor for his helpful comments on my draft introduction. But, even a book of 'free' contributions involves much behind-the-scenes work, so I would like to thank Anne Martin for all her help in typing the many letters to contributors/publishers etc., and for typing the bibliography. Without her cheerful assistance, editing this would have been a much more difficult task. I would also like to thank Kim Pickin and Sean Magee at Basil Blackwell for their friendly, encouraging and efficient work on this project. Finally, on behalf of the contributors I would like to express our thanks to Claire Andrews for her meticulous work in copy-editing the book.

My hope in gathering these contributions together is that they will encourage thinking about how the discipline has developed in Britain and the United States, and further to force us to consider the reasons for any differences we might observe. As the real world of international relations turns increasingly bleak, it is timely to remember that our study of the subject can never be simply empirical and value-free: for this reason, a reassessment of how the discipline has developed as it has in the two communities highlights this crucial nexus between academic enquiry and the wider political and economic environment.

STEVE SMITH
Norwich

Introduction

STEVE SMITH

The very diversity of the international political system implies that the nature of international relations will be perceived differently by different groups. The variety of religions, cultures, moral and ethical systems and histories ensures that there can be no universal view of the main issues of international relations. The world looks a different place in, say, Calcutta than it does in Moscow, Kabul, Tehran or Kansas; the structure of the states-system means that people in different countries will have contrasting views of what the most important issues are, and of how these are to be dealt with. This volume is concerned with exploring in detail the ways in which the subject of International Relations has developed, and has been studied, in two academic communities – those of Britain and the United States. (Throughout, the use of the words 'international relations' refers to the activity in the world, and the words 'International Relations' to the academic discipline.)

Initially, it must be pointed out that these are by no means chosen as natural contrasts! In fact, even taking into account the European countries, we would expect that Britain would be more like the United States in terms of how International Relations is defined and studied than any other state. So, this book does not aim to choose two opposites, only to choose two states where there seem on the surface good reasons to expect that the subject may be studied in a similar way. After all, reasons of language alone mean that contact between the two academic communities is relatively easy. The links between the British International Studies Association (BISA) and the US International Studies Association (ISA), and the participation of academics from BISA/ISA at the annual conferences of each other's association, bear this out. Hence, this volume is concerned with examining the extent to which the subject has developed, and has been studied, along the same lines in the two communities. As such, it will focus on one of the most prevalent views about the discipline, namely that it is possible to delineate a British tradition in International Relations, which can be distinguished from the American approach.

Central to the rationale behind this book is the common notion that the Atlantic represents a powerful divide in the subject of International Relations. This argument contends that the numerous major controversies in the discipline have been largely restricted to the US academic community. For example, the major debates in the history of the discipline in the twentieth century have been those between idealism and realism, realism and behaviouralism, and behaviouralism and post-behaviouralism. All these have been basically confined to the US academic community. Furthermore, even the recent controversy about *what* is to be studied has been almost exclusively an American debate. Whereas idealism, realism, behaviouralism and post-behaviouralism were concerned with how the subject should be studied, and in this sense related exclusively to age-old assumptions about power politics, the recent transnationalist attack on this tradition has argued that the content of the subject has altered. Hence, transnationalism, by concentrating on economic factors, and especially the North–South cleavage, attacks the military-based assumption implicit in the East–West orientation of the previous paradigms in the subject. Now, the important point is that the British academic community has been almost entirely isolated from these discussions, so that it can be (and often is) argued that there is an identifiable British way of studying the subject, and this has remained essentially unchanged throughout these debates. The one exception to this general rule – the so-called 'Great Debate' between, initially, Kaplan and Bull – explicitly concerned methodology and epistemology.

However, this volume is not designed to argue any one line over this issue; rather its aim is to examine the extent to which the two academic communities have progressed along parallel or divergent paths. Of course, there are a number of cogent reasons for believing that the subject has developed and been studied in a very similar fashion in the two countries.

The first is that the two communities have ready access to each other's literature; this allows the straightforward transfer of information and theory. A second argument is that this access has led to a cross-national development of theory. Rather than theory developing independently in the two communities, it has undergone a process of transatlantic cross-fertilization. The subject can be seen to be studied in a variety of ways which cut across national boundaries, and which reflect general theoretical orientations rather than a geographical division. Thirdly, both states have had similar problems to deal with since the subject of International Relations emerged as a separate discipline. Each is a nuclear power, and both are central members of the NATO alliance. Each state has been a major power during this century, with involvement in two world wars, and, since 1945, a similar orientation to the major military adversary. This has meant that each academic community has been engaged in explaining essentially similar problems in external affairs. Finally, the two countries are similar in terms of internal political organization and economic orientation: to be sure there are major differences, but each is a liberal democratic capitalist state with common sources of, and constraints on, foreign policy: for example, electoral constraints, public opinion and economic considerations. For these reasons, the two communities can be seen as most likely to develop along similar lines. Certainly the four factors of language, theory, external issues and economic and political structure apply to the two states to a far greater extent than is the case with any of the other leading powers in the international system.

On the other hand, though, there is a powerful case that contends that the two communities have developed very differently, and study the discipline in different ways. Thus, rather than the major division in the two academic communities being a theoretical/methodological one, the divide is seen as being a national one. The first reason for this is the argument that the two countries have had quite separate political, economic and cultural experiences, experiences which have been *crucially* different since 1918. For example, the fact that each is a nuclear power hides vast differences between their military strategies and the technical capabilities of their weapons. Similarly, great power experience has been notably distinct: British experience was as a great power in a multipolar world, US experience has been in a bipolar one; each of these systems imposing different constraints, and offering different opportunities.

Secondly, the two states have in recent years been faced with different internal and external political and economic problems. To see the two states as, since 1945, responding to the same world is over-simplistic; the external demands of the British and American economies are quite unrelated, and the decline of British power and its internal effects have no real parallel in American experience. According to this line of argument it is unsurprising that transnationalism had such an impact on the US academic community, given the nature of the economic and political problems facing that country at the time (the early 1970s) the approach was first developed.

A third reason concerns the ways in which US and British academics are trained. In the United States there is much greater stress on numeracy and on the breadth of education. This is very unlike the training given to British academics, which, especially at the graduate level, tends to involve far less quantitative techniques, and is much narrower in focus; the Ph.D. programmes at British and American universities illustrate this very clearly. The difference in training automatically takes the two sets of scholars in different directions, as a comparison of the contents of the journals of BISA (*Review of International Studies*) and the ISA (*International Studies Quarterly*) shows: the latter publishes far more quantitative material than the former.

Fourthly, the academic communities are themselves dissimilar in terms of structure and modes of operation. Although a generalization, it remains true to say that US academics are under far more pressure to publish, and to be innovative in their publishing. Given the popularity of quantitative techniques in the last two decades, this has led to innovation being concentrated along quantitative lines, for example in the extension of the use of quantitative techniques into previously unchartered areas, or through the extension of the techniques themselves. Certainly the last few years of *International Studies Quarterly* bear out this line of argument. The result is that US journals tend to be criticized in Britain for being far too concerned with quantification, at the cost of content. The British tradition enables academics to publish after a considerable period of mulling over ideas: though this means that British academics can be criticized in the United States for their relatively poor publishing record and for the lack of explicit theoretical and methodological consciousness in their work.

A fifth reason concerns the nature of the links between government and academia. In the United States there is far more contact between academics and policy-makers than there is in Britain. Not only is this illustrated in the prevalence of research institutes, serving to bring the two communities together, but there is also direct contact between them as individuals move from being academics to being policy-makers and vice versa. Indeed, it can be added that government in the United States is more interested in the output of academics than is the case in Britain; it also funds academic research more directly.

Despite the fact that the same language, and often the same concepts, are used, a sixth reason for a difference in the two communities concerns access to information in the two countries. Whatever its limitations, the Freedom of Information Act places American scholars in a fundamentally different position with regard to obtaining information than their British counterparts; such a distinction reinforces any predispositions in the academic communities to study rather different aspects of the subject.

However, the major reason for the divergent approaches in the two countries derives from their distinct intellectual climates. The subject of International Relations has grown up in the United States in an academic environment conducive and responsive to social science methodology. Indeed, International Relations in the United States has proceeded in a fashion that is essentially similar to the other social sciences. In Britain, the subject had its roots in the study of philosophy, law and history. Given the different policies of the two states towards international involvement in the inter-war years, the subject only expanded markedly in the United States after the Second World War; this, of course, was precisely the time when social science was developing. Further, the roots of the subject in Britain have been strengthened by a resistance to social science among British academics generally.

It can thus be argued that there is a very large gap between the basic orientations of the two countries towards the study of International Relations. This gap precludes the automatic transfer of academic work in one country to the academic community of the other, and, more saliently, significantly retards progress in the discipline.

However, it is important to stress that these two blanket assertions (that the subject is studied in essentially the same way in the two countries or that it is studied in very different ways) need to be qualified. Different sub-fields of the discipline may have developed in different ways, and thus fit one or the other model more closely. Certainly, it would be surprising to find a uniform pattern across all the sub-fields.

This point leads me to the approach adopted here. Each of the following chapters takes as its focus a specific (and major) sub-field of the discipline and examines the way in which it has developed and been studied in the two countries. Established specialists in the field analyse the literature and offer a description of the distribution of views, as a basis for an explanation in terms of wider academic, political and historical factors. The book's aim is to explain the development of the subject on both sides of the Atlantic. The book will also provide evidence of the extent to which either of the general arguments holds; whether, that is, the division is primarily national or methodological. Such a concern raises the question of why divergence has been more marked in some areas than others, and hints at the issues which need to be tackled if cumulative research is to develop.

The book contains nine chapters on the major sub-fields of International Relations. These chapters are preceded by an introductory chapter by William Olson and Nicholas Onuf, which examines the development of International Relations as a discipline, pointing to the major debates, approaches and 'landmark publications'. The final chapter also has a rather different focus. In this, Steve Gill looks at attempts to combine different national views on International Relations in the Trilateral Commission; whereas other chapters look at the study of the subject, Gill's chapter considers an actual example of the ways in which various attitudes (from the US, Japan and Western Europe) have been dealt with in the Trilateral Commission's attempts to create elite consensus.

This volume is based on the assumption that the question of how the study of International Relations has developed and been studied in Britain and the United States is extremely important. Much has been asserted on this point, but this book is the first attempt to analyse the issue on the basis of detailed case-studies of specific sub-fields. Such an analysis should enable us to understand more clearly the history of the discipline in the two countries and hint at an explanation of why the actual development and method of study has adopted the patterns outlined.

1

The Growth of a Discipline:
Reviewed

WILLIAM OLSON AND NICHOLAS ONUF

> *Yet the fact remains that Mr. [Woodrow] Wilson (because of the rude precisions of the Jusserand Memorandum) and Mr. Lloyd George (in view of his amazing predilection for the unexpected) both rejected, and indeed resented, any written formulation of what, or how, or when, they were supposed to discuss.*
>
> *The effects of this disinclination on their part were deplorable in the extreme.*
>
> Harold Nicolson, 1933, p.103

The late Sir Harold's devastating conclusion contains a lesson obviously less related to the respective British and American nationalities of the two statesmen than to his enlightened despair about preparation for the intelligent discussion of international affairs after the First World War. If half the motivation for developing a new kind of study was the preservation of peace (which has not been achieved), surely the other half arose from recognition of the need for a different approach to the organization and understanding of knowledge about the relations of states (which has been achieved). At a time when the future of humanity seemed to depend upon mastery of the subject, the ways in which

'The Growth of a Discipline' was the title of an essay by William Olson which constituted Chapter 1 of *The Aberystwyth Papers: International Politics 1919–69*, edited by Brian Porter (1972) on the occasion of the fiftieth anniversary of the founding of the first chair in International Politics at University College of Wales, Aberystwyth. The present essay revises and updates that chapter; portions are reprinted with permission of Oxford University Press.

international relations had hitherto been analysed proved inadequate. A new discipline was born because it had to be.

What Discipline?

One distinction needs to be drawn at the outset in any developmental analysis of the discipline called International Relations, and that is the contrast between the qualitative and quantitative aspects of its development. It is tempting to measure growth using criteria that can be quantified and conclusively demonstrated. Statistics can be gathered showing the number of courses given. How many professorships, degree programmes and students are there? What new textbooks and journals have appeared? But this gives us only scant or even misleading guidance about the true nature of the development of the discipline. Quantified summaries of what has occurred can be interesting, and may even provide clues to the nature of progress. Yet they can also be depressing. For example, administrators point with pride to the growing cadre of professionally trained people in this field (indeed graduate numbers in several professional schools in the United States are impressive), but what roles do these graduates assume in the field after their academic training? While some move on to doctorates (usually in the conventional disciplines), most go into diplomatic careers, the civil service, law, banking or business. This kind of assessment therefore gives only a limited view of disciplinary growth. Some of the increases may not reflect growth at all, but may be evidence of the pedagogical split between professional schools, with the placement of students a primary concern, and academic courses no different in character from those in, say, art history. This split is codified in the US to the extent of separate professional societies: the Association of Professional Schools of International Affairs, and the International Studies Association and its national affiliates.

From a qualitative point of view, not only has the field been defined – it has been redefined, again and again. Despite the magnitude of change since 1919, it would be difficult to argue that this necessarily represents progress, because scholars' interests have gone in so many different directions. Many of the paths along which leaders in the field thought the subject was moving, say thirty years ago, have been dramatically altered by some leaders today, and the contrast between the 'growing points' of International Relations in 1919 and 1969, when *The Aberystwyth Papers* appeared, is staggering. Even the fifteen years between the first and second versions of this essay mark great changes. There is now, and has been for a long time, constant challenge, criticism and counter-attack.

What are teachers of International Relations trying to accomplish? Are they working to advance the field through their students, or aiming for something quite contradictory to that incremental intellectual process, satisfying the state by producing civil servants and diplomats to pursue its national objectives? Or have they yet another purpose: serving the cause of peace or other cosmopolitan values? These are all very different aims, and they cannot be made one merely by asserting that the intention is to produce diplomats as well as scholars, and enlarged awareness in everyone.

As an academic subject, rather than a professional training, the field has had to face one of the most difficult problems of establishing any discipline, that is the question of separateness from other disciplines. This was solved at Aberystwyth from the start by establishing a Chair and a Department of International Politics, but in many universities it remains unresolved to this day. The prevailing feeling in the United States appears to be that this is not an important issue. While interdisciplinary degrees in International Relations, formed from offerings in existing departments, continue to proliferate in undergraduate studies, some of the few, separate Ph.D. courses have actually been abolished in the last fifteen years. This attitude, that what matters is the subject-matter of International Relations and not where the subject-matter is located institutionally, may have had a critical effect on the intellectual development of the discipline. Scholars who want to follow careers in this field must realize that they will probably work in departments of political science and must therefore be political scientists first, and only secondarily specialists in international relations. It might seem that a strategic mistake was made early on by not insisting on separate international relations departments, but was there really a choice? Would-be disciplines have always had to establish their integrity as such before gaining institutional recognition, and this International Relations was ill-prepared to do. Finding another disciplinary home was the inevitable – and irreversible – alternative.

What indeed is a discipline? Though some regard it as unimportant, this question continues to be a matter for considerable debate. Here, the distinction must be made between 'discipline' in the formal sense, implying a subject with particular characteristics that distinguish it from others, and the more informal interpretation that suggests the systematic study of subject-matter, with or without the 'credentials' of separateness. One can go back to Machiavelli for an attempt to be systematic in the way one looks at social phenomena (indeed, Georg Schwarzenberger of the University of London once characterized him as 'the founder' of the science of international relations (1951, p.11), but if one seeks to delineate the features of this discipline which are distinct – fundamentally distinct – from those of other social science subjects, it is not only difficult to do so but controversial as well.

Harry Howe Ransom has suggested what some of these distinguishing points *ought to be*: first of all, a distinct subject-matter; secondly, agreed-upon abstractions or models; thirdly, concepts uniquely adapted to the analysis of international behaviour; fourthly, a specialized vocabulary, with precise definitions; fifthly, standardized analytical methods allowing re-testing or replication of initial analysis; and finally, a central system for cataloguing, evaluating and communicating research and its results (1968, p.369). One might usefully take these criteria and examine how far specialist work in International Relations and the other social sciences meet these requirements. Such a dual test might reveal a set of characteristics shared by all social sciences, with distinctions between particular subjects being less significant than is commonly thought. It may be true that criticisms made of International Relations as a discipline can to some degree be levelled at other disciplines as well. International Relations might therefore more profitably be regarded as an 'inter-discipline'. This would concede that, while such study may not qualify as a separate subject, it does reflect an increasingly coherent orientation which integrates the contributions of the other social sciences in a special way.

Definitions of International Relations may provide more clues to growth than debates about the term 'discipline', especially if one examines representative definitions, in their briefest and most fundamental forms, over the period since International Relations began to emerge as a separate subject sixty-five years ago. At the outset, a book appeared which presented a novel organization of existing knowledge, *Diplomacy and the Study of International Relations* (1919), by D. P. Heatley, lecturer in history at Edinburgh. Admitting that 'history does not give much encouragement to the promulgators of schemes of Perpetual Peace', Heatley divided his book into sections on diplomatic history, international law and ethics, but made no attempt to define the term 'international relations'. In 1922, however, James Bryce provided the simple statement in the opening pages of his *International Relations* that he was dealing with 'the relations of States and peoples to one another'. By 1944 Grayson Kirk and Walter Sharp declared that their purpose in preparing *Contemporary International Politics* was to 'explore and examine those fundamental forces which in the authors' view are most responsible for the motivation of foreign policy, schematically considered'. Ten years later, Hans J. Morgenthau and Kenneth W. Thompson, in their book *Principles and Problems of International Politics,* argued that the 'core of international relations is international politics, and . . . the subject matter of international politics is struggle for power among sovereign nations.' In *Contemporary Theory in International Relations* (1960), Stanley Hoffmann asserted that 'the discipline of international relations is concerned with the factors and the activities which affect the external policies and power of the basic units into which the world is divided.' More recently, in writing of International Relations as a science, John Burton described its concern 'with observation and analysis, and with theorizing in order to explain and predict the operations and processes of relations between states, and of the world system as a whole' (1965, p.5).

The differences and similarities between these definitions, which span a period of over forty years, are equally striking. One crucial distinction lies in references to the rationale for the study; whereas the earliest cite peace as the purpose, the latest seek rigorous procedures to achieve understanding. This is a profound change not because scholars today are less devoted to peace than their counterparts were fifty years ago, quite the contrary, but their devotion to peace is separate from their devotion to scholarship and now takes a different form. Whereas thirty-five years ago there was hope of permanent and universal peace in a new order of international organization and law, there is now an acceptance of the likelihood of continued tension and uncertainty which a number of distinctive disciplined perspectives can perhaps comprehend but not change.

Does all this mean that despite its possible failure to gain recognition, International Relations has developed a certain orthodoxy? As early as the 1960s, Burton thought this was implicit in the discipline's preoccupation with state power and interest. In his attempt to evolve a general theory, he started with an inclusive most writers today would agree with P. A. Reynolds's distinction between International Relations (which studies all 'boundary-crossing transactions of whatever nature among whatever units') international politics (embracing 'behaviour of, and interactions among states') and international studies (which contains 'both of these, but also all studies that would illuminate or have a bearing on them') (1975, pp.6–7, 9). Evidently we have built a mansion with many rooms and expansive grounds.

Major Phases

Five overlapping phases of development seem to suggest themselves. The first was the historical phase, during which students endeavoured to explain how the present had been formed from the past. This was combined with a legalistic approach, which saw states increasingly implicated in a complex set of rules of their own devising. The First World War demonstrated the political as well as disciplinary limitations of historical and legalistic methods, not only for an understanding of international relations but also for their improvement. As C. K. Webster said in his inaugural lecture as Wilson Professor in the University College of Wales:

> This is the first Chair of International Politics founded in this country, and though in other countries there are professors whose duties are akin to mine, there is no general acceptance of the principles of the study. Indeed, even if such principles had existed before the Great War, that event has so sapped the foundations of International order, and changed so remorselessly our conceptions of International Relations, that a recasting of our ideas would be necessary. But of course no ordered and scientific body of knowledge did exist in 1914. Perhaps, if it had, the catastrophe might have been averted; for its mere existence would have been proof that men were thinking about very different things than actually were occupying their attention. (1923, p.4)

The second phase was one of organization in which an emerging discipline had as its foundation the ordering of the world through the new international institutions resulting from the peace settlement at Versailles. This approach, in the face of the challenge to the League system by expansive dictatorships, gave way to a third phase, based on the analysis of great power interplay. During this exciting and disastrous period, military strategy, often within the context of the pseudo-science of geopolitics, came to fascinate many students of International Relations. After a brief return to another institutional phase, as the United Nations rose like a phoenix out of the ashes of the Second World War, a fourth phase developed, overshadowed by the cold war and coloured by controversies over the place of ideology in the study of world politics. As the bipolar nature of this second post-war era appeared to dominate world politics, so did the language of 'realism' – of state power and interest – dominate public policy and scholarly discourse.

The mid-to-late 1950s marked a new phase of sanitized realism. The basic assumptions of realism – the autonomy of state actors, maximizing behaviour in the name of national interest, necessary competition for scarce values, concern for stability in a conflict-prone system – were not only unchallenged at this time, they were hidden from view amid claims that International Relations *could* have the value neutrality appropriate to the positivist frame then and (to a somewhat lesser degree) still prevalent in the social sciences. Value neturality could obtain, that is, if the underlying concepts of International Relations could be rendered in a purely abstract form, if these abstractions were assembled into generalizations possessing the explanatory and predictive characteristics of powerful theories in natural science, and if suitable tests employing quantitative methods could be derived from the logical entailments of posited theoretical relationships. Apparently a discipline could only exist if it was based on science in the strictest sense of the term. To the extent that the first post-war generation of scholars weaned on Morgenthau (at least in the US) endorsed assumptions proper to realism, there was indeed a consensus that International Relations could aspire to standing as a discipline in its own right, as defined by science.

The realist 'paradigm', as we have come now to call such consensual but largely unspoken agreements on theories giving meaning to day-to-day scholarly activities, assured those involved that their world of discourse was 'real' and important; that theoretical, empirical and policy-relevant work was justified under an informal division of labour; that cumulative knowledge, theoretically and procedurally grounded, spelled progress in the Enlightenment tradition that underlies all scientific and technolog-ical endeavour since the 'scientific revolution' of the sixteenth and seventeenth centuries. Needless to say, the power of this view, which made International Relations a discipline as well as a vocation, exercised its greatest influence in the United States. Rapid expansion of the universities, the success of the German ideal of doctoral training and research so much reinforced by emigré professors like Morgenthau, and the willingness of US elites to accept, even to relish, the responsibilities of being the world's greatest power and promoter of peace and prosperity (an enduring dimension of the national psyche) – all these factors contributed to the rapid growth of International Relations and to its institutionalization during the 1950s and 1960s.

One fissure in the US consensus on a science-based, power-oriented International Relations was immediately observed; J. David Singer (1961) defined it as 'the level-of-analysis problem'. Macro-level, systemic thought, much influenced by sociology, and the micro-level behavioural work, influenced in its turn by psychology, might be defended as necessary and complementary aspects of a normal science paradigm, just as theory and experimental science constitute any discipline in the positivist mould. In practice, the quest for an underpinning theory on the one hand and the dogged pursuit of testable propositions on the other played on temperamental differences among individual scholars, emphasized methodological pluralism, highlighted the substantively fissiparous character of International Relations, and sorted scholars into seemingly hostile camps arranged on two sides of a great divide: systemic theory versus behavioural science.

The aridity of conceptual development for its own sake, the inflated nature of high theory claims, and epistemological challenges to the organic imagery of most systems-level thinking, condemned theory to an earlier eclipse than science. There are today few theorists working in this paradigmatic tradition, Kenneth Waltz and Robert Gilpin serving as lonely examples. Procedurally based science has fared better, if only because it can respond to criticism with plausible efforts to rectify procedural inadequacies. As to charges that it is nothing more than trivial, mindless empiricism, the safe reply is always that the shape of cumulative knowledge can only be seen retrospectively. (For the classic debate on this topic, see Young (1969), and Russett (1969).)

The deeper flaw in the realist/science paradigm was not discovered so readily. The realist position on power and interest, and the scientific value of detachment were called into question by the war in Vietnam. Yet revisionist historians and insurgent sociologists came to this realization first. International Relations, with its comparatively conservative frame of reference established by political science, only slowly responded to disquiet over the US role in the war, and then in a variety of ways.

Some scholars challenged the normative implications of realism, and called for a misnamed 'post-behavioural' phase that would restore concern for peace and world order to its central position. Peace research in the US tended to be much influenced by social psychology and its interest in frustration, aggression, misperception and cognitive distortion. Many European peace researchers, steeped in Marxism, were openly hostile to positivist science. Their willingness to brand America an imperial power alienated some US scholars even though they too had reservations about realism, struck others as rhetorical and inconsistent with the scholarly need for careful expression, and seeped into the consciousness of yet others, strengthening their incipient radical views. World order studies were rooted in a progressive legal-institutional tradition that most students of International Relations thought naive and unlikely to achieve its stated task of devising a plausible strategy for moving from the allegedly moribund 'war system' to a world order that optimized liberal and humane values. The diverse threads of these radical schools lacked a conceptual loom of the same scope and power as realism, and they were not brought together, even loosely, until the last few years.

Other scholars challenged the substantive assumptions of realism head-on. The importance of actors (multinational corporations, terrorists, religious faiths, ethnic groups, etc.) other than states was asserted. These assertions opened up the field of International Relations but cost the discipline its definition. The realist preoccupation with power, defined for all intents and purposes in military terms, was also challenged. A multiplicity of issue areas, with distinctive instruments of power and inhibitions on their use, replaced the homogeneous picture given by realism. Once this alternative view was acknowledged, it was easy to attack realism for underestimating the interdependence of states which had so many cross-cutting interests and constraints on the free use of their power in all arenas.

Arguably, these challenges to realism constituted a revival of the Anglo-American liberal tradition of functionalist and legal-institutionalist thought, cleansed of excessive faith in universal institutions like the League, and adapted to the complex, bureaucratically defined features of contemporary international life. In Britain, there was a corresponding revival of interest in David Mitrany's work and admiration of John Burton's 'cobweb' imagery of world societal relations. Transnational, interdependence and issue area arguments do seem to have a coherence lacking in peace research. They appeal to the many 'moderate' scholars in the US and Britain by supporting detente and accommodation on North–South issues. The resuscitation of this tradition of thought, so prominent a hundred years ago, has been strengthened by the rediscovery that international economics are extremely significant politically.

The most notable development of the last decade has been the institutionalization of a new field of International Relations called international political economy, which combines attention to economic matters, acknowledgement of non-state actors, interdependence and issue areas. It also involves the claim that a better version of realism is now possible – one that sees states like the US using its great power in specific issue areas such as international finance through the emplacement of the Bretton Woods system to sustain its position; and sees that the shift in power, as a function of world capitalist developments, away from the US since, say, 1965 or 1970, has resulted in significant changes in the capacity of the American government to manage the international financial 'regime' (as evidenced by the abandonment of the gold standard in 1971). In the US Robert Keohane and Stephen Krasner are especially identified with this highly sophisticated neo-realism; in Britain Susan Strange is pre-eminent. Pulling in the other direction, away from any affiliation with realism, is the Marxist version of international political economy, from which liberal scholars increasingly draw their insights. Thus dependency theory, theories of imperialism and assessments of the crises and contradictions of late capitalism have intruded into the discourse defining international political economy as a field of International Relations.

If Anglo-American liberalism shows signs of merging with a revised realism, we must not conclude that this spells a new era of disciplinary consensus. On the contrary, the consolidation of the subject of international political economy as a coherent field parallels the redefinition of the old realism as national security studies. The nuclear peril, detente's deterioration, the conservative tide of opinion in the Anglo-American world resulting in the Reagan and Thatcher governments, the willingness of defence and intelligence agencies to contract out studies of national defence problems, the striking if perverse intellectual power of much strategic and deterrence thinking all contribute to realism recapturing its geopolitical origins in the Second World War and insure its relevance for those inclined towards a relatively conservative world view.

We are seeing perhaps the permanent bifurcation of International Relations into two sub-fields, reflecting the antinomy of the main intellectual traditions in the subject: Anglo-American liberalism, with its attachment to rationalism–instrumentalism and functionalism but without necessarily endowing these theories with ameliorative consequences; and Continental reason of state, reinforced by a sense of implacable conflict in a world ever more capable of inflicting harm. If the fifth phase was the erosion of the discipline's substantive and epistemological harmony between realism and science, then the next phase, perhaps already under way, will be the evolution of these two vital and growing fields – international political economy and national security studies – as disciplines in their own right, distinguished on substantive, ideological and (as they progress) procedural and institutional grounds.

Changing Elements

International Relations therefore can hardly be said to have developed by a series of logical steps, with each advance leading systematically to still greater discoveries and insights in orderly progression. Rather, it has been subject to fundamental re-examination as changes in world politics and trends in allied disciplines have invalidated approaches which had earlier seemed both useful and intellectually legitimate. Yet one can identify, in reviewing landmarks in the literature, a fairly high degree of consensus during the discipline's period of rapid growth concerning what the most respected scholars have set forth as the principal elements for study. So whereas 1919 marked a fumbling for ways of comprehending and controlling the relations of contending power centres, and 1969 the high point, the last fifteen years betray uncertainty and slippage, for good and sufficient reasons. Twenty years ago, F. H. Hinsley thought that the study of International Relations was 'still in the state in which biology was before Darwin' (1963, p.6). Today, the vice-chancellor of Cambridge might say, 'before Linnaeus'.

Careful study of world politics certainly began before the end of the First World War, as Stephen H. Bailey pointed out in 1938 in his discussion of the origins of International Relations (1938, pp.1–16). But, though one could point to diplomatic history, or to international law, or even to the beginnings of political science, nothing which could be remotely described as a distinct subject in international relations existed. Perhaps we are not all historians because of the reluctance of diplomatic historians, like many other practitioners in that field, to deal with contemporary problems. The demands of the discipline of history in terms of evidence could simply not be met by those dealing with contemporary affairs who were unwilling to wait fifty years for archives to become available. In law, there were certain underlying assumptions which limited the application of legal methodology to the development of International Relations. Anglo-American international lawyers of that period tended to rely upon a case-study approach, and only some tentatively and reluctantly were prepared to move from precedent to prediction. Political science was at that time emerging as a discipline on the Western shores of the Atlantic, a process which to this day is incomplete in the United Kingdom and only recently undertaken on the continent.

What must never be forgotten in assessing the emergence of International Relations is that it grew out of a fervent desire to understand and therefore to find ways to control world politics in order to prevent future wars. Rationalist-instrumentalist theories about human potential and the techniques for harnessing it were drawn straight from the Anglo-American liberal internationalist tradition of the nineteenth century and invested with Wilsonian fervour in the League of Nations. The failure of the League system inevitably gave rise to charges of misplaced idealism and legalism from students of International Relations. The stage was set for power politics and its analysis.

In terms of the new literature, strategic studies began to take the place of the study of international institutions, even before the outbreak of the war. Partly because of and partly as a corrective to Haushofer's work, geopolitics was the fad of the day. In the midst of the war, Harold and Margaret Sprout produced an important reappraisal entitled *Foundations of National Power* (1945), based on a syllabus utilized in the training of young naval officers. Before his untimely death, Nicholas Spykman won respect and esteem for geostrategic perspectives, developing one of the most effective team-research enterprises ever to appear, in the form of the Yale Institute of International Studies. Despite the fact that immediately after the defeat of the Axis Powers there was to be a renewal of the emphasis upon international peace and understanding, analysis of the make-up of national power had already become a central feature of International Relations.

It was as natural for a rebirth of idealist internationalism to occur at the end of the war as it had been for strategic and power analysis to flower during that war. But the period of enthusiasm for and almost exclusive concentration upon the United Nations and UNESCO's humanistic programme to treat conflict as a problem of misunderstanding or mental pathology was a very brief one. The disappearance of the improving thrust of the earlier post-war phase marked the fact that the world had fundamentally changed. Just as one must never forget the atmosphere of 1919 in understanding how and why the discipline started up in the way it did, so one must never lose sight of the fact that the tensions of the cold war prevented a lasting return to the optimism of the 1920s by practitioners and scholars alike. This cold war phase was influenced for a time by an ideologically laden geopolitics, which lingered on in the preoccupation with protracted conflict. More important was the shift by leading scholars away from broad analyses of the balance of power to a more restricted focus on national policies and decision-making. Frederick Sherwood Dunn and his co-workers at the Yale Institute of International Studies led the way, joined by such diverse institutions as Morgenthau's Center for the Study of American Foreign and Military Policy at Chicago, and a post-war Air Force offshoot, the Rand Corporation, on the west coast. Later, the (now International) Institute of Strategic Studies in London became one of the most prestigious manifestations of this approach.

The next stage of development reflects the generalizing aspirations of theory. Theoretical positions put forward so strikingly in what George Liska (1966, pp.5–11) called 'the heroic decade' (1955–1965) now seem untenable and even pretentious as *theory*. Their lasting value has been in conceptual and taxonomic clarification: steps necessary to bring International Relations level with the study of biology as it stood between Linnaeus and Darwin. The organic imagery of systems thinking makes the comparison with biology more apt than Morton A. Kaplan's grandiose claim that International Relations, after the pattern of positivist science, was awaiting its Galileo (1961, p.6). Would-be Galileos, with significant support from the US government and the assistance of modern computing, began large research programmes involving the gathering and analysis of vast amounts of quantitative data. Science depends on reliable measurement; the science of International Relations would create its own measured reality. However such an ambition could not succeed to the extent needed to convince the sceptics, and those toiling to create the conditions of science became increasingly isolated from the rest of the International Relations community.

The largest research programmes (Charles McClelland's World Events Interactions Survey, at the University of Southern California, J. David Singer's Correlates of War Project, at the University of Michigan, and Rudolph Rummel's Dimensionality of Nations Project) employed a substantial number of graduate students as research assistants. The quantitative skills and commitment to International Relations as a science acquired by students working on all such programmes had lasting effect. Many of these individuals now occupy faculty positions throughout America and, to lesser extent, Britain. They may be the greatest long-term legacy of the era of research programmes, which came to an end with the playing out of the Vietnam war and government support for such research. A scientific orientation is now an institutionalized part of the discipline. In the US it is strongest in the public universities in the east. (Curiously, this pattern is to be found in the social sciences as a whole.) But the fact that professors in the old, influential private universities of the east are called on for policy advice in Washington aggravates this tendency. A similar phenomenon can be observed in Britain, where interest in International Relations as a science is stronger in the 'redbricks', while Oxford and Cambridge cling to their traditional commitment to international history and international law.

The most recent phase represents a return by *some* academics to the universalist and normative preoccupations of the discipline's founders. The emergence in the last decade of peace and world order studies on a scale sufficient to warrant academic institutionalization – journals, degree courses and the rest – may well make these the proper successor to International Relations as a claimant-discipline, truer to International Relation's original aspirations and orientation than either of the barely coexisting and increasingly self-contained International Relations fields of international political economy and national security studies.

Diverging Ideals

Obviously, these overlapping phases of growth, stressing in turn history and law, institutions, strategy, national policy, conceptual development and science, and now renewed ideological considerations, acknowledgement of the subject-matter's complexity, and concomitant field differentiation within the discipline, are distinct neither in time nor in scope. None of them has fully disappeared (nor should have done), nor is any of them predominant. Each is simply suggested as one of the 'growing points' of the subject over a period of years since 1919 (Fox 1968, pp.97–116).

To consider those decades in a different way, several ideals may be said to have motivated professional analysts in the discipline. They were neither necessarily consistent nor simultaneous in time with one another. The first of these was the ideal of purpose, which characterized the approach of many people on both sides of the Atlantic, an ideal of world statecraft which saw analysis as the servant of peace and international understanding. In some ways, the second ideal, the ideal of discipline, was contradictory to this, because it insisted on looking at the world as it was rather than as it should be. In a sense, this contradiction was divisive. In another sense, however, the disciplined attitude helped to develop a consensus among scholars, at least during the subject's expansive period, concerning the character and scope of the subject-matter. Closely tied to this second ideal was a third, that of political realism, based on the insistence that the study of international relations involved the analysis of power and the national interest. Along with this, one sees the beginnings of the important new ideal of science, in the nineteenth-century sense of a systematic undertaking. This was quite different from, but led to, what was to emerge twenty years later in the methodologies of positivist science. These were to be adapted for an understanding of international relations not only from other social sciences, but from natural science as well. A fifth ideal (though some have regarded it as a curse) is that of eclecticism, the widespread willingness and even demand to utilize the wide range of the social sciences, the humanitites, distinguished journalism, and even sophisticated novels (such as Harold Nicolson's *Public Faces* of 1933) in seeking an understanding of the forces at work in world politics.

Perhaps one reason for the delay in accepting International Relations as a discipline lies in what has been recognized from the beginning, that the subject impinges upon and draws from so many other subjects, each with its own disciplinary characteristics. We have always been experts in the art of borrowing, something which is both a strength and a weakness. In one of the earliest treatments, *An Introduction to the Study of International Relations* (1916), several British authors representing different disciplines – history, law, economics, and philosophy – endeavoured to apply their insights to the subject. Six years later Bryce observed that International Relations was a vast discipline covering every branch of the principal human sciences – ethics, economics, law and politics. Quincy Wright's survey in the *The Study of International Relations* (1955) counted more than a dozen contributing fields of practical and theoretical analysis. More recently, other related fields such as comparative politics and area studies, and public goods, social choice and game theory have entered the scene. The approaches and methods of the behavourial sciences have been particularly influential in the analysis of the determinants and dynamics of state relations. Yet sociologists and psychologists themselves have only occasionally occupied a significant place in the study of International Relations.

This may not always be so, however. The extraordinary interest among younger, post-Vietnam students of International Relations in the sociologist Immanuel Wallerstein's 'world-systems' concept, which is greatly influenced by neo-Marxist studies of imperialism and dependency, poses the possibility of an institutionalized branch of sociology (sometimes called macrosociology) parallel to International Relations in political science. The central position of Marx in the development of sociology as a self-conscious discipline matches the place of Machiavelli in political science, and helps to explain the parallel evolution of radical and conservative International Relations traditions in sociology and political science respectively. Even with regard to power, a central concept in the study of International Relations by political scientists, sociologists have made frequent and significant contributions (see Blau, 1964; Lukes, 1974; Wrong, 1979).

Ecology may be a different case. As early as the late 1960s scholars like Robert C. North drew attention to world problems that transcended national boundaries, such as the population explosion, environmental degradation and racism. Many of these concerns were crystallized in the popular as well as the academic consciousness by the publication of the Club of Rome's first report, *Limits to Growth* in 1972. The uncomfortable forecast of the collapse of civilization in the West within a matter of decades, if nothing were done to curb its exponential industrial growth, caused a sensation. Repudiation of the report by economists, who often hold a redemptive view of technological innovation, and scepticism by political scientists (including International Relations specialists), who felt the report was politically naive and who tend to be equilibrium-minded, like economists, in their conceptual concerns, has resulted in a focus of activity dominated by systems engineers and computer modellers called global modelling. Without purporting to replace International Relations, global modellers attempt to reconceptualize the planetary situation (as do sociologists) even more broadly than students of International Relations, by including all circuits of human activity and social arrangements of import to the dynamics of global capitalism.

Another field – national security studies – which has different (and mixed) disciplinary anchors and empirical referents, and yet is parallel to International Relations, thrives in the current climate of concern over nuclear weapons. Physicists, engineers, meteorologists, physicians and theologians are all lending their expertise in a virtual explosion of reports on the nuclear situation. The fusion of disciplinary perspectives in the heat of passionate concern tells us how quickly distinctive fields can emerge under propitious circumstances. The report of the Harvard Nuclear Study Group (1983) also suggests that academic respectability has already been conferred on these efforts and, inasmuch as two of the group's members are prominent International Relations specialists, that a *rapprochement* with International Relations is welcome.

A further point of high-level interdisciplinary attention has been the worsening material conditions for large populations in the non-industrial world, with the crisis in North-South relations both contributing to and precipitated by this situation. The role of economists in discussions about international development tends to overshadow that of International Relations specialists trained as political scientists. Nevertheless, the propensity for interdisciplinary teams of agronomists, hydrologists, demographers and so on to use highly visible political figures like Willy Brandt (the Brandt Commisssion) makes their work part of the International Relations tradition, by being interdisciplinary and by locating themselves, however imperfectly, in a tradition of public discourse which has always been a frame of reference for International Relations: consider the place of Thucydides and Machiavelli in our sense of what International Relations is about. It remains for International Relations professionals to 'recapture' in a disciplinary sense, subject-matter of such importance that it has 'escaped' into the realm of public debate where all people of professional standing, and high reputation, feel equally competent to engage. This is not to suggest that International Relations specialists should suppress such debate on the grounds of superior knowledge, but that they should guarantee its value to public policy by pointing out the limitations of arguments voiced from a professionally narrow or less well-informed perspective.

One may well conclude from these recent trends outside International Relations that professionals from other disciplines, by virtue of their sometimes innocent concerns, are demarcating the frontiers of the discipline for those of us within it. Our reception of these endeavours, wary or indifferent, contributes to problems of 'boundary maintenance', to borrow a systems concept. Is International Relations narrowing as a result? A different interpretation is possible – one that admits to increasing disciplinary interdependence. Frontiers are no longer set by fiat. In Clifford Geertz's words, this is a time of 'blurred genres' in social thought (1983, pp.19–35). Supporting this view is the pattern of interdisciplinary interests now emerging among younger International Relations scholars like Richard K. Ashley, David Earle Bohn, Friedrich V. Kratochwil, John Ruggie and Roger D. Spegele. They are exploring interpretive sociology, hermeneutics, linguistic theory, literary criticism, the study of discursive practices, and aspects of modern philosophy. These tendencies are not easily discriminated, for they represent a wave of interest among social scientists in several disciplines in what is indeed an interdisciplinary movement in the humanities much influenced by Continental thought. If, as it appears, our access to the humanities is no longer mediated by the discipline of history, then we are likely to be affected by modernist sensibilities in art and literature far more than in the past. Post-positivist inclinations will gain substance and support.

A sixth ideal is suggested by the new, interdisciplinary movement within post-positivism: the ideal of a cosmopolitan discipline in which adepts from many cultures enrich the discourse of International Relations with all the world's ways of seeing and knowing. This ideal is no doubt implicit in the global aspirations of the International Studies Association, but an international membership indicates the successful diffusion of the Anglo-American cognitive style and professional stance rather than the absorption of alien modes of thought. As teachers, we find many talented students with non-Western backgrounds deeply resentful of a discipline they see as smug and parochial in its attitudes to the world. If coherence within International Relations is finally a product of Anglo-American nurturing, disciplinary and cosmopolitan ideals may never be reconciled.

Landmarks in the Literature

Any list of suggested landmarks in the growth of the discipline is bound to be controversial, so varied and vast is its literature, and what follows is not a move to pass judgement on these particular works. They may or may not be the 'best'. It is rather an attempt to show that each has either contributed something new and useful at the time, or has had a significant impact on thinking about International Relations as a disciplined study during the twentieth century.

Paul Reinsch, *World Politics* (1900), represented a pioneering bid to develop a comprehensive overview of international society, based principally upon a critique of imperialism, then a subject of hot debate between the two great political parties in the United States.

A. J. Grant et al., *An Introduction to the Study of International Relations* (1916), was perhaps the first text to use the term 'international relations', with contributions from economics, law, strategy, and government as well as history, but with no particular attempt to integrate them.

D. P. Heatley, *Diplomacy and the Study of International Relations* (1919), drawing upon diplomatic history, the law of treaties, and the literature of philosophy and politics, served as an excellent example of the desire to inform public opinion concerning the techniques and requirements of diplomatic practice.

James Bryce, *International Relations* (1922), regarded history as the only 'guide to a comprehension of the facts as they stand, and to a sound judgement of the various means that have been suggested replacing suspicions and enmities by the cooperation of states in many things and their good will in all', and thus expressed the prevailing British view that the key to peace in the future was an understanding of war and peace in the past.

Parket T. Moon, *Syllabus on International Relations* (1925), brought together colleagues from several disciplines to produce one of the first comprehensive and systematic attempts to subdivide the field in an interdisciplinary way (into the areas of history, economics, law, politics) with precision and in detail.

Frederick L. Schuman, *International Politics* (1933 and six subsequent editions), using lengthy historical interpretations, depicted world politics as a system and, as suggested by the famous chessboard endpapers, a game.

Harold D. Lasswell, *World Politics and Personal Insecurity* (1935), was a provocative and early move to devise a psychologically oriented framework for political inquiry.

Edward Hallett Carr, *The Twenty-Years Crisis, 1919–1939* (1939), made a seminal contribution with a realist critique of prevailing approaches based on international law, morality and organization, even though its author did not endeavour systematically to do more than suggest alternative formulations.

Quincy Wright, *A Study of War* (1942), was the first large-scale application of social science methodology to the study of international conflict and remains a massive achievement which has yet to be equalled.

David Mitrany, *A Working Peace System* (1943), was the classic statement of functionalism, a major theme in Anglo–American liberal thought.

Karl Polanyi, *The Great Transformation* (1944), described the rise of the self-regulating market as a unique historical institution and set out its relation to British international policy and 'the hundred years' peace', 1815–1914. Its rediscovery in the mid-1970s, along with Albert O. Hirschman's *National Power and the Structure of Foreign Trade* (1945), which analysed Germany's use of foreign trade as an instrument of policy, fuelled the rise of international political economy as one of the discipline's main thrusts today.

Hans J. Morgenthau, *Scientific Man v. Power Politics* (1946) made a devastating attack on Anglo–American liberalism's rationalist assumptions and set the stage for *Politics Among Nations* (1948 and subsequent editions). This was the most influential textbook of the early post-war period and is thought by many, if not by most, to have redirected those working in the field from idealist advocacy to realist analysis.

Karl W. Deutsch, *Nationalism and Social Communication* (1953), pioneered the charting of social transactions to study trends in integration and interdependence.

Richard C. Snyder et al., *Foreign Policy Decision-Making* (1962), showed the relevance of aspects of sociology, communication theory, social psychology, and organizational behaviour in advancing an entirely new perspective on how to approach the study of international relations.

Quincy Wright, *The Study of International Relations* (1955), was, according to W. T. R. Fox, 'The most comprehensive and systematic inventory of the theoretical and practical disciplines which shape the contemporary study of the subject', and represented a monumental contribution which could be even more useful if revisions were made to show the advances of the past fifteen years.

Morton Kaplan, *System and Process in International Politics* (1957), constructed six possible international systems, specifying the conditions under which each was likely to persist, with the use of esoteric language which itself represented a historical contribution to the growth of the discipline.

Kenneth N. Waltz, *Man, the State and War* (1959), analysed the views of classical political theorists and others on the nature and causes of war, using three principal themes or images: the nature and behaviour of man, the internal organization of states, and the international anarchy.

Lewis F. Richardson, *Arms and Insecurity* (1960a) and *Statistics of Deadly Quarrels* (1960b), posthumously collected essays written over three decades by a British meteorologist, who produced compelling mathematical models of arms races and statistical analyses of the frequency, characteristics and correlatives of organized violence.

Thomas C. Schelling, *The Strategy of Conflict* (1960) inventively employed game theory to explore a variety of situations involving conflict, co-operation and uncertainty.

James N. Rosenau (ed.), *International Politics and Foreign Policy* (1961, 1969a), collected contemporary scholarly materials of particular value for (post)graduate instruction.

Klaus Knorr and Sidney Verba (eds), *The International System: Theoretical Essays* (1961), appeared first as a special issue of *World Politics,* in which younger scholars decisively mapped the conceptual concerns of International Relations.

Raymond Aron, *Peace and War* (English translation, 1966), set forth the complementary concepts of 'rational schematics' and 'sociological propositions' as the basis of International Relations theory, dividing the subject-matter into three levels of conceptualization: sociology, history and praxology (or normative and philosophical considerations).

Harold Guetzkow et al., *Simulation in International Relations: Developments for Research and Teaching* (1963), was a pioneering and influential alternative theoretical approach which, in attempting to simulate interaction between states, utilized both human participants and computer calculations in an innovative methodology.

F. H. Hinsley, *Power and the Pursuit of Peace* (1963), manifested unusual interest and capability by a leading historian of

International Relations in dealing with state relationships on a theoretical level without abandoning clarity of language.

John W. Burton, *International Relations: A General Theory* (1965), was a sweeping critique of orthodox power theory and its assumptions and policy implications, which set forth interdependence, decision-making, non-alignment and non-discrimination as viable theoretical foundations of international society.

Herbert Butterfield and Martin Wight (eds), *Diplomatic Investigations: Essays in the Theory of International Politics* (1966), was a collection of papers by British authors which combined historical sociology and conceptual analysis; by exemplifying an older tradition of thought it provided a useful counterpoint to American approaches to theory.

J. David Singer (ed.), *Quantitative International Politics* (1968), was the first book-length presentation of the so-called data-based studies of international politics, employing many of the new techniques and methodologies.

Graham Allison, *Essence of Decision* (1971), devised three models to explain US decision-making in the Cuban missile crisis, including one giving primacy to bureaucratic alignments and commitments.

Immanuel Wallerstein, *The Modern World System* Vols I and II (1974 and 1980), with two further volumes projected, drew on Marxist theories of imperialism and dependency and the Annales school of social history to interpret the evolution of the capitalist world economy, and the relations of states in the world's core, semiperiphery and periphery, since 1450.

Hedley Bull, *The Anarchical Society* (1977), spelled out a 'Grotian' answer to the question, 'How is order maintained in world politics?'

Robert O. Keohane and Joseph S. Nye, *Power and Interdependence* (1977), combined a critical review of realism's emphasis on military power with an assessment of power relations in different issue areas each with its own distinctive resources, practices, rules and institutions.

Kenneth N. Waltz, *Theory of International Politics* (1979), offered a restatement of realism that was structurally oriented and self-consciously indebted to microeconomic thought.

Johan Galtung, *The True Worlds* (1980), formed a Norwegian peace researcher's synthesis of a number of recent trends which was conceptual, structural, transnational, value-oriented and genuinely global all at once.

The Discipline's Debates

In a literature whose scope is exceeded only by its variety, none but a panel of judges wiser than the authors of this chapter could possibly 'rate' the value of any given contribution to the discipline, especially at a time when originality is increasing both methodologically and geographically. Another reason why it is difficult to write a history of the discipline lies in the healthy, if at time acrimonious, debates which have characterized its development. Two 'landmark' lists, prepared, for example, by the editors of any two of the subject's scholarly journals, would no doubt be strikingly different, and whether the two could agree on any but the earliest literature is certainly open to question.

The debates themselves are useful in assessing the growth of International Relations. What have various proponents argued about over the decades since it began to assume an identity of its own? It was perhaps inevitable that the presumed eclecticism of some of these disputants would become an early target for attack because most of the early writers in the field were historians. History's methods and emphasis on the past soon proved inadequate to meet the need for contemporary analysis and forecasts. Therefore historians who (like Grant in 1916 and Heatley in 1919) endeavoured to deal with international relations were soon obliged to call upon colleagues in other fields, as did Moon several years later. Zimmern made a virtue of this necessity in his plea to the 1935 University Conference on International Relations for an overview of the subject which would draw from and contribute to many disciplines both within and outside the social sciences. Critics who favoured a precise and focused approach were convinced that this move, by bringing too much into the net, would violate the proven canons of an academic discipline. Without unity and coherence, International Relations would be, in Schwarzenberger's words, 'nothing more than an ill-assorted conglomeration of disjointed pieces of knowledge' (1951, p.8). Yet the dilettante overtones of the word 'eclecticism' disappear when the expression 'interdisciplinary approach' is utilized. The two terms are hardly interchangeable, but can it not be argued that this general attitude made analysts of international relations among the first to perceive the value and the necessity of visualizing the social sciences as a whole? The attitude of intellectual receptivity still prevails. What has changed, however, is that, whether its home is in history, political science, sociology, or psychology, the study of

International Relations itself is infinitely more disciplined and more certain of its limitations than it was in its early and middle phases. Eclecticism is not dead, but it is more respectable than it was in its new, and more sophisticated multi-disciplinary garb. The precision–eclecticism debate may be over, but International Relations and the social sciences in general have profited enormously from it.

A more crucial controversy was the debate between the idealist internationalists and their realist critics. It must never be forgotten that the discipline was born at the end of a war to end wars and was designed self-consciously to contribute to that noble end. 'Peace' through institutionalized legal order was the theme of the 1920s. By 1933, when the League's structure was beginning to show signs of stress, the first of several editions of Schuman's historico–power analysis of the Western state-system appeared. Devoid of sentiment, it did not concern itself particularly with attacking any other school of thought. It was Edward Hallett Carr's brilliant realist critique of utopianism, published on the eve of the Second World War, which both focused and ended the debate. Morgenthau, however, felt obliged to end it again (albeit in his own way) in the immediate post-war years, with his demolition of the analytic attitude and progressive beliefs of 'Scientific Man'. When *Politics Among Nations* and the cold war together ushered in a new era in the history of International Relations (one as an analysis, the other as a historical phenomenon), the realist–idealist debate had, for all practical purposes, ended, for in the face of world events the idealist position could no longer be convincingly maintained. In retrospect, there was very little debate. Scholarly proponents of the Anglo-American rationalist–instrumentalist tradition disappeared from the scene, taking refuge in largely autonomous and unfashionable tributary fields such as international law and international organization. Others concentrated their attention (and their hopes) on the nascent integration of Europe, for which they developed elaborate models. As integration stalled, so did integration studies; integration theorists became interdependence theorists, and the issue was revived in a different guise.

Yet another debate took place (and was especially heated in the years after the Second World War), between the generalists and the specialists, particularly the regional or area specialists. In the United States, this tension was exacerbated, if not engendered, by two institutional intrusions into the process of determining the compass and focus of international studies. One consisted of government agencies, secret and otherwise, in pursuit of personnel and promoting research through grants for the new research organizations which mushroomed after the war. The other came from the grant foundations, which, by deciding which universities were to receive support for what kinds of research and teaching, tended to determine the direction of the development of the discipline and especially its subdivisions. To cite but two examples, both Russian studies in the late 1940s and African studies in the 1950s and 1960s received encouragement in this way. A number of area study centres still exist, for example at Columbia University, where under the umbrella of a professional School of International and Public Affairs no less than eight regional institutes compete for funds, students and prestige. In the United Kingdom St. Antony's College, Oxford, founded in 1948, has become a leading centre for regional studies.

The controversy tended to revolve around the charge by International Relations specialists that regionalists lacked the theoretical rigour associated with disciplinary commitments. Regionalists retorted that most of them did have disciplinary commitments, that these were to modern history and anthropology rather than to political science, and that they placed higher value on detailed study of a particular part of the world than on an a priori decision on what is important based on prevailing theoretical warrants. This debate merged with a more general debate (the only dispute about International Relations as a disciplined activity) between the advocates of theory and science in the positivist tradition of natural science, and the proponents of history, policy-makers relying on accumulated wisdom and historicists working to identify the ineffable features of whole epochs. This debate flourished in the 1960s and, crudely speaking, seemed to pit the Americans against British scholars. Despite the conviction and intellectual force on both sides, a major confusion marred the controversy and subsequent appreciation of it. The debate was not about behaviouralism – a name associated with the Chicago school of political science, which held that the study of politics must concern individual human behaviour, not formal institutions. While some exponents of theory were also behaviourally inclined, and drew their inspiration from political behaviouralists like Harold Lasswell, most were systemic in orientation. They drew inspiration from structural-functionalism and general systems theory – traditions allied to behaviouralism. The conflict between theory and science, though papered over for purposes of debate, was aggravated by the level of analysis problem, which acknowledges different modes of discourse for system and action, individual and behaviour.

To the extent that behaviouralism examined the political implications of behaviour through its aggregate expression in voting or trade, for example, it lent itself to statistical analysis and to the use of mathematical models. But behaviouralism is not necessarily quantitative, as Lasswell's *World Politcs and Personal Insecurity* reveals. Systematic phenomena can also be treated quantitatively, but this is procedurally far more difficult and is rarely done. If there is one element that a systemic approach has in common with the theory-science position, it is that all concepts should be stated as rigorously as possible, so that a means of measuring them can, in principle, be devised. Since conceptual clarity is a value which historians can accept (providing it does not lead to obscurantism), there is no real debate on these grounds. The remaining difference was succintly captured by J. David Singer's 'N/V ratio (Singer, 1966, p.14). He observed that in studying problem-areas, theory-science partisans tend to favour the analysis of a large number of cases in which only a few related variables could be identified, while history-wisdom partisans preferred by contrast to examine large numbers of variables studied in one or two comparable cases. The difference is one of substantive interests, which pre-ordain epistemological choices, methods, and, undoubtedly, conclusions.

Despite claims of victory from both, neither side prevailed. Indeed neither party could, because no one wished, quite rightly, to surrender judgement on what was important in, and about, the subject-matter of International Relations. Instead the debate petered out, with a general understanding, at least in the US, that advanced students needed to learn the technical skills associated with positivist science, so that they could choose their substantive interests and working styles without the limitations of ignorance.

Discipline for What?

The debate between science and wisdom has assumed a baleful afterlife, at least as far as the US is concerned. It takes the form of a tension between the academic discipline of International Relations, where conceptual activity is the ideal, and the world of public policy, where wisdom gained from experience is preferred. The concerns of academics appear both distracting and naive to policy-makers and advisers. If early hopes for the predictive capability of theory and science had been borne out, such reservations could be more easily crushed. But academics have given up claiming that their methods will be useful for prediction in the near future, and the empirical work of the last two decades contains too little material suitable for policy purposes. Academic International Relations has chosen integrity over ersatz relevance, and policy-makers proceed with no greater assistance than they received from Carr and Morgenthau or, for that matter, from Machiavelli. Who knows what other ghosts inhabit the huge, largely descriptive literature on world affairs outside the disciplinary pale?

Indeed the influence of Morgenthau (along with Henry Kissinger) on the public policy community in Washington remains tangible and pervasive (Hicks et al., 1982, pp.288–93). Yet the mid-1970s saw a revival of thought on interdependence, not only in scholarship but also in public policy, courtesy of Jimmy Carter and his 'educators' on the Trilateral Commission like Zbigniew Brzezinski. The Carter government's 'discovery' of the North–South axis of world politics, its sensitivity to interdependence and issue-area dynamics, and its human rights convictions all indicate the resurgence of the Anglo-American liberal tradition of a rationalist-ameliorative orientation, not just as a scholarly fashion, but as the appropriate stance of a global power. Both realism and idealism are misnomers for the major choices facing the United States. Should it attend to its responsibilities in the manner of Germany, or Britain, in the nineteenth century? Realism would prefer the Germany of *raison d'état*; idealism, when stripped of its Wilsonian moralism, the British model of control through indirection and issue differentiation. While it is arguable that the British scheme should be the more congenial to America on cultural grounds, the appeal of the German model lies not merely in the fact that it prefigured the Kissinger style in public policy, but in its dramaturgy of power and confrontation. Regrettably, scholars decline to formulate their own concerns and choices in such sweeping terms as these (unless they reject both positions), and so the contemporary half-submerged debate between partisans of international political economy and national security studies is inadequately seen as a refined version of a debate which only intermittently breaks in on public awareness in the US, but which in fact determines some of the most meaningful policy choices a global power can make.

Contemporary specialists are proud of having shed the sentimentality which they feel characterized the early years of the study of international affairs. Yet is there not a danger now that, instead of a window through which the world may be seen more clearly, our many approaches may be more like a looking-glass in which we see only ourselves deeply engaged in controversies which are less and less intelligible to governments and politicians on whose judgement survival depends? As Quincy Wright has observed, 'It is intriguing to consider whether all this study provides any better basis for predicting what the world will be like in the year 2000 than The Book of Revelation provided for the year 1000' (1969–70). and that may depend on whether we remember, or forget, the ideal of purpose. If we remember, from what appears to some to be a state of array may emerge a new stage of integration, redefinition and renewal. If we forget . . . .

2
Strategic Studies

LAWRENCE FREEDMAN

I

Military strategy is not usually an area for academic study. Until recently the great strategists have all been practitioners – generals or their more erudite subordinates reflecting on the nature of their craft. They were highly suspicious of civilians who sought to offer them advice on the proper conduct of war. Within the universities wars needed to be studied only because history could not be understood without reference to their occurrence and outcome. Few were disposed to study wars so that future campaigns might be prosecuted more successfully, and by the time it had become apparent that the military were unlikely to develop effective strategies without outside advice, most academics were sniffy (to say the least) about associating themselves with military affairs. Even when these affairs became too important to ignore, academics often only involved themselves on the assumption that their purpose was to check for potential errors that might be made by the military rather than to guide them to greater efficiency.

The use of violence to settle disputes must inevitably constitute an affront to communities committed to solving society's problems through the application of reason (although it does not require much experience of academic life to appreciate the limits to the role of reason). Over the past few decades academic inhibitions have evaporated and the study of strategy has become popular and almost respectable. The dangers of the nuclear age and the novelty of the military situation provide obvious reasons for the growth of strategic studies. A fascination with high technology may provide another. However, it would be wrong to underestimate the attraction of strategy as an intellectual exercise in itself. The essence of strategy is the need to make decisions in the face of anticipated decisions from an opponent, and it is this competitive element that adds spice to the subject. Interdependent decision-making can be found in most human activities. The essence of military strategy is that the relevant decisions entail the manipulation of instruments of violence.

Strategic studies can be defined as the study of the use of military means to achieve political ends. In practice the emphasis may range from microscopic analysis of the military means to macroscopic assessments of political ends, but it must always involve some sense of the relationship between ends and means. The main methodological issues in strategic studies tend to revolve around the proper balance between the 'soft' factors of politics and culture and the more 'hard' factors of technology and force structure. The most controversial issues may have a technical side to them – such as the most appropriate means for measuring forces or the calculations of weapon 'lethality' – but by and large they reflect political divisions within the wider community. When it comes to withstanding the sharp if often transitional political pressures which regularly afflict strategic studies, common sense is usually a more reliable shield than methodology.

Strategic studies attracts interest as a subject area, not as an academic discipline in its own right. It is populated by people who already specialize in one subject or another and believe this to be the source of their own distinctive contribution to that subject. At certain times specific disciplines have come to the fore (for example, natural science in the 1940s and economics in the 1950s) but none have established lasting dominance so the legacy is somewhat eclectic.

Drawn to the subject because of its worldly importance, practitioners of strategic studies tend to betray an understandable desire to influence the course of events. Because, at least in the United States, elaborate mechanisms have been developed for exercising such influence, this tendency is much more pronounced than in other areas of academic endeavour which are also relevant to public policy.

The result of all of this is that academics work more *for* the strategists, to help them employ military power effectively, rather than making a study *of* the strategists, to look at how military power is in practice put to use. This at least is the case in America. Even in countries which have traditionally approached the study of military matters the tendency is to accept this as the ideal type.

Interest in the practice of British strategic studies focuses only on the extent to which it diverges from the American model. However, as we shall see, there is a distinctive tradition in Britain and this has resulted in far greater continuity of thought than in the United States. Moreover, it was the American community which diverged from the British, rather than the other way round.

II

It is tempting to use stereotypes when comparing the practice of strategic studies in Britain with that in the United States. The Americans mass-produce strategists while the British remain satisfied with a small number of craftsmen. The Americans are preoccupied with technology while the British pay more regard to politics. The Americans continually look to the future while the British never forget the past. Such judgements, while not wholly unfair, do justice neither to the quality nor the diversity of much of American strategic writing nor to the extent to which some of its worst features would have been happily copied in Britain if only circumstances had permitted.

It is certainly difficult to explain the evident differences solely by reference to intellectual traditions. For example, one of the leading exponents of the sort of 'new wave' strategic studies favoured in the United States but generally deplored in Britain is an expatriate Englishman (see Gray, 1982). To take another example, one of the most persuasive defences of the general practice of American strategic studies was made by the British (or more properly Australian) scholar who also provided the sternest review of trends in American theorizing on international relations (Bull, 1968). Equally, it was one of the founding fathers of American strategic studies who weighed in with one of the most effective critiques of later developments in the subject that he did so much to help make respectable (Brodie, 1966).

It is political structure which has really had the greatest effect on strategic studies – for in each country the subject has developed according to the requirements and restraints laid down by those responsible for making security policy. To understand the differences between the two countries, therefore, we need to look at their respective political structures.

The most striking difference lies in the relative size of the two strategic studies communities. Those who have some official part to play in the formation of American policy – in the branches of the executive, the military, the large congressional staffs and the many who advise on policy on a contract basis – must be in the thousands. Given the turnover in personnel in all these agencies, those Americans who might feel able to comment authoritatively on strategic matters must now number in the tens of thousands. In addition there are hundreds of academics who have managed to avoid participation in government but who still feel able to teach the subject. There are many others involved through a variety of pressure groups and public interest bodies, not to mention those who work for manufacturers. A large number circulate around all these categories. When brought together in what is loosely – and somewhat erroneously – known as the strategic studies community, the number of people in the United States who have dabbled in strategic studies is simply enormous.

Sheer size ensures the American community international prominence and provides it with its most striking characteristics. The proximity to policy-making emphasizes the practical dimension of the studies that might not otherwise be so pronounced. By contrast the numbers involved in Britain cannot be into four figures – especially if one excludes the military. A security apparatus manned by a professional civil service with a high degree of continuity that allows slight scope for outside intervention – plus of course a somewhat slighter world role – does not encourage the development of a distinctive and extensive stategic studies community. In particular the lack of an 'inner-outer' system which allows for movement between the public and private sectors means that there are relatively few people outside government able to ask the most pointed questions, and the prevailing cult of official secrecy has led to a general paucity of high-quality information with which to work. Although matters have improved recently, especially concerning information, there remain formidable obstacles to the development of any serious input into policy-making, obstacles which discourage many academics from even making the attempt (see Freedman, 1982).

The relevant university departments in Britain tend to call themselves anything but strategic studies. They study defence, arms control, international security, peace and even war – but rarely strategy. Because the British community lacks political clout it is correspondingly less vulnerable to political pressures. This has been less true in recent years because of the intense political debate generated by the protest movements from which few academics have been able to remain aloof.

A key point, however, is that it is extremely difficult to sustain the notion of two distinct communities. Because of the close connection with the world of policy, the fact that it is comparatively well-funded, and that its very nature involves a certain amount of travel, there is truly an international community in strategic studies. If it has a headquarters it is in London (at the International Institute for Strategic Studies), although the focus of activity is Washington. The journals have an international circulation and at national meetings there are often foreign guests. The problems they address involve a sensitivity to policy-making in more than one country. Certainly for those from outside the United States it is absolutely essential to be fully cognizant of the Washington 'scene'.

This requirement has been found to be less than onerous in Britain. Visits to Washington are usually rewarding and rarely demanding, given the relative openness of the American system. There is always someone involved in policy-making to talk to and the language is approximately the same. It is an interesting thought, the development of which would be well beyond the scope of this chapter, that the ease of access to information in Washington may be partly responsible for the comparative insensitivity to the prevailing moods in Bonn or Paris. The need to take account of general attitudes within countries other than one's own is less pressing in the United States and is perhaps therefore honoured more in the breach than in the observance. Nevertheless, the strategic studies community is truly international in its composition and attitudes, and while it is still largely organized along national lines there are clearly established networks that transcend national boundaries. It is therefore necessary when considering strategic studies in the US and Britain to look not only at the way in which the two political structures have shaped the study of strategy, but also at how the two communities have influenced each others' development.

III

Before the Second World War the United States had produced few writers on military affairs. Only Mahan had achieved an international reputation. The inter-war years were hardly conducive to the study of war. The prevailing isolationist mood dampened interest in the possible sources and character of war. Indeed, the legal bias in the American approach to international relations practically ruled out the subject once war itself had been declared illegal by the Kellogg–Briand Pact of 1928 (Kaplan, 1983). When the United States was finally drawn again into war in 1941, it was historians who were best placed to instruct their countrymen. The most remarkable testimony to their efforts in this regard is the famous textbook edited by Edward Mead Earle on the *Makers of Modern Strategy* (Earle, 1943). As Earle noted in his introduction:

> Only two American professional military officers are discussed in this book – Admiral Mahan and General Mitchell. This is small representation for a people which has been preoccupied with war, to a greater or lesser degree, since the first colonists landed on our shores. The reason is, of course, that our significant contributions to warfare have been in the fields of tactics and technology, rather than strategy. (p.ix)

The only other significant attempt to come to grips with the nature of modern war was led by Quincy Wright at Chicago. His monumental *Study of War* (Wright, 1942) serves as an empiricist reproof to the legalistic treatment of the subject still prevailing on the eve of the Second World War. It was followers of Wright, and in particular Bernard Brodie, who undertook some of the first sustained analyses of the strategic consequences of the new atomic weapons. With a few colleagues at the Yale Institute of International Affairs, Brodie wrote the first important work on nuclear strategy – *The Absolute Weapon* (Brodie, 1946).

This book identified most of the major themes of the nuclear age, including the central concept of deterrence. However, it did not attract a great deal of attention and Brodie's achievement is now recognized largely with hindsight. The Yale group was also unusual. By and large the American universities did not immediately acknowledge, in the relief at the war's end, the importance of their country's new-found power and international responsibilities. Those interested in hard research soon found a home in the new and powerful non-profit corporations of which RAND (funded by the Air Force) became justifiably the most notorious.

RAND first forged what was later to become mainstream nuclear strategy. Its links with the Air Force are clearly significant. The work was undertaken from the start with the needs of policy to the fore. Working with classified material and producing reports intended for senior policy-makers gave American strategic studies its distinctive character right from the start. Even when the subject at last became established in the universities later on in the 1950s and a serious academic community developed, many of the stars were soon creamed off by the think-tanks, and many of those who were not wished that they had been. Nevertheless, up to that point the running (at least in public) was still being made by historians and political scientists.

In Britain, an interest in military affairs was much more firmly established. Centuries of preoccupation with the European balance of power had helped to develop a keen sense of the workings of high politics and the role of military force in shaping international relationships. Military history was not wholly respectable. However, the Chichele Chair of Military History was established at Oxford at the start of the century with Spenser Wilkinson as the first occupant. After the First World War the Chair of Military Studies was established at King's College, London, largely because of a belief in the need to understand the character of modern war in order either to prevent it, or at least to ensure that if there was to be fighting it would be with less of the murderous intensity of the previous war. Although the chair was not filled following the retirement of the first incumbent – General Maurice, it was revived in the 1960s by Michael Howard, who had established the Department of War Studies in 1953. Primarily a military historian, Howard soon found himself drawn into the developing debate on defence.

What is interesting is the extent to which the most serious early thought in Britain concerning nuclear weapons came from those close to policy-making circles. The difference was that this advice was not well received by the policy-makers and no clear channels were developed to draw on work undertaken by people with one foot outside the official sphere. Those concerned – such as Blackett – were almost forced to become dissidents. As Foreign Secretary, Bevin commented after reading a long Blackett memorandum: 'he ought to stick to science' (see Gowing, 1974, pp.115–16).

It is instructive to note the extent to which academics did not play a part in the early British debate. Liddell Hart, the doyen of British defence analysts and an incisive early commentator on the strategic significance of nuclear weapons (see Liddell Hart, 1946), never enjoyed a university post. The debate was led by former military officers such as Air-Vice-Marshall Sir John Slessor and Rear-Admiral Sir Anthony Buzzard (see Slessor, 1954; Buzzard, 1956). As a young MP, Denis Healey made his name as a defence specialist. After discussions with Blackett and Buzzard, Richard Goold-Adams wrote a pamphlet for the Royal Institute of

International Affairs on limited war which made a major contribution to the Western debate (Goold–Adams, 1956).

Although some ideas in this pamphlet might prove embarrassing now – particularly the advocacy of the large-scale deployment of 'tactical' atomic weapons – it was, nevertheless, well within the pragmatic tradition which became the most prominent feature of British literature. A warning not to rely too heavily on nuclear weapons became a regular theme. This injunction first came from Blackett, with his suggestion that the new atomic bombs were not going to be as decisive in warfare as was commonly predicted at the time. This was largely because of their limited yield (which in the 1940s was still equivalent to the destructive power of a Second World War air raid) and their comparative scarcity (see Blackett, 1948).

By the mid-1950s neither of these conditions still applied. The cause of moderation now rested on quite opposite arguments, that with the arrival of quantity production of thermo-nuclear weapons capable of apparently unlimited destruction there was little point in investing in a vast surplus capacity. More important still was the arrival of Soviet nuclear power which for obvious reasons of range impressed itself on Britain before the United States. The Soviet capability was seen to lead to a nuclear stalemate that would soon negate American superiority and whatever political benefits were presumed to flow from that superiority.

The second plank of the moderate platform was therefore the need to recognize that the function of strategic nuclear weapons would be solely to deter those on the other side, and that limited war capabilities would be vital if the West was to respond effectively to the most likely forms of aggression. This theme has persisted for three decades. It appears in the work of most of the main commentators in subsequent nuclear debates, for example Zuckerman (1982) and Carver (1982).

As already mentioned, the third element in the moderate case – the relative enthusiasm for tactical nuclear weapons – did not survive. Having featured rather extensively in British writing in the 1950s, there was virtually no discussion of these issues until they were revived in 1977–8 with the 'neutron bomb'. Zuckerman appears to have played a major role in the early 1960s in persuading policy-makers of the danger of relying too much on these weapons, although they continued to figure prominently in official pronouncements. By the 1980s, even government statements reflected the widespread dissillusionment with nuclear weapons.

IV

It is important to recognize that up to the late 1950s the American debate was not markedly different from that in Britain. Most of the articles and books published were opposed to official policy. Those writers who led the debate – Kaufmann, Kissinger and Osgood as well as Brodie – were by and large schooled in history and politics. They were preoccupied, as were their British counterparts, with the relationship between political ends and military means in the nuclear age. Here also the emphasis was on the limitations imposed on Western strategy as a result of the development of a balance of terror.

Over this period British and American academics were not working in isolation. They were regularly corresponding, reviewing each others' books, and taking on each others' ideas. For example, Bernard Brodie wrote to Liddell Hart in 1957 to say that he had become a follower of his a few years before on learning of the unprecedented power of the new thermo-nuclear bombs. (quoted in Bond, 1977, p.196). Senator John Kennedy also used an enthusiastic review of Liddell Hart's *Deterrent or Defence* as a vehicle for his own views when campaigning for the Presidency in 1960 (*Saturday Review* 3 September 1960).

British influence on official American policy was also evident. The writings of Sir John Slessor and the British Chiefs of Staff study of 1952 were an input into the American policy of massive retaliation – at least they were intended to have an influence (see Freedman, 1981, pp.79–81). At this time the British were even holding their own in nuclear weapons design (see Simpson, 1983).

V

Of course, it tended to be the case that the British were responding to American developments rather than the other way round. But they were still in touch, and there was a common set of issues and a common mode of discourse. However, towards the end of the 1950s the two communities began to drift apart. As already indicated, the British style and themes remained reasonably consistent throughout our period. The changes were largely on the American side. What were they?

The basic change was in the character of the strategic environment. The problems were becoming even more difficult and perplexing. Once American policy was widely perceived to have failed to appreciate these perplexities, there was an explosion of intellectual activity. With the development of Soviet retaliatory forces increasingly making the US nuclear position weaker, the most important question was whether or not real political let alone military leverage could still be extracted from a substantial nuclear stockpile.

In the United States, at least, it began to be doubted whether conventional approaches to such questions, relying as they did on a combination of common sense, historical experience and reasonable sources of information, could cope with the wholly novel situation which presented itself.

It was then that the full potential of American strategic studies came to be felt. For a start, the American social sciences were generally in a self-confident and innovative mood. As part of the 'behaviouralist revolution' an attempt was under way to ape the natural sciences and produce a more precise understanding of the working of human society than anything that had gone before. This involved both straightforward empiricism and ambitious model-building, designed to provide a framework for the information gathered by the empiricists. These forces were at work in strategic studies. The systematic analysis of all aspects of the strategic environment that had been under-way at think-tanks such as RAND since the 1940s began to be publicized. The most significant example of this was the publication, in the post-Sputnik scare, of Albert Wohlstetter's seminal article 'The Delicate Balance of Terror' (Wohlstetter, 1959). Thereafter any detailed discussion of the nuclear balance had to be both rigorous and sensitive to technical nuance. The need to discuss nuclear issues in terms of the properties of individual weapons put a premium on being extremely well-informed, and this strengthened the hand of those who either had access to classified sources or were prepared to wade through the specialist journals.

The alternative to operating at this micro-level was to operate at an equally innovative macro-level. Here the idea was to return to first principles in order to work out the paradoxes of the nuclear age. What, for example, constitutes rational behaviour when the choice to be made involves either the loss of vital interests or embarking on a course of action that could well lead to devastation? Was there a way of using nuclear weapons, recognizing their frightful destructive power, and perhaps employing them for bargaining purposes? Questions such as these were explored with great vigour in the late 1950s and early 1960s, usually without much reference to the immediate political situation, by a number of writers, most notably Thomas Schelling (Schelling, 1960).

All this was brought together in what became known as the 'new strategy', and it was to this that the smaller and somewhat less rigorous British community responded. The response was mixed. It was hard not to be impressed by the sheer volume of resources devoted to the subject and the *élan* with which it was conducted. These were both envied and admired. However, there were a number of powerful objections that hindered emulation.

Objections were apparently made largely to the abstract methodologies. Certainly there was a strong indication that many of the trends in American strategic studies were viewed in Britain with a combination of distaste and disbelief. The authors of one of the offending American volumes quoted a complaint 'that in the thermo-nuclear age military strategy begins to look like a game of chess without a chess board, that its mental construction and strategic anticipations are made in a world in which Kafka meets Lewis Carroll'. The editors added: 'this viewpoint is especially prevalent in England' (Knorr and Read, 1962, pp.v–vi). Liddell Hart wrote to an American inquiring about his interest in game theory: 'I find that the jargon used by its exponents is more puzzling than illuminating. It also leaves doubts in my mind about the value of deductions drawn from it' (quoted in Freedman, 1981, p.307).

However, the reaction was more than a conservative disdain for intellectual fashions. It has to be remembered that much of the original work on operational analysis had been undertaken in Britain and that there was plenty of experience of the application of the scientific method to military affairs. The most important attacks on the methodological presumptions behind much of the new American strategy therefore came from such past-masters of British operational analysis. Blackett challenged the assumptions behind Wohlstetter's claim that the balance of terror could be considered delicate (Blackett, 1962); Solly Zuckerman attacked the attempts to come up with general plans for the actual conduct of nuclear war (Zuckerman, 1962). So it was not the case that the British simply took fright at this sophisticated methodology; these critiques posed important methodological questions.

Nevertheless, it was the case that the British reaction reflected a rather different opinion concerning the likelihood of nuclear war. The tendency in Britain was to assume that 'the bomb' was so powerful that it would be too big a sledge-hammer for most of the international nuts that might need to be cracked, and that it would be neutralized by the adversary's possession of a similar weapon in any conflict among the great powers. It was thought that nuclear war was such a horrific prospect that political leaders were going to steer well clear of any actions that might result in such a catastrophe, whatever the promises and subtle calculations of the strategists. As the resultant caution introduced a profoundly conservative force into international affairs, all the West needed to do was ensure that everyone stayed in awe of the bomb's destructive power. Elaborate analyses of what could be done should deterrence fail were both alarmist in their presumptions and misleading in their detail, especially when it came to devising ways to use nuclear weapons sensibly in combat.

So, while it is true that the British were not well placed to mount the sort of intensive micro-analyses upon which so much of the American debate was based, those in a position in Britain to assess the value of such analyses doubted whether they were worthwhile. Nor is it the case that the lack of comparable analyses precluded British academics from exercising influence on policy-makers. As early as 1962, Laurence Martin described the method by which influence is exercised by outsiders on insiders (and vice versa) in Britain. Writing of the then Institute for Strategic Studies (the International was added later), Martin observed:

> From time to time the I.I.S. is used for briefing sessions in which official information is confidentially conveyed. This is thought to serve the dual purpose of broadening support for policies which are based on information not suitable for general dissemination . . . In return the audience receives more substance for its unofficial assessements and may presumably hope that its own views may not be without influence on the officials. (Martin, 1962, p.34)

To the extent that the British tradition stresses the importance of putting strategic issues in a broader context, exchanges of this nature make a lot of sense. They have also become more regular and more widely based since the 1960s, although they remain somewhat exclusive. For example, in some critical security issues in which Parliament was only barely involved (there were no debates on nuclear weapons policy from 1965 to 1980), there was little material available for a widespread, open debate and no opportunity to develop more radical approaches. Furthermore the essentially conversational mode of communication in Britain precludes the introduction of hard technical analysis. Both of these features can be contrasted with the more fluid and open American debate which is much more receptive to hard analysis and radical ideas (albeit more often from the right than the left). The British approach encourages the sense of continuity and broad judgement that are the hallmarks of its national policy-making in security affairs.

Thus we might usefully compare the American and British strategic studies communities during periods of essentially stable policy-making when security issues are not occupying the centre of the political stage. To some extent the comparisons fit the stereotypes mentioned earlier. The American tendency is to gravitate towards a strategic technocracy, in which policy-making is supported by a vast constellation of advisory groups, consultants and lobbies supplying a wealth of material on second – and third-order questions of policy. The British gravitate towards a more exclusive discussion of a vague and unsystematic form of first-order grand strategy, unsupported by technical analysis and inclined (in 'stable' times) to be preoccupied with maintaining stability. As has already been said, these tendencies reflect differences in political structure. It has also been argued that the development of a strategic technocracy in itself was very much a function of the American political system. The existence of such a technocracy is the anomaly; the lack of it, in the United Kingdom, is the norm. Otherwise, both countries can boast similar academic communities interested in the general relationships between the military and political aspects of international affairs.

VI

However, in recent years events have conspired to disrupt the established patterns of policy debate. This is not simply a reference to the anti-nuclear movements, although clearly these have a large part in the changing picture. Since the mid-1960s American security policy has been subject to severe challenge: first from the opponents of the Vietnam war and then from the opponents of detente. This has led to the politicization of many of the key issues in the security debate with the strategic technocrats providing the concepts and the jargon with which most of the political discussions have been conducted. However, the technocrats have been unable to sustain the debate, especially as the Reagan administration attempted to handle a number of complex foreign policy issues, including relations with the Soviet Union, as if they were no more than technical military problems. This has led to the resurgence of a more broadly based strategic studies, critical of the simple assumptions that appeared to lie behind much of the administration's thinking (see Draper, 1983; Wieseltier, 1983).

In Britain it took much longer for security affairs to become politicized. The public controversy, largely concerned with the introduction of cruise missiles, took the debate away from the specialists. What was interesting was that the radical critics of established policies demonstrated a technical competence that was in marked contrast to that displayed in the 'first wave' CND (Campaign for Nuclear Disarmament). One reason for this was a consciousness of the criticism of the 'first wave' for its strategic ignorance. They were supported by academics familiar with the American literature which was used to make technical as well as moral and political charges against the new weapons (see Roberts, 1983; Smith, D. 1983). Not surprisingly, there was a convergence between those in the United States who saw in the new weaponry a potential for strategic breakthroughs and protestors in Europe who believed such breakthroughs to be extremely dangerous (see Dando and Rogers, 1984). Both were ready to acknowledge the potential of the new weapons while sceptical analysts could take a more relaxed view.

Simply because European nuclear issues have become more complicated in recent years, they can now only be appreciated with a degree of technical knowledge and a sense of the intricacies of the NATO debate that has not been necessary in the past. It would be going too far to say that the British government has recognized this, although it has made a real effort to provide a full background to its decisions on the national nuclear force (Ministry of Defence, 1980, 1982). The American example has also helped to increase expectation of more high-quality information. What is less clear is whether this extra information has been matched with a higher quality of analytical effort. Familiar and straightforward concepts such as 'first strike' and 'limited war' are often deployed in a rather uncritical manner, even in support of radical arguments. It also has to be recognized that academics take pleasure in demonstrating technical competence and second-guessing the professionals on their own ground.

However, it may be that the unsatisfactory nature of the nuclear debate in general reflects the development of the issue itself. Nuclear strategy has progressed about as far as it can, and it is unreasonable to expect further innovation. Much writing on nuclear matters is now political commentary – not surprisingly, given the political controversies surrounding nuclear weapons and the intricate diplomacy involved in arms control. Moreover – again understandably given the way that these matters are dealt with in public – the debate has increasingly focused on the possibility of deterrence failing. This was never a particularly useful way of looking at nuclear policy; it presumed that the basic objective of current policy could not be met and ignored the context in which policy was framed, with the alliance dimension most neglected. The postulate of a failure in deterrence invited harrowing descriptions of the destruction of a way of life. Events leading up to this destruction were described not by reference to crises in international politics, but to the weapons and tactics available to both sides. The source of catastrope was seen to be either the arms race itself, or the influence of mischievous and misleading strategic theories which imagined operations that could produce an outcome recognizable as victory. In the United States the hawks worried that the Soviet Union could imagine such operations; in Europe the doves were concerned that America was actively preparing for limited nuclear war. As both superpowers denied such intent, the issue soon degenerated into charges of mendacity and malevolence. Academics either joined in the debate as partisans or sat on the sidelines bemoaning the lack of intellectual content but unable to counter the spread of well-informed prejudice.

Partly as a result of the difficulties of sustaining a nuclear strategy revealed by the debate, and partly because of a need for a fresh area of inquiry, interest is now shifting towards conventional strategy. With a few notable exceptions, this move has been led by the Americans, despite the fact that conventional strategy is of crucial importance to the military situation in Europe. Moreover, conventional strategy is less suited to speculative academic analysis than are nuclear issues, and it may be that the intrinsic American strengths in dealing with detail will ensure American pre-eminence once again. There is, after all, nothing in Europe to compare with the military reform movement in the United States.

However, the growing debate on conventional strategy has taken its cue from the nuclear debate and has again concentrated on the implications of a failure in deterrence and the consequent conduct of military operations. It is, of course, much easier to imagine conventional weapons being used; they are in regular use all over the world. So there is a disposition to treat conventional strategy solely in terms of tactics, logistics and technology. These are all matters which cannot be ignored and which are embarrassingly unfamiliar to a generation of academic strategists brought up on nuclear weapons and without military experience of their own. But sensitivity is also needed to the political role of conventional deployments – for example in Germany; the problems of alliance formation and disintegration at times of tension will have a major impact on the order of battle. It is also necessary to draw on history to understand the dynamics of conflict. The challenge for the strategic studies community on both sides of the Atlantic will be to ensure that the discussion of conventional strategy is put in its full political, economic and historical context.

I have argued that both the British and American strategic studies communities started off with a shared interest in relations between the political and the military spheres, and that the Americans developed a strategic technocracy that diverged from this pattern, while the British continued to follow established lines. Although there has been a resurgence of broader thinking in the United States as it has been found both difficult and unsatisfactory to handle the nuclear debate in purely technical terms, the sheer quantity of technocratic material produced and the way the nuclear issue has been presented has militated against a focus on such factors as politics and history. This has even been the case in recent years in Britain, and the rediscovery of conventional strategy may aggravate the tendency. Academics working in a highly politicized area are more likely to find themselves responding to the prevailing treatment of their subject than providing the intellectual framework to which politicians and other interested parties must respond. In contemporary circumstances the risk is that the debate will downgrade precisely those factors which are in the end most important and with which academics are most capable of dealing. The task for strategic studies will be to rediscover its traditional strengths and then to reinsert them into the public debate.

3
Foreign Policy Analysis

STEVE SMITH

Of all the sub-fields of International Relations, foreign policy analysis appears to support most strongly the contention that there are distinctive British and American approaches to the subject. To an extent these reflect more general differences between the two academic communities, but the direction of the study of foreign policy in the two countries clearly diverged in the 1960s. The paradox is that academics on both sides of the Atlantic use the same works, and often the same concepts, to explain common problems and phenomena, yet this frequently leads to radically different explanations revealing very different epistemologies. This chapter seeks to examine the nature of this paradox.

Of course, the necessary proviso must be stated: foreign policy analysis in Britain and the United States involves a variety of approaches to the subject. It is an over-simplification to talk of two rival and mutually exclusive academic communities. Reference to an Atlantic, or geopolitical, divide within foreign policy analysis is to name only one possible dividing line. There is also a methodological difference which separates the two communities.

The major United States journals highlight the extent to which foreign policy analysis is undertaken in a variety of ways in that country. Indeed journals such as *World Politics*, *Foreign Affairs* and *Foreign Policy* tend to treat foreign policy in a style similar to that which prevails in Britain and many important American figures in foreign policy (for example, Hoffmann, George and Allison) seem to accept this epistemology. However, while the geopolitical

This chapter was originally published in an amended form in *Political Studies*, 31 (4), December, 1983, pp. 556–65. It is reprinted here by kind permission of the editor and the publishers, Butterworths.

divide must not be overstated, it cannot be ignored. If the two academic communities are examined it is clear that there is in the United States a very powerful and productive school for analysing foreign policy behaviour that has no real counterpart in Britain. In this way, it makes sense to study the two communities in terms of geopolitics. This will not paint the full picture, but will locate a central area of difference.

Throughout this chapter these two ways of interpreting foreign policy will be referred to as approaches. The most obvious term for describing them might seem to be Thomas Kuhn's word 'paradigm', but this is surrounded with such conceptual confusion that, for the sake of clarity, I have used 'approach' instead. In this way, neither stance will be seen as a paradigm in Kuhn's sense, nor as an ideal type. The chapter will attempt to outline the two approaches, trace their development and offer an account of why they have developed in this way. Finally, it will discuss the epistemological issues raised by these diverging views.

In the United States the approach that concerns us here most resembles the school dubbed by Charles Kegley as the Comparative Foreign Policy school (Kegley, 1980, p.1). Although Kegley includes a wide range of authors and viewpoints within his definition, the most explicit examples of this perspective have been the Inter-University Comparative Foreign Policy Project (ICFP), based on Jim Rosenau's pioneering work on pretheory (Rosenau et al., 1973), the Interstate Behavior Analysis Model (IBA) of Jonathan Wilkenfeld et al. (1980) and the Comparative Research on the Events of Nations Project (CREON) of Maurice East et al. (1978). More generally, its roots also lie in Jim Rosenau's work on the comparative study of foreign policy (Rosenau, 1980a) Pat McGowan and Howard Shapiro's 1973 survey of the field (McGowan and Shapiro, 1973) and the yearbook of comparative foreign policy studies published by Sage (*Sage International Yearbook of Foreign Policy Studies*, 1973–83).

Whereas the comparative approach has been dominant, if not predominant, in the United States, it has had no real success in the United Kingdom. Furthermore, to the extent that this method has competed with a more historical, case-study approach, the historical approach has been far less developed in America than in the United Kingdom. The different emphases reflect diverging views on the value of using social science methodology to explain foreign policy behaviour.

The epistemological basis of the comparative approach is quite explicit: it is that foreign policy can be best explained by treating it as a phenomenon common to all states. While on the one hand, this is its clearest point of departure from the British approach, on the other it is the kind of claim made by many of those working to understand human behaviour. In essence, the argument is that the foreign policy of any state is to be defined in terms of its conformity to certain phenomena. So that while the policy of any specific state will vary from issue to issue and from time to time, the same analytical tools can be applied to explain that policy as are used to explain the policies of other states. This particular approach to the field therefore searches for common structures and processes in a variety of countries, utilizes an explicit set of analytical techniques, and stresses the need for cumulative research, so that work undertaken by different authors may be combined to increase understanding of foreign policy behaviour.

The best example, for both paradigmatic and historical reasons, is Rosenau's pretheory (Rosenau, 1980b). This article had a massive impact on the subject-area, and represents the founding statement of this approach. The main objection that Rosenau had to the extant literature was that it did not lend itself to the scientific study of foreign policy. He started from the belief that foreign policy, as a subject, had been both exhausted and neglected and that it was too easy to exaggerate the rate of progress. The reason for this was that: 'Rare is the article or book which goes beyond description . . . Even rarer is the work that contains explicit "if-then" hypotheses' (Rosenau, 1980b, p.119). Foreign policy analysis lacked 'comprehensive systems of testable generalizations that treat societies as actors subject to stimuli which produce external responses. Stated more succinctly, foreign policy analysis is devoid of general theory' (Rosenau, 1980b, p.119). Indeed, the prevailing approach at that time was incapable of leading to such a general theory precisely because it stressed the idiosyncracies of each state; each study used its own concepts and techniques, making comparative analysis virtually impossible.

Rosenau's central point was that this tendency was not inherent in the material. While his specific response to this situation – his pretheory – is well known, it is more salient for the purposes of this chapter to concentrate on the reasons for Rosenau's move towards a scientific approach. He noted two main shortcomings in the approach to foreign policy dominant at that time: one philosophical, the other conceptual.

He saw that the philosophical shortcoming arose from the lack of similarly analysed materials, and this prompted him to devise a means of rendering the materials comparable in his pretheory. More generally, he argued that it was impossible not to have a pretheory since to operate otherwise would imply that foreign policy behaviour was completely random. As he pointed out, 'while it is thus impossible to avoid possession of a pretheory of foreign policy, it is quite easy to avoid awareness of one's pretheory and to proceed as if one started over with each situation' (Rosenau, 1980b, p.135). This philosophical shortcoming therefore involved causation, for existing theories did not specify causal links between independent and dependent variables. The conceptual flaw was derived from a lack of agreed concepts; thus, even if the philosophical problems were overcome, there would still be no accepted concepts with which to arrange the data.

This argument seems to underlie the comparative foreign policy movement in the United States; it is, above all, a plea for a social scientific approach to the study of foreign policy behaviour. Of course, there have been many developments within this framework, but it remains true that this orientation lies behind them all. Certainly, Rosenau's own article on pretheory was central to the development of this approach, as even a cursory glance at the contemporary literature shows. At a general level it provided an intellectual direction for those dissatisfied with the domination of case-studies and diplomatic history; at a sociological level, it provided a tremendously heuristic ideal-type, which gave a sense of purpose and hope to a large number of researchers; more specifically, it was the epistemological core of the ICFP project.

Therefore, in tracing the development of the American approach, the publication of the Rosenau pretheory article in 1966 is a crucial date. Following this, there was a proliferation of ideas, with the most cohesive belonging to those who based their work on the pretheory and sought to develop it into a theory (Rosenau, 1974). Rosenau himself attempted to do this in his work on adaptation (Rosenau, 1981), but had little success (Smith, 1981). The proliferation of thought was mirrored in the publication of the McGowan and Shapiro volume noted above (McGowan and Shapiro, 1973), and in the advent of the Sage yearbook. But it was not until the late 1970s that it fully demonstrated its variety, with the major publications of the IBA and CREON projects. Nevertheless, Rosenau could claim in the mid-1970s that 'developments in the comparative study of foreign policy over the last seven years amply justify the conclusion that those engaged in the enterprise have nurtured a field into existence' (Rosenau, 1975, pp. 24–5). Even more triumphantly, Rosenau declared in 1976 that 'all the evidence points to the conclusion that the comparative study of foreign policy has emerged as a *normal* science . . . Our differences now are about the small points' (Rosenau, 1976a, p.369).

Since then, Rosenau has, to a large extent, modified his claims. In an article published in 1976 he wrote: 'it appears that this process [of knowledge building] may be grinding to a halt in the scientific study of foreign policy. While I do not retract from the argument advanced elsewhere . . . that considerable progress has been made in the field over the last ten years, the long-term trend towards convergence seems to have slowed and, even worse, there are more than a few indications that we are going our separate ways' (Rosenau, 1976b, pp.1–2). More recently, he has argued that new approaches are needed since the subject-area is in a 'muddle' (see Rosenau, 1979; Smith, 1980).

The explanation for Rosenau's contradictory assertions in the mid-1970s lies in the fact that ICFP disintegrated in 1974. Two points can be made here: first it is clear that the ICFP, based as it was on the Rosenau pretheory, did represent an extremely coherent approach to the explanation of foreign policy behaviour. Secondly, the most recent publications from the IBA and CREON projects indicate that the orientation is alive and well. It has, of course, moved on considerably from pretheory, and is now centred around the quantitative analysis of the variables necessary to explain foreign policy, but it still retains the epistemology of the United States approach.

As Kegley has recently commented: 'Those present at the creation of the comparative foreign policy (CFP) paradigm shared a cluster of assumptions that seemed to justify – indeed, demand – a declaration of independence from pre-existing approaches to the study of foreign policy . . . The declaration accepted one set of epistemological prescriptions and rejected another' (Kegley, 1980, p.1) Although Kegley discusses in detail the problems facing the comparative foreign policy school, he nevertheless concludes that he has provided 'good reasons for denying claims to the effect that the CFP paradigm is lost. It is preceding, even advancing, however haltingly and non-self-assuredly' (Kegley, 1980, p.29).

The British approach to the analysis of foreign policy stands in marked contrast to the comparative approach. Indeed, when Kegley contrasts the comparative method with the method that it succeeded, he seems to be balancing the comparative approach with the British perspective (Kegley, 1980, pp.1–2). For example, comparative foreign policy's dissatisfaction with existing studies seems to refer to the way the subject is studied in Britain. It is also clear that the features of comparative policy Kegley describes, are exactly those the British approach is critical of.

Hence, whereas the comparative approach stresses regularity, British analysts assert the uniqueness of the foreign policies of states and the need to use different approaches and methodologies for the analysis of each one. Rather than generating knowledge by the creation of falsifiable hypotheses and testable evidence, the British approach emphasizes intuition and insight.

The British method is clearly reflected in the works of Northedge and Wallace. In his widely used text on international politics, Northedge argues for the uniqueness of foreign policies:

> in the final resort . . . there is really no alternative to the consideration of the state as a unique entity. Apart from certain superficially similar physical features, it remains true that no two states . . . are exactly like each other. We may enumerate all the standard aspects of foreign policy, but in the end the nature of that state and its attitudes towards other state-members of the international system will elude us unless we have done something to penetrate its unique cast of mind, the product of quite unique historical experiences. (Northedge, 1976a, p.175)

More specifically, William Wallace explicitly eschewed comparative analysis in trying to understand British foreign policy. He claims that a rational-actor approach to decision-making 'assumes a degree of simplicity and certainty in the process of decision-making which does not obtain in real-life situations' (Wallace, 1975, p.6).

But the British orientation is most explicitly illustrated in a recent series of books on comparative foreign policy analysis (Wallace and Paterson, 1978; Clapham, 1977; Adomeit and Boardman, 1979). From the start each book seems intent on a comparative approach, yet in no case do the subequent pages live up to this expectation. In one book, there is not even a concluding chapter to examine the comparisons that might be drawn from the separate empirical studies; indeed, the content of the individual chapters themselves quite undermines the claims of American theories (Wallace and Paterson, 1978). In the other two books, although both have a conclusion, each points to the problems of using comparative theories and methodologies. Adomeit and Boardman recognize:

a need for more, and not fewer, detailed case studies of foreign policy behaviour . . . comparative analysis carried out in a classical mould of international relations would produce different results from work carried out by a researcher committed to 'scientific' norms; but there is advantage in such diversity. Comparison, then, does not call for simple-minded rambles through the coincidental similarities of a complex world. (Adomeit and Boardman, 1979, p.159)

The British approach to foreign policy analysis is based on explicit epistemological prescriptions. Knowledge about the foreign policy of a state is to be obtained by a detailed study of the state's history; this allows the scholar to unearth the specific historical and cultural factors that have made that state unique. Although it is accepted that there are some similarities in the way foreign policy is made in different countries, it is argued that these obscure the important fact that each is unique.

Models and theories, by fitting empirical material into rigid categories, fail to get to grips with the unique combination of factors that results in the foreign policy of a state being as it is. Above all, the quality that divides good scholarship from bad is the 'understanding' of the state revealed by the academic. This, of course, requires not evidence and theory, but insight and imagination.

On this basis, British academics have a field-day with much of the comparative foreign policy literature. In two recent articles, Berridge has unequivocally dismissed comparative analysis (see Berridge, 1980, 1981; Smith, 1982). He writes that 'much of what passes for "International Relations" is nothing more than the pseudo-science of Diplomatic History and thus different from the latter only in quality' (Berridge, 1981, p.79). In one article he takes Northedge severely to task for addressing himself to this approach when Northedge is 'only too alive to the bankruptcy of this pseudo-science of diplomatic and military history' (Berridge, 1980, p.84). He claims that the 'preoccupation with foreign policy analysis has led to an intellectual dead-end predetermined by the nature of its historical subject matter, as well as by the scientific methodology which it has misguidedly leased' (Berridge, 1980, p.82).

That there are two quite different schools of thought concerning foreign policy behaviour is clear; the reasons for this are more difficult to establish. The basis for this divergence probably lies in a much wider phenomenon, namely the popularity of the social sciences in the United States. Stephen George, discussing International Relations generally, has argued that the widespread use of scientific method in America derives from a specific historical circumstance: this was America's sudden involvement in great power politics after the Second World War. He writes: 'Because the United States was traditionally isolationist, the problems which now presented themselves to the government of the U.S.A. were novel problems. American statesmen were innocents in the international arena, but suddenly they were cast as the main actors on its stage. In this situation, they turned to the country's academics to supply them with formulae which would enable them to solve the problems of the world' (George, 1976, p.29).

The belief in the power of scientific methodology arose, argues George, because of the existence of three dominant analogies. Firstly, there was the analogy with natural sciences, which had allowed the US to 'control' nature as evidenced by the atomic bomb. The second was the analogy with cybernetics, which had increased the material wealth of American citizens, and allowed international relations to be seen as a network of communications which could in principle be controlled. Finally, there was the analogy with economics and management. These had allowed American businesses to bestride the world economy; why should not a similar approach allow the US to dominate the international political system? [1]

The popularity of the scientific method also derived from its earlier achievements in the other social sciences. As Kegley has argued: 'The CFP research orientation was part of a much larger intellectual movement, deriving stimulation at its incipience from these wider developments in the social sciences' (Kegley, 1980, p.2). Echoing George's comments, he noted the importance of the policy-maker's need for information: 'The demand of policymakers for knowledge that was more than merely heuristic . . . also facilitated the search for methodological innovations able to provide that knowledge . . . non-systematic and non-comparative approaches were perceived increasingly as inadequate to account for foreign policy phenomena' (Kegley, 1980, p.3).

In short, comparative foreign policy gained recognition (and funds) because, on the one hand, it was able to appeal to politicians who needed ways to comprehend a new, and bleak, international environment, and on the other, it benefited from the success of scientific methodology in other social sciences. As an example of the former, it is interesting to note the concern over the degree of policy-relevance in much modern comparative work (see, for example, Wilkenfeld et al., 1980). With regard to the latter, it is clear that the pioneers of comparative foreign policy saw their field as having failed to undergo the modernization of methodology that had occurred in the other social sciences, a feeling very evident in the early works of Rosenau.

The British approach to foreign policy analysis started from a strikingly different perspective. At an academic level, social science methodology has never taken root in the discipline to the extent that it has in the United States. British academics have traditionally been sceptical about scientific methods, preferring the age-old disciplines of history and philosophy (from which, of course, International Relations emerged in Britain). The dominant values of British International Relations are therefore rather different from those in the US. As George has noted, these values, of individualism, elitism and traditionalism 'were translated into a history which saw individuals as the motive force of world affairs, concentrated on Great Men and focused on the foreign policies of particular states' (George, 1976, p.35). The study of foreign policy was really an art, not a science; knowledge evolved from insight, not theory. Above all, the dominance of a philosopy of idealism denied the utility of theory, except in so far as it allowed the academic to re-create the thoughts of the decision-maker.

On a wider level, the links between the British foreign service and the academic community are quite unlike those in the US. For one thing, the lengthy history of British foreign policy has underlined the need for an understanding of that history in explaining foreign policy. Britain's long experience with international politics has also led to a focus on practical, procedural methods for dealing with foreign policy issues. Once again, foreign policy is seen as an art, requiring imagination; theories are of little practical relevance. This point has been well illustrated in a recent debate between a former foreign office official and a leading British foreign policy analyst (Cable, 1981; Frankel, 1981).

This background has been reflected in the absence of any demand from politicians for an academic analysis of the general principles and theories of foreign policy, In particular, there has been no significant partnership between policy-makers and academics in Britain, with the exception of the Royal Institute of International Affairs, and nothing of the kind of movement from academic to policy-maker that so characterizes the US foreign policy community.

These two factors – the general hostility to social science methodology and the nature of the British foreign policy community – seem to stand in marked contrast to the prevailing tendencies in the United States and thereby seem, in part, to account for the divergence between the two countries.

Of course, both American and British approaches can claim to have advantages over the other, and, as such, must be seen in terms of a much larger debate on methodology. However, it is important to realize that differences between them reflect not only distinct intellectual traditions but also the relative standing of the two states. The United States, as a world power, has to respond to world problems in a way not demanded of Britain. This clearly results in a managerial view of international relations: world problems require management, thereby opening the door for the use of techniques that have served US business so well. For Britain, its history, combined with its current status, produce an altogether different form of behaviour, stressing the importance of mediation and negotiation, forms of interaction that fit in with the view of international relations as an art.

To this extent, the paradox becomes more easily understood because the two communities are no longer seen to be dealing with the same phenomena; even common problems are analysed using different methods and theories that seem to identify the orientation of each state's foreign policy. Ethnocentrism pervades the two communities. The divergence reflects two very different intellectual traditions, and reflects a fundamental division over epistemology and methodology. Thus, whereas the British analyst looks for specific historical knowledge to explain a state's foreign policy, the US analyst will search for regularities, believing these to be inherent in the material. While the British analyst will be cynical about theorizing, the American will point to the weaknesses of a 'common-sense' view of foreign policy, and refer to the often mutually exclusive assumptions contained in such works. To this extent the two are not participants in the same scholarly enterprise. The way forward from this position is to be found in what is the central task of all academic activity, the task of explanation. If it is accepted, as surely it must be, that the prerequisite of any theory of foreign policy behaviour is its ability to explain that behaviour, then the way of assessing the utility of these two approaches lies in a comparison of their explanatory power.

Even so, there is still the problem that exactly what it is that needs to be explained is defined wholly differently by the two communities. For the British analyst there is no point in trying to explain the foreign policies of all states; they are not comparable. For the US analyst, although you can move deductively from explanations of foreign policy *per se* to the explanation of one state's foreign policy, this is to be on the basis of generally applicable theory. As has already been stated, these differences reflect the markedly distinct intellectual traditions of the two countries and remain the major stumbling block to any reconciliation. In part the problem is that for the British approach it is comparison as such which is impossible; this makes discussion of the appropriate methods entirely secondary. Without an admission that comparative analysis is possible the two schools will remain far apart.

In conclusion then, the divergence between the two communities derives from a set of academic and a set of institutional factors. To this extent, they do not share similar problems, nor do they see the task of foreign policy analysis in the same way. The major cause for the differences between them would seem to lie in the separate intellectual traditions of the two communities and, without some convergence at this level, the two schools seem set to follow their own, distinct paths.

Indeed a more pessimistic development might follow from the continued fall in popularity of the comparative foreign policy analysis approach in the United States (see Smith, 1985). It has been on the decline since the mid-1970s, with the foreign policy of the Reagan administration encouraging a return to a realist, state-centric analysis. The theoretical deficiencies of this analysis are overshadowed by it seeming exactly the right approach to a world once again divided by military issues. The paradox is that the current international system, with the dominance of both economic and political-military cleavages, requires theories of foreign policy behaviour to be more sophisticated, rather than less.

4
The Methodology of International Relations

MICHAEL NICHOLSON

The methodology of International Relations concerns not the study of international relations itself, but the ways and methods by which the discipline is studied. However, what is studied and how it is studied are clearly interdependent issues. Certain methods are appropriate for answering certain kinds of questions, but if these questions are themselves thought to be illegitimate for some reason or another, the methods become superfluous. This is not merely a pedantic clarification. There are fundamental disagreements among scholars of International Relations concerning the very nature of the knowledge we can have about the international system – or indeed any other aspect of social behaviour – and this necessarily permeates the study of the discipline, involving discussions about what we think the discipline is.

While this chapter specifically concerns the study of International Relations, it could well be written about political science in general. My examples would clearly be different were I dealing with the whole of political science, but the underlying argument would be unaffected.

Roughly speaking, we can say that there are some scholars who regard social scientific methods as appropriate tools for analysing International Relations, and some who do not, the latter relying instead on the so-called classical methods. Social scientific methods work on the basis that there are large classes of events to which common nouns are properly applied, and that the scope for the classification of things as 'similar', or 'the same' in crucial respects is relatively broad. Classical methods assume that classes of events are small, and that analysis should be carried out on an *ad hoc,* case-by-case basis, with relatively narrow scope for generalization (though presumably some degree of generalization must be thought possible, or common nouns would not be used at all). Conceivably there is some separate, distinguishable Marxist methodology, but I shall discuss this issue later.

Those who believe that the scope for generalization is limited, will clearly use the methods of the historian or of any analyst who focuses on particular situations. Those who are ready to generalize, however, have a broader set of tools at their command. If classes of events are thought to be significant, they need to discover the size of those classes (for example, how many wars occurred in a particular period of time), record any interesting sub-classes (how many of those wars were fought by single states and how many by states in alliance with each other), and perhaps look to see whether different classes are related (did countries in an alliance fight more often than countries which were not). The point I am trying to make is that what is necessary for any social scientific analysis is that data should be collected in an appropriate form, namely in the form of statistics and measurements or, more generally, in the form of classes of events which are deemed 'similar'; for clearly without the facts in such a form we can do nothing. The collection of such data has cost a considerable amount of effort in the recent past.

The social scientific method also involves the belief that the world is structured and that events follow a pattern rather than occurring haphazardly. The 'hypothetic-deductive method', widely used in the natural sciences, works on the principle that some generalizations are true and that the consequences of these can be anticipated by making a chain of logical deductions. The theory then stands or falls as a whole, for if some of the deductions are found to be untrue when tested against the evidence, then something in the initial postulates must also be false. Thus the task is one of theory construction, where theory is applied to classes of events and not to isolated single events. In a general sense, then, there is the assertion that social behaviour is something which can be analysed in the same way as the behaviour of inanimate objects. Whether this is true or not is of course a fundamental question which runs through the whole of the philosophy of the social sciences. (For a classical anti-social science statement, see Winch, 1958; for an extreme scientific position, see Hempel, 1965. With specific reference to International Relations, see Reynolds, 1973, and Nicholson, 1983.)

It is commonly held that the social scientific approach is predominantly a North American one, whereas the classical approach is predominantly British. This might be regarded, with justice, as a very Anglocentric view of the discipline, particularly inappropriate considering the subject-matter as agreed by scholars of all philosophical predispositions; but I must refer such critics to the title of the book, and hence the implied brief to which I write. With some qualifications, I think this characterization of the practice of the discipline within the two countries is justified. The importance of scholars working in the social science tradition seems to be greater in the United States than in Britain. However, these are differences of emphasis only. Further, I must confess that my justification for this assertion is intuitive and is not based on hard data.

Nevertheless, it seems to be the case that a higher proportion of United States scholars work in the social science tradition than is the case in Britain. As a consequence of this, expertise in that particular method is more respected in that country, and teaching as well as research reflects this emphasis. However, while I do not think that this is an accident (and, for reasons that I shall discuss below, the degree of difference can easily be exaggerated), I would assert it to be an accident that one of the doyens of the classical tradition was Hans Morgenthau (see Morgenthau, 1978) from Chicago, while one of the founders of the social science tradition was Lewis Fry Richardson, an Englishman who never went to the United States in his life. In fact Richardson's work was largely neglected in his lifetime, and his books, edited by Americans, were published posthumously (see Richardson, 1960a and 1960b). His significance was first recognized in the United States, where he is still more highly regarded than in Britain. However, there are too many American scholars in the classical tradition for it to be regarded as a purely British preserve, while the social sciences have crept into all but the most resilient quarters in Britain.

I

At this point, I wish to elaborate my assertions about the underlying presuppositions of a social science of international behaviour. It is, after all, as well to understand the argument fully before attempting to discern systematic national differences in approaches to the methodology of International Relations. Suppose an analyst considers the hypothesis that wars occur in cycles; that is, that there are periods in which wars begin, followed by periods in which only a few wars start. Having recorded all the wars that arise within a particular period of time, the analyst will then carry out statistical analysis to determine whether any apparent concentration of wars during that period could, in all probability, be attributed to chance, or requires a positive explanation. Richardson believed that he had, in fact, demonstrated the randomness or chance hypothesis (Richardson, 1960b). This raises two problems. The first is the technical problem of what techniques can be used to detect randomness in time. For this particular problem there is little disagreement about what are the appropriate techniques. However, there is then the more fundamental question of whether wars are a sufficiently uniform category of events to be handled in this way. Our statistical techniques may be impeccable, but if they are applied to data which are incommensurable in relevant respects then the results are, in the strict sense of the word, meaningless: that is, they are not false, they are nonsense.

To illustrate this point more precisely, let us consider another category of behaviour where there seems to be little dispute about the suitability of statistical analysis, namely road accidents. These are relatively clearly definable events; if a person is injured there is rarely any doubt as to whether the injury was sustained in a road accident or in some other way. Occasionally there may be doubts about whether an apparent accident is deliberate or not, but this must apply to a small fraction of the total number of accidents. There are further occasions where it may be difficult to decide whether an incident should be regarded as one accident or more, as in a motorway pile-up. Again these are not a large proportion of the total. In many parts of the world the data on road accidents is good, for few go unreported or, conversely, get reported twice.

It would be widely agreed that we can properly categorize a road accident in the south west of England in 1983 and one in north of Scotland in 1963 as similar events. If they are similar in many respects then it is proper to look for systematic differences. We can consider the subsets of accidents, whether a driver was under the influence of alcohol, was in a particular age group, whether the car was of a certain age and so on, to see what conditions appear to increase the chance of an accident. But we can only usefully carry out such analysis if we accept that the basic set we begin with can be regarded as a common category of behaviour in some important senses of the word. This is accepted in the case of road accidents, along with the fact that in many countries the data on them is tolerably complete.

Let us compare this with the phenomenon which understandably and properly absorbs much of the attention of International Relations scholars – war. Consider the wars that have taken place in the world since the start of the nineteenth century. We should be careful to distinguish between practical questions and theoretical questions. A desirable quality, if not an absolute requirement, of statistical analysis is to have a complete set of data, or at least to have good reason for assuming that missing facts occur on a random and not a systematic basis. There are difficulties with this in certain parts of the world and indeed it is possible that some wars have not been recorded, or are incompletely described in some pertinent respect, failing to give the number of fighting on each side, for example. However, for the nineteenth century this is no longer a serious worry, and while the data may not be up to the standard of contemporary road accident data in many states (though far better of course than road accident data in the earlier part of the same period), the efforts of various compilers give us confidence that the data is tolerably complete and appropriately categorized (see Richardson, 1960a, 1960b; Wright, 1942; and Singer and Small, 1972).

However, let us return to the difficult question of deciding whether the common noun 'war' in fact denotes the same sort of activity in different contexts. In what sense, for example, is the American Civil War the same sort of activity as the Second World War? In the case of the Second World War, how many wars were there? Could it be regarded as a collection of several wars fought simultaneously (at least after 1939), or was it just one war (see Holt et al., 1978)? When did it start? The year 1931 would gain some advocates; 1936 would be favoured by many Spaniards and some Europeans, particularly those on the political left; September 1939 would have the approval of most of Europe, and of Europhile Americans; but 1941 is the official date in the Soviet Union, while some Americans might even insist on 7 December, 1941. If one sees the Second World War as a collection of wars this is not disturbing. If it is thought to be a single event then it is problematic. But if it is to be regarded as several wars, how many wars were there? Was Britain at war with Vichy France (it did, after all, sink its fleet)? Laval appeared to think so, but many Vichy, including probably Pétain, seemed to think of Britain as a future, if somewhat distasteful, ally. But I think I have made my point. When there are allies in a war there can be some ambiguity as to whether they are fighting the same war for the same purposes and whether the whole event can be regarded as a unity. Presumably Britain and France, despite different global aims, can be seen in this light in the First World War. With other allied forces the case is much more problematic – the USA and USSR in the Second World War being prime examples.

To illustrate my point above I have taken one of the most difficult examples. All accidents are similarly unique. We could assert that a twenty-car pile-up on a motorway was just as different from an incident in which a car collides with a cow on a country road, as the Napoleonic wars (usually put in the plural interestingly enough, unlike other good candidates for the category of a multiple event) are from the Korean war, or either from the Zulu wars. Most social events, or natural events outside the laboratory, are extremely complex and we should perhaps not be too struck by the heterogeneity of mankind in its more lethal methods. It is possible that the common factor is the killing of human beings and that the rest is relatively incidental.

However, the point I wish to emphasize is that the methodology we use to analyse events is not just a matter of taste; it also depends on one's view of the world, and the assumption that at least some sub-categories of war (if not all) can appropriately be regarded as common phenomena. Ultimately, whether we wish to classify some things as similar or not is a metaphysical rather than a scientific issue. We can, however, hope for some consistency. It seems that some people of the classical persuasion will accept accident statistics without a qualm, but will express great concern at handling war in the same way. It may be that wars are more heterogeneous than accidents (if any criterion for heterogeneity could be devised) but the problem is similar. Hence, for those who would accept the legitimacy of the former but not the latter, I think it is appropriate to ask for reasons which must support the argument that wars have gone beyond some boundary of heterogeneity which makes social scientific analysis inappropriate. However, I see no reason why this should be so.

As remarked earlier, a broad view of the possibilities of categorizing events leads on the one hand to the generation of data in classes and on the other to the generation of theories of processes, where theories are not simply haphazard collections of generalizations in which the hypotheses are about classes of events, but are logically interconnected generalizations. This tradition is strong in, say, economics but relatively new in International Relations, with Lewis Fry Richardson as its progenitor, but with subsequent developments again occuring primarily in the United States (see Rapoport, 1957, and Newman, 1956).

This tradition in the social sciences is often called the deductive theory or formal modelling tradition, and is obviously intimately bound up with the statistical tradition as it relies on the same methodological presuppositions. One simply searches for generalizations spurred on by a mixture of faith and common sense, hoping that statistical regularities will confirm one's suppositions about social behaviour. In this case one has isolated generalizations which are of use, but which are unrelated to anything else. Deductive theory involves setting up certain postulates about a behaviour and seeing what can be deduced from them, and then testing the system of postulates and deductions as a whole. This sort of analysis is widespread in economics. 'Economic theory' normally refers to theory which is carried out in this methodological framework. It is important to note that as far as this sort of methodology is concerned, there is no distinctive American or British school in economics. The grip of deductive theory in other disciplines is more tenous but does exist, for example in psychology.

The tradition of formal modelling introduced into political science and International Relations, by Richardson in particular, owes some of its origins to the natural sciences and surprisingly, perhaps, to biology. This surprise might dwindle when we recognize that scholars in that field were themselves involved in the task of trying to put biology on a more formal basis. Formal modellers used mathematical techniques to describe biological processes, commonly patterns of change. Lotka in Chicago in *Elements of Mathematical Biology* (see Lotka, 1956), was a pioneer, as was D'Arcy Thompson (a Scotsman) in *Growth and Form* (Thompson, 1917). Rashevsky, also from Chicago, wrote and worked extensively on the development of mathematical models and made a foray, perhaps not entirely well advised, into the social sciences with *The Mathematical Biology of Social Behavior* (see Rashevsky, 1951, 1968). Despite the naivety of much of the material, it is nevertheless intriguing to read for its attempt to link social behaviour with psycho-physics and indeed its endeavours to deduce much of the former from the latter. Rashevsky makes deductions from a parsimonious set of postulates to reach extravagant, rich, if regrettably often preposterous, conclusions.

His attempt to build social sciences out of psycho–physics, while not intrinsically outrageous, remains an impossibly ambitious programme at the present time. His ignorance of a great deal of the work carried out in the social sciences gives the book a refreshing charm. While his project lies substantially undisturbed to this day (perhaps fortunately), the methodological principle of using mathematical methods to pose and answer questions to which these methods had not earlier been applied has most certainly flourished. In economics it has, of course, always been there and many of the mathematical practitioners in International Relations owe an explicit debt to the economic tradition. However, in a more general social science tradition these styles of approach were drawn on and developed by various scholars, perhaps particularly by Herbert Simon. *Models of Man* is a relatively early collection of his papers in which he applies mathematical methods to many fields of social behaviour (but not International Relations) and rivals Richardson in his bold mathematical imagination (see Simon, 1957). Also in this tradition is Richardson who, like Rashevsky, came in from the outside with scant knowledge of the social sciences (though in the inter-war period when Richardson was doing a lot of his work, the social sciences, it should be remembered, were at a noticeably earlier stage of their development) and with great verve applied the techniques with which he was familiar as a distinguished meteorologist to the problems of violence and war – or, as he referred to them, 'Deadly Quarrels'. Unlike Rashevsky, whose impact was on a relatively few people like Simon and Rapoport (Rapoport, 1960), Richardson is quite properly regarded as being significant in his own right and is widely cited. It is generally accepted that his *Statistics of Deadly Quarrels* and *Arms and Insecurity* are seminal works in the deductive theory of International Relations (Richardson, 1960a, 1960b).

In his deductive models, Richardson posits a relationship between various variables and then observes the consequences of such relationships being true. In his most important model, the models of an arms race, he suggests that the rate of rearmament of a state is positively influenced by the level of a perceived opponent's arms, and negatively influenced by the level of a state's own arms. He poses this in the form of a differential equation: $dy/dt = ax - by + c$, where y and x are the level of arms of two countries and a, b and c are constants (the d is an operator of course). By taking this equation, along with the equation for the other state, Richardson is able to make all sorts of interesting, and sometimes counter-intuitive, statements about arms races. Notice, however, that this model posits a relationship which seems plausible, without going further back and deducing that relationship from a set of goals which the state decision-makers are presumed to follow. This relationship is the starting-point of the analysis. In this way it is reminiscent of various trade cycle models in economics which proceed in the same way. For example, investment is seen as a function of the change in consumption over the same preceding period (a relationship called the accelerator), without going further back into the relationship to deduce it rigorously from a prior set of goals (though the accelerator follows from the profit maximizing assumption, and at full employment and under a wide variety of cost conditions). These models are known as *process models*.

However, there is another type of formal model used in International Relations which posits that all actors pursue some sort of goal (though it might be rather vague and flexible and embodied in some cover-all concept like 'utility') and then works out the consequences of following these goals under various conditions and in a 'rational' manner.

It was from this persepctive, and explicitly in the social science traditions, that the 'Theory of Games' was devised. Originally published in 1944, but gaining in impact after the war, *The Theory of Games and Economic Behavior* (Von Neumann and Morgenstern, 1953) rapidly established itself as a classic, not only in economics but in all areas of the social sciences. It was essentially a theory of interacting decisions and concentrated on the problem of making decisions in a conflicting environment where the participants were regarded as rational. As its names implies it marked a major change in the form of analysis. In Richardson's models, the cognitive component was relegated and the emphasis was on the consequences of taking decisions according to particular rules, without analysing decision-making as such. Indeed Richardson described his arms race model as the analysis of what happens if people do not stop to think. In the theory of games it is supposed that actors have goals which they pursue according to certain principles, even if the environment in which they make their choices might be seen as unduly narrow.

The significance of the theory of games for a whole host of decision-making problems was quickly realized. The theory as it stood was couched in mathematical terms which were not readily accessible to many economists (much less to decision-makers), but in due course more simplified statements of the theory were made, conspicuously in one work of exposition which has become a minor classic in its own right – *Games and Decisions* by Luce and Raiffa (1957). The relevance to International Relations was obvious, at least after a gap of some years during which the theory was slowly absorbed into the general intellectual consciousness. It was in America that the first interpretations appeared. Close on one another came Schelling's *Strategy of Conflict* (1960), Boulding's *Conflict and Defense* (1962), and Rapoport's *Fights, Games and Debates* (1960). All three dealt in some detail with the theory of games, while Schelling's book was devoted primarily to game theory. Schelling's work was critical in a number of ways. In general he thought that classical game theory relied too much on mathematical considerations, whereas he believed that contextual issues were also relevant in practical situations. For example, a river might be regarded as a boundary even if it did not divide an area strictly in two parts, whereas two equal parts might, from a mathematical point of view, be regarded as a kind of natural division. The mathematical considerations of the theory of games were usually somewhat more sophisticated than this – part of Schelling's complaint was that they were too sophisticated.

All three books have acquired considerable status as classics, and can still be read with profit and not merely as historical curiosities. Schelling's book was received in Britain with some caution and even a little embarrassment. Schelling might be called a liberal conservative and be said to be in the business of arms control rather than peace research (two terms I wish to keep a little vague). His message was therefore well received among liberal conservatives in Britain, who were nevertheless unhappy that congenial conclusions should be reached by uncongenial methods. Hedley Bull (1977), would-be scourge of behaviouralism and other noxious doctrines, claimed that the results could quite easily have been derived without the rest of the apparatus, which convinced those who wished to be convinced, but failed to convince those who were enthusiastic about the method, if less enthusiastic about the conclusions. Rapoport and Boulding were both strongly in the peace research tradition, both hoping, if in Rapoport's case rather pessimistically, that science could be called in to save the world, whose continued existence seemed to them, as to many others, to be problematic.

The question is, of course, was it an accident that all three writers were American (though only Schelling was born in America while Rapoport subsequently re-emigrated)? Was that more or less important than the fact that none of them was an International

Relations specialist, and that all had professional concerns in more than one discipline?

While Schelling, albeit critically, was trying to draw out from the abstract and sometimes abstruse structure of the theory of games something which was more readily interpretable in terms of the international system, Boulding and Rapoport were doing the same, but were also endeavouring to amalgamate the two traditions of formal modelling, and direct them towards the analysis of the international system. Karl Deutsch, a German-Czech immigrant to the US who unusually in this area (and for that time) had a formal training in political science, had earlier analysed the problem of nationalism (1953) in a social scientific framework and subsequently carried out a substantial amount of work in the social science tradition (see Merritt and Russett, 1981). At roughly the same time, Guetzkow in Chicago was introducing the techniques of mixed man–computer simulation into International Relations (Guetzkow and Valadez, 1981), while the major data collection programmes were getting under way: for example David Singer's project on the correlates of war (Singer and Small, 1972). These were major efforts to expand the statistical data available on the international system which, despite the heroic efforts of Quincy Wright (1942) and Richardson (1960a, 1960b), were then, but not now, woefully inadequate.

II

These developments were alien to all but a small number of scholars in the British community of International Relations, but it is as well to remember that they were scarcely welcomed by a considerable number of US scholars either. The idea that International Relations was being practised in the United States by a community of social scientists is grossly misleading.

It is possibly better to ask not whether there is a specifically American approach to International Relations, but rather, why has the social science tradition in International Relations flourished better in the United States than in Britain? As stated earlier I would accept that the social science tradition has developed more fully in North America than in the United Kingdom, therefore the question becomes a proper one and also an interesting one. One possible answer is simply that it is entirely accidental that formal methodologists have tended to be American. It is not foolish to suggest that the equal numbers of traditionalists and scientists at least in the United Kingdon are quite fortuitous. There are relatively few International Relations scholars in Britain, a small enough group for chance to play a significant role. However, while I think this could be an important factor it is surely not the only consideration. We must try to offer further reasons for the greater significance of science methodology in the United States.

The mind-game of speculating how Karl Deutsch or Anatol Rapoport would have fared if they had come to Britain instead of the United States in the immediate pre-war years is intriguing. That the result of this mind-game, in the case of this author, results in them going at some stage after the war to the United States is, of course, as much a comment on the mind of the author as on the state of the world. Given this, I wish then to suggest non-accidental reasons why this should be so.

A variant of the accident hypothesis would be that it was not an accident of people but of money. During the 1950s and 1960s the American universities were wealthier and more ready to take the risks which novel approaches to International Relations (or anything else) involved. In its brief moments of glory, in what now seems to be regrettably like a ten-year abberration, the British scene was also innovative and ready to break away from established academic conventions. It would be too cynical to suggest that money alone is the key to an innovation, but there is no doubt that it helps.

It is also argued that the underlying reasons for the success of social scientific methodology in the United States is that since 1945 (or really since 1949) the United States has accepted a role as one of the major world powers. (This was in marked contrast to the views of the inter-war period when many Americans hoped that the rest of the world would simply go away.) As a result, there is said to have been an urge to develop a way of looking at the international system which would be useful in pursuing this role. This is only partly true. British journals and British conferences seem to be more immediately policy oriented than their American counterparts, which would incline one against this point of view. There is, for example, little in the work of Rapoport or Boulding which affords any practical hints for the would-be policy-maker. They argued strongly that, by understanding the structure of the international system, we might be able to alter it and render it less lethal. I think none of the scholars in this tradition thought this would be an easy or a quick job; indeed, quite the contrary.

Nevertheless, behind the caution of the social scientists

commonly lay the belief, reminiscent of nineteenth-century optimism, that scientific knowledge was a necessary if not a sufficient condition for progress. A significant group of British academics was temperamentally opposed to this. The opposition divides into two logically independent, but possibly psychologically related, points of view: firstly a general attitude of pessimism, and secondly a distrust of the social sciences, perhaps in any field, and certainly in International Relations. The pessimism is most clearly shown in the work of Martin Wight (see Wight, 1977, 1978), who appeared to hold the view that the international scene was totally wicked, but that there was little we could do about it. It is not the fact that Martin Wight was British that is relevant here – this could surely be an accident – but the fact that he had an enormous impact on many British thinkers, who appear to have been particularly influenced by his doctrine of Christian pessimism. The distrust of social science is not logically related to pessimism. As I have already pointed out, whether one thinks the methods of the social sciences are applicable to the study of social behaviour in any significant degree, and in particular to the study of very complex social systems such as the international system, depends in part on one's view of the nature of social behaviour, and the nature of social knowledge. There are doubtless many cheerful scholars who deny the possibility of a social science of international behaviour, while many social scientists, like Rapoport, are pessimistic about the future of the world. However, there is some tendency for these two views to go together. Clearly, a social scientist offers some form of hope for restructuring the world. The hope may be for something in the distant future, far too distant for it to have any current relevance, and possibly after the nuclear doomsday has already occurred, making it irrelevant. The knowledge is not here yet but the social scientist believes that it is researchable. The sceptics argue that it is not researchable, because it is not knowable. If one is determined to be pessimistic then one is unlikely to be sympathetic towards novel approaches. The scepticism of many British academics in International Relations inhibits the progress of the discipline. There is a fine balance between the scepticism which forces the purveyors of new methods to justify their techniques, and the scepticism which finally makes those purveyors give up in disgust and go in search of a warmer reception elsewhere.

III

Another tradition of thought within International Relations could be called the radical tradition – sometimes loosely called the Marxist tradition, though its link with Marx is tenuous. From a methodological point of view it is not clear that there is anything specifically different about this tradition – no particular dialectical method, for example, seems to be apparent. In the writings of people such as Galtung, (a Norwegian in origin) the methodology is clearly that of the social sciences (see Galtung, 1975, 1976, 1978). The interest of radical scholars has been to direct academics towards different problems in International Relations – towards dependency and asymmetric relations in particular, and away from the traditional concern of all schools with the great power conflict. This is not a methodological issue but a question of focus. It can be a source of disagreement among scholars, quite apart from their methodological position, and thus falls outside the scope of this chapter. However, it is worth remarking that much interesting work in this tradition, though often written in the English language, has been carried out outside Britain and the United States.

Throughout this chapter I have discussed the question of international political behaviour: what people do, what they ought to do. There are other questions concerning international political obligation and the right of sovereignty which are more in the domain of classical political theory applied at an international level. Though obviously dealing with international relations these issues involve different kinds of questions and methodologies for looking at these problems, and I do not intend to examine them here. There is a group of scholars, in one way or another associated with the London School of Economics, who are particularly involved in this work, but whether this is a specifically British way of looking at these problems and whether it is a particularly British concern, I am not able to say (see Donelan, 1978; Mayall 1982). Most of these scholars in fact share a scepticism about social scientific methods, and share both this scepticism and an interest in problems of obligation with the older classicists in the British tradition. However, a coincidence of views is not inevitable. A concern to investigate the nature of the ethical obligation for rich countries to provide economic aid to poor countries can be an issue of interest to an ardent social scientist and an ardent classicist. The issue of their different methodologies does not apply, though there are occasions where it seems to be implied that they do. Indeed, I have argued elsewhere that the more control one has over the environment, a control that the social scientist at least hopes for, then the more complex are the ethical problems. If one has no choice, then the question of making the correct choice from an ethical or from any other point of view is redundant.

The perceptive reader will have sensed a sympathy on the part of this writer (who is British) for the social scientific approach, rather casually called the American approach. That it is known as an American approach is due to the fact that this method is more respected and practised in America than in Britain but, beyond this, its national origins are unclear. I would in fact like to think of myself as in the tradition of writers such as Rapoport, Boulding and Simon, and, from earlier on, Richardson and the mathematical biologists. From a national point of view the tradition is a mixed one, with Americans well represented, but it is not a group that has been unduly troubled by problems of nationality. As mentioned earlier, the important point is that these scholars have also been untroubled by the boundaries of professional disciplines. The characteristic of the social science approach is that it has not been so much interdisciplinary but adisciplinary. Inasmuch as the social scientific development of International Relations has flourished more in the United States than in Britain, it can be attributed to greater willingness to tolerate the disciplinary eccentricity than is the case in Britain, except, perhaps, during the British universities' brief period of affluence.

Whether these national attributes are correct or not, they are rather impressionistic speculations. I have adduced little hard evidence, and in the last analysis, I do not regard them as important. What is important is that not all scholars are distracted by the immediate policy issues from the task of endeavouring to build a more soundly based social science of conflict behaviour, with the aim of reducing, and perhaps eliminating, some of the less savoury aspects of human social conduct. I believe that the arguments that such a science is in principle impossible are weak ones, but, if they turn out to be true, they are to be deplored rather than gloried in. In my experience, there is greater enthusiasm for social science in the United States than in Britain, an enthusiasm which seems to me to be wholly laudable.

5

The Systems Approach

RICHARD LITTLE

The systems approach to the analysis of International Relations has been so exhaustively attacked and defended that it seems, on the face of it, gratuitous to use this topic as a vehicle for exploring the Anglo-American divide. If conventional wisdom is accepted, then the nationalistic responses have been defined so clearly and with such monotonous regularity, that any attempt to plough the furrow again is to invite bored indifference. Yet, at the risk of seeming deliberately provocative, I want to argue that the prevailing conception of systems thinking is inadequate, and that the presumed attitudes of the British and American academic communities are inaccurate. It is necessary to reassess the nature of systems thinking and the role it plays in Britain and the United States. Once this is done, the evidence suggests that the significance of systems thinking for the analysis of international relations has been both underestimated and misunderstood.

Ever since its formation as an independent discipline, International Relations has been dominated by academics working in the United States. In this respect, International Relations is different from most social sciences. Although Americans now play a vital role in virtually all academic disciplines, the origins and seminal developments in subjects such as economics and sociology must be sought beyond the confines of the United States; the Scots and the French, the Germans and the Italians must all be represented in any account of how these disciplines have emerged. In the case of International Relations, on the other hand, it was the Americans, in the period after the First World War, who did most to foster the nascent discipline. Subsequent developments make familiar reading. An initial phase of utopian thinking gave way after the Second World War to an era of realism, when the Americans came to terms with the immutable fact of power. Having absorbed this lesson, a new generation of Americans, observing the pervasive influence of behaviouralism, made serious attempts to establish the scientific credentials of International Relations. Systems theory was to provide the master plan for this new venture.

According to this American view of how the discipline has developed, the role of the British has, with a few notable exceptions, such as Carr (1939), been peripheral. However, it is acknowledged that it was the British who mounted the rearguard assault on behavouralism. Although there were plenty of Americans who were unhappy with the way the discipline was developing under the behaviouralists, it was from the shores of Britain that the criticisms were most clearly articulated. But the Americans successfully managed to absorb these criticisms. The tactic employed was to argue that the traditionalists and the behaviouralists must exploit each other's work. As Knorr and Rosenau put it, the traditionalists should 'employ rather than deplore' the quantitative findings of the behaviouralists, while the latter should 'use rather than abuse' the qualitative insights of the former (1969, p.18). By casting the debate in this light, the two schools of thought were seen to be compatible rather than competitive.

The British never accepted that the debate could be resolved in this way. But as far as the Americans were concerned, the debate was over. British academics continued to snipe on the sidelines and to mock the naivety of the American behaviouralists who ventured across the Atlantic, but because of the American hegemony, criticism was stemmed until the Americans themselves recently began to question the methodological and epistemological assumptions which underpin behaviouralism and systems thinking (Spegele, 1982).

It is ironic, yet wholly predictable, that International Relations, of all disciplines, should appear in the words of one observer to be 'as American as apple pie' (Gareau, 1981, p.779). The dominance of the United States is undeniable, but the effect of their position in the discipline has, almost inevitably, been scarcely appreciated. Nevertheless, the consequences have been important and unfortunate. In the first place, as a result of the inconclusive way in which the debate between the behaviouralists and the traditionalists was resolved, the philosophical assumptions of both positions were left largely unexamined. This has meant, in the second place, that both schools of thought have operated on the basis of some quite crucial misconceptions. For a start, both have accepted that there is a natural equation to be drawn between systems thinking and a scientific approach to analysis. Furthermore, adherents to behaviouralism and traditionalism have uncritically accepted a positivist conception of science. Although positivism is a notoriously difficult idea to pin down, at the very least it presupposes that the task of science is to develop theory which can be evaluated using scientific method. Behaviouralists assume that positivism has a crucial role to play in the social sciences, while traditionalists argue that social science requires its own methodology. Nevertheless, when attacking behaviouralism, trenchant British critics, such as Reynolds (1973), invariably accept the validity of the positivist conception of science.

It is almost certainly true to say that when the British and Americans were discussing the merits and demerits of behaviouralism, they were unaware of the ferment going on among philosophers of science about the nature and status of science. The positivist view was accepted by default. Although attempts have been made (Keat and Urry, 1975) to explore the major rivals to positivism, such as conventionalism and realism, the implications of this debate have hardly touched International Relations. Kuhn's idea of a paradigm (1970) has been examined as in every other discipline, but the full implications of his conventionalist view of science have never been explored, perhaps because, as Vasquez (1983) has argued, there has been an absence of competing paradigms. Moreover, the realist conception of science has never been considered in International Relations; realism only denotes power politics.

The overall argument of this chapter can now be made clear. It seeks to invert the conventional view that systems thinking has been an exclusively American phenomenon designed to establish International Relations as a science. The argument will be developed in three parts. First, there will be an examination of the role played by systems thinking in the United States. It will be suggested that although the influence of systems thinking was initially very important in the American approach to International Relations, the long-term effect of positivism has been to undermine the relevance of systems thinking. Second, there will be an examination of the role played by systems thinking in the United Kingdom. Here it is suggested that the historicist and idealist approaches to the discipline have served to reinforce the significance of systems thinking. Finally, in the third section, it will be suggested that in recent years a new world systems approach has developed. Although this new school of thought has had a major impact on a variety of social sciences, its influence on the study of International Relations in Britain and the United States has been slight. It is argued that this is due to lack of interest, because the world systems approach presupposes a realist view of science and is, therefore, at odds with both idealism and positivism. It is concluded that the discipline on both sides of the Atlantic could benefit by looking more closely at this approach and the related realist philosophy of science.

Positivism and Systems Theory in the United States

The study of International Relations in the United States has been preoccupied with systems theory ever since the late 1950s, when the first attempts were made to put the discipline on a scientific footing. The link is not coincidental. Advocates of systems theory have consistently argued that their approach provides the only possible basis for developing a science of international politics (Kaplan, 1957; Waltz, 1979). This assertion, however, can be contested. Within the social sciences, there have always been two competing epistemological positions. One, variously referred to as reductionist, individualist or behaviouralist, seeks to develop explanations at the level of the participants in a social system. The other, identified as holist, collectivist or systemic, seeks to develop explanations at a higher, more abstract or structural level of analysis (O'Neill, 1973). Although early advocates of a scientific approach to the study of international politics tended to opt for the latter position, they failed to spell out its full implications. Indeed, McClelland argues that Kaplan's exposition (1957), 'served both to popularize and render mysterious 'systems theory' (1970, p.73). Both the popularity and the mystery have persisted.

The role of systems theory in the American study of International Relations raises three questions which will be all examined in this section. First, why did the desire to develop a scientific approach to International Relations establish such a firm grip in the United States, given its failure to secure more than a tenuous toe-hold in the United Kingdom? Second, why did the Americans adopt a systemic rather than a reductionist approach in their endeavour to set up a science of International Relations? The decision is particularly significant because the behavioural movement in the social sciences which emerged after 1945 tended to favour reductionism. Third, what is the current status of systems theory among American specialists in International Relations? The move to develop a science of International Relations described in this section will be referred to as positivism rather than behaviouralism, because it will be argued that American social scientists of both holistic and reductionist persuasions have tended to draw upon a positivist conception of science.

The Rise of Positivism

It has been generally recognized that International Relations was one of the last bastions of traditionalism in the United States to hold out against the advances of positivism. To a large extent this can be explained by the influence of diplomatic history and international law on the origins of the discipline. They encouraged the belief that the essential elements of International Relations were fully comprehended. Problems in the international arena arose not because of an absence of understanding, but because of conflicts of interest. The role of diplomacy was to manage these conflicts, and the role of law was to help reform the system. The study of International Relations was restricted to providing a retrospective analysis of international conflicts using a historical method.

In the post-war era, as the realists made their mark on the discipline and the study of International Relations became more firmly established, there was growing dissatisfaction among the younger academics with the influence of the historical method. They wished to make a greater contribution to the understanding of contemporary events, and the historical method, far from helping in this exercise, seemed to pose an obstacle. As McClelland noted, while historians insisted they had the 'best possible access to this area of knowledge', the absence of the kind of documentary evidence which was crucial for their methodology meant that all they could produce was, at best, 'journalistic descriptions of high quality' (1958, p.230).

Others must also have experienced this frustration. But why only in the United States did the community as a whole respond by rejecting traditional methods and opening its arms to the methods of natural science? There is no straightforward answer to this question, except to show, as Crick has done, that the desire to use scientific methods not only to understand social reality, but also to bring about change, is deeply rooted in the American tradition. As Crick puts it, from the end of the nineteenth century, '"progress" and "science" become the master-concepts of a distinctively American social thought' (1959, p.38). Crick relates his thesis to the development of political science, but there is no doubt that specialists in International Relations were all part of the same tradition. From this perspective, therefore, what needs to be explained is not the adoption of positivism but the earlier attraction of realism. As Weltman argues, it is the 'brief flowering in the United States of so antipathetic an outlook as realism with its denial of progress and of the utility of scientific rationality which is the curiosity requiring explanation' (1982, p.37).

In the majority of the social sciences, according to Crick, Americans had for most of this century seen science as the 'technologist of progress' (1959, p.68). Scientists were depicted as problem-solvers, moving diligently and systematically to uncover the mysteries of the natural world. An important aspect of problem-solving was the ability to predict behaviour, and closely associated with prediction was the capacity to manipulate and control. Although philosophers of science have dismissed the suggestion that science presupposes a predictive ability (Toulmin, 1961) as Crick notes, for American social scientists prediction has frequently been regarded as 'the most important criterion of a genuinely scientific theory' (1959, p.179).

It is not difficult to see why those Americans dissatisfied with the historical method would be so attracted by this image of science. The dissatisfaction coincided with the emergence of nuclear deterrence and crisis diplomacy. It seemed obvious that if it was possible to develop a predictive capacity then the danger inherent in crises involving two nuclear powers could be reduced. At the same time, once international affairs were understood more fully, it would be possible to precipitate more permanent reforms. One of the most remarkable admissions relating to this belief in the potential for prediction, and reflecting aims derived from science fiction, has come from Rummel, the author of a complex cross-national factor analysis, who noted that 'of course, anyone in the know must realize that the Dimensions of Nations project has been designed to provide the same mathematical forecasts Hari Seldon provided his followers in *Foundation*' (1976, p.13). (In his novels, Seldon provided accurate predictions of events many years in the future.)

In addition to the excitement generated by the prospect of

predicting the future and staving off a nuclear holocaust, there was a more prosaic reason for the attraction of positivism. It relates to the fact that academia in the United States is a highly competitive enterprise. It quickly became apparent in the post-war years that, as in the natural sciences, behavioural research required extensive funding so that individuals and institutions came to be assessed by their capacity to generate research grants. Prestige was soon related directly to the size of grants given to an institution. If International Relations hoped to maintain the position it was beginning to establish in the post-war era as an independent branch of the social sciences, then there was no alternative but to develop a positivist orientation.

The Rise of Systems Theory

If the influence of positivism was irresistible to academics in International Relations, then the emphasis on a systemic approach, is, at first sight, more surprising. After the Second World War, positivism in American social science adopted a reductionist, or as it was then called, behavioural focus. The reason is not difficult to identify. During the first half of the twentieth century there had been major advances in research techniques, statistical methods and technology. These three factors all facilitated the task of quantification. It now became relatively easy to measure and compute research findings on human behaviour. Nevertheless, some of the new enthusiasts did recognize that this emphasis on 'micro' activity created a problem. Eulau asked in the context of political science, for example, 'how meaningful statements about large systems can be made on the basis of inquiry into the behaviour of individual political actors?' (1967, p.46). However, he concluded optimistically that there was no logical reason why the analysis of complex systems could not be reduced to an analysis of their constituent members (1967, p.48).

However, this new breed of behaviouralists quickly began to run into criticism. It was argued that a fascination with statistical techniques was creating the illusion that quantification in itself was sufficient to generate scientific understanding. Unfortunately, the technical language associated with statistics fostered the illusion. Statisticians talk about 'significant relationships', 'explaining variance', 'controlling for a variable', and using an 'independent variable' for the purpose of 'prediction'. Significance, explanation, control and prediction all have technical meanings, which do not correspond to those in everyday use. Nevertheless, there was a tendency to translate the technical meaning of these terms into daily usage, giving the impression that the research being done was much more significant, in the non-statistical sense, than was actually the case. The research was attacked because it reflected barefoot empiricism and lacked any kind of theoretical formulation.

Holists and reductionists in the social sciences have always acknowledged the importance of theory in developing explanations. Moreover, they have tended to draw upon a common positivist conception of science – often without recognizing that there are other ways of characterizing science. A very clear exposition of positivism, which acknowledges that its roots can be traced back to the idealism of Kant, has been provided by Waltz. For him, the scientific enterprise involves the establishment of laws and theories. Laws 'identify invariant or probable associations' and represent 'facts of observation' (1979, p.56). Theories, on the other hand, are purely speculative and are designed to account for the existence of laws. Theories are not circumscribed by facts and can include concepts which only make sense in terms of theory. It follows that 'theory is not an edifice of truth and not a reproduction of reality'. Instead, it is a 'picture mentally formed of a bounded realm or domain of activity' (1979, p.8). Positivists have gone on to assert, moreover, that theories are necessarily 'underdetermined' by facts. As a consequence, it is perfectly possible to develop more than one theory to fit the same set of facts (Hesse, 1980).

Positivist critics of behaviouralism, therefore, focused on its failure to develop theory. It was to empiricism rather than reductionism that objections were made. Nevertheless, when searching for a way of overcoming the problems of empiricism, social scientists were drawn towards holism, which relies on the properties of a system, such as stratification or integration, to account for the behaviour of individuals. So, for example, the holist might wish to account for the different rates of suicide by relating suicide to the level of integration to be found in different communities. Integration is a non-observable property and constitutes a theoretical concept because it is an idea formulated by the analyst.

By the time International Relations began to shed its traditionalist image, criticism about the empiricist nature of behaviouralism was widespread and there was self-evident concern to ensure that the discipline should not be tarred with the empiricist brush. Adopting a holistic approach seemed to offer an obvious solution. Holism in other areas of social science was identified by a concern with the social system, and so it appeared that a holistic approach to International Relations could be achieved by studying the international system. The idea of an international system was already well established in the discipline and can be traced back to Grotius, who considered it necessary to view interactions among states from a holistic perspective (Wight, 1977, p.217). Moreover, concepts such as bipolarity and balance of power, which have traditionally been used to describe the international system, are obviously holistic formulations (Vasquez, 1983, p.80). There seem to be good grounds, then, to suggest that International Relations had always been drawn towards holistic explanations. This view has been endorsed by Frankel, who asserts that 'anybody who has systematically reflected about the nature of international reality will find much that is familiar to him in the systems analysis approach and may even discover that he has been employing it, like Moliere's Mr Jourdain when he discovered that all his life he had been employing prose' (1973, p.33). In their efforts to avoid empiricism, therefore, the new school of positivism adopted an approach which was perfectly familiar to the traditionalists in International Relations.

The Current Status of Systems Theory

In a recent survey of International Relations, Waltz (1979) concludes that almost none of the work carried out by the American positivists has succeeded in developing a systemic explanation. Given the vast number of studies that have been conducted ostensibly using a systems approach, this is an astonishing claim. Nevertheless, Waltz insists that although systems terminology is frequently used, these studies invariably resort to reductionist explanations. If Waltz's assessment is correct the question must be raised as to why so many social scientists have gone astray. One possible answer could be that positivism breaks down the distinction between holistic and reductionist explanations and as a consequence, paradoxically, Waltz's assessment is thereby confirmed, in the sense that the explanations are not systemic, and invalidated, in the sense that positivism nullifies the distinction between reductionism and holism.

In making this point, it is necessary to recognize that positivism is only one way of characterizing science. According to positivists, theory involves a set of ideas which transcend observation. In attempts to explicate further the essential dimensions of positivism, questions have been raised about the ontological status of the concepts which appear in theory. Harré, for example, argues that concepts such as a gene in genetic theory become 'nothing more than cyphers within the logical system, serving a formal role in binding together the laws into that system. To ask for the empirical meaning of a 'gene' as an entity would be a mistake, for its role is purely logical' (1972, p.54). One view of positivism has gone on to suggest that these theoretical entities should be given ontological priority over our observations (Spencer, 1982). But a more persuasive line of argument is that the effect of idealism on positivism is to collapse the distinction between epistemology and ontology. In other words, the key concepts used in a theory exist only in our mind, so that we cannot attack a theory on the grounds that the basic concepts are unable to be identified by observation. For the positivist, theory building depends upon establishing concepts for which there are no direct empirical referents. By the same token, these concepts are denied any ontological status (Williams, 1981). The purpose of theory is not to replicate reality, but to help us to explain it.

The influence of idealism is also apparent in the positivist's approach to systems analysis. For the positivist, a system is not endowed with any ontological status. It is not possible to touch or observe a system. It is an idea which the positivist uses to make sense of observed regularities. There is no economic or political system 'out there' to be discovered. Both of these systems only exist in the mind of the analyst. A system can best be defined as 'a picture mentally formed of a bounded realm or domain of activity' – Waltz's definition of a theory. For the positivist, there is no distinction to be drawn between a theory and a system. Moreover, because their components are mental products, without ontological status, it becomes perfectly possible to extend economic concepts to the political domain. For the positivist, there is no problem about establishing, for example, an economic theory of democracy (Downs, 1957). The use of economic concepts to explain political action has proved particularly irritating to anti-positivists (Morgenthau, 1970). This positivist takes it for granted that a theory developed in one context can be extended to another; a contagious theory of disease, for example, can be used to account for the spread of rumours. The reason, as Harré has pointed out, is because theoretical concepts are 'nothing more than cyphers'. This idea provides the basic impetus for general systems theory (Bertalanffy, 1971).

This line of argument suggests that the positivist view of theory transcends the distinction between holism and reductionism. So, for example, the positivist is quite happy to contemplate the theory of cognitive dissonance (Festinger, 1962) expressed in 'reductionist' terms to account for the behaviour of individual decision-makers in international politics (Axelrod, 1976), and in 'systemic' terms to account for change in international alliance patterns (Harary, 1961).

It makes no sense from a positivist perspective, therefore, to argue that there has been a failure either to accord the international system an ontological status (Little, 1977), or to develop an holistic explanation of International Relations (Waltz, 1979). If the argument set out here is correct, then, from the positivist's point of view, any description of an explanation as either holistic or reductionist fails to appreciate the true nature of theory. For the positivist, the use of systems terminology does no more than reflect a linguistic preference. Consequently, as Weltman notes, the use of systems in the American literature only denotes 'an inter-relationship' (1973, p.100). It follows, then, that a systems approach has had little effect on the study of International Relations in the United States since the emergence of positivism other than as a source of confusion.

Idealism and Systems Thinking in the United Kingdom

In comparison to the United States, the International Relations community in the United Kingdom is tiny, although it has grown substantially during the last twenty years. In contrast to the United States, there have been no pressures to develop a behavioural focus. Nevertheless, a few members of the community have shown an interest in moving the discipline along this track. A sympathetic analysis of the behavioural developments in the United States was provided by Frankel (1973); Reynolds (1971) produced an imaginative textbook which was organized around the divergence between a reductionist and a holistic approach to analysis; and Burton (1968) made extensive use of systems terminology in an early attempt to articulate the distortions and counter-productive consequences of a state-centric view of the world. However, there was little contact between these scholars and they were never likely to generate the support that was necessary to change the direction of International Relations in Britain.

There is, however, a more integrated group of academics in Britain who have been identified, albeit in the most caustic terms, as constituting a school of thought (Jones, 1981; Suganami, 1983). The school can be said to have originated with Toynbee, who, as Thompson has shown, developed a distinctive view of the subject, depicting it as 'Janus-headed': 'One type of international relations is that among communities within a civilization; another is among the civilizations themselves' (1956, p.372). This view of the discipline was accepted and propagated by Wight, an associate of Toynbee. It was not until the late 1950s, however, that there was a self-conscious attempt to establish a school of thought. At the prompting, ironically, of the Americans, a group was formed in Cambridge called The British Committee on the Theory of International Politics. Once formed, it was soon recognized that the group had the potential to develop an approach which was quite distinct.

The committee set itself the task of inquiring into the 'nature of the international state system' (Butterfield and Wight, 1966, p.11). Expressed in such bald terms, it is difficult to imagine how they hoped to distinguish themselves from other schools of thought. Indeed, the identifying features of this school have never been spelled out; they only emerge from an examination of the work completed. This work reveals at its centre a notion of explanation which, although idealist in form, operates at the opposite end of the spectrum to positivism. These academics had no difficulty in accepting that the task of the natural scientist was to develop theory which could account for observed regularities. Theories, in other words, resided in the mind of the analyst. Such an approach, however, is considered nonsensical in the context of social reality, where it is only possible to understand behaviour by examining the ideas of the people whose behaviour is being observed. The British Committee, therefore, was working from an idealist perspective associated with writers such as Teggart, with whose work Toynbee was certainly familiar (Thompson, 1955). Teggart advanced the conception of 'idea systems as a basis for the comparative study of man'. He argued that when we come to compare 'the differing groups that go to make up the human population of the globe, the distinguishing feature of any group will be, not its language, implements, or institutions, but its particular idea system, of which these other manifestations are varying expressions'. He went on to assert that:

Without exception, the products of human activity are expressions or aspects of the entire mental content of the group or individual. This mental content, moreover, is not to be conceived of as a mere assemblage of disparate units placed in juxtaposition, but as cohering in an idea system. Ideas are not simply accumulated or heaped up; on the contrary, every 'new' idea added not only modifies, but is in turn modified by the existing system into which it is incorporated. (1977, p.281)

In this way, a states-system must be formulated in terms of an idea system. The task of the theorist is to examine the components of this idea system and to show the relationship between behaviour and ideas. The positivist alternative of establishing analytical models is firmly rejected in favour of a 'commitment to the exploration, in as ordered manner as the evidence permits, of the thought already embodied and at work in practice' (Keens-Soper, 1978, p.40).

In addition to the idealist aspect of their approach, the committee was also influenced by historicism, which asserts that the customs and beliefs of any group are the product of historical experience. To understand these beliefs the essential task of the analyst is to 'penetrate the thought world of other times and places' (Bebbington, 1979, p.92). The committee accepted this position and acknowledged the great danger of misinterpreting reality, as the result of a failure to understand the ideas which were governing that reality. It follows from this, moreover, that the task of the analyst can never be completed, because as our ideas change, so it becomes necessary to reassess past ideas. Failure to do so can lead to misunderstanding and false explanations. It has been argued, for example, that analyses of attempts to establish deterrence in the 1930s in Britain have been distorted because of a failure to appreciate that there is little relationship between the current understanding of deterrence and the idea which prevailed in the 1930s (Smith, 1978). The importance of historicism in the group was stressed, in particular, by Butterfield (1931, p.9).

As far as the British Committee was concerned, therefore, the study of international theory involved an examination of the way ideas have affected international activity. An understanding of theory was seen to deepen as knowledge of these ideas was extended, and as the range of ideas increased. There was, as a consequence, also a commitment to comparative analysis. It was not considered sufficient to examine only the ideas associated with the European states-system.

For the British Committee, a states-system was an idea which emerged when states acknowledged the legitimacy of each other's existence. The complexity of the states-system was determined by the complexity of the ideas developed by its members to ensure that the system endured. While the committee acknowledged that there were a number of different states-systems, it was also asserted that the European states-system had generated the most sophisticated body of ideas. The balance of power, diplomacy, international law and sovereignty were all ideas which had only really flourished in the modern European states-system. Moreover, it was also argued that these ideas had only evolved slowly and with difficulty. Wight showed, for example, that the Greeks had failed to develop either a conception of international law or the balance of power (1977). The task of the theorist was to identify when these ideas emerged and to show how behaviour was affected before and afterwards. Butterfield, for example, has discussed how important it is not to impose our conception of the balance of power onto periods before the idea developed. He argues that: 'Since an idea can sometimes be illuminated by studying its negative, it may be useful to illustrate the effects of the absence of the doctrine of the balance of power' (1966, p. 153). He proceeds to explore how international politics looked to diplomats and analysts who had as yet failed to formulate the balance of power idea. In this way, he is able to reveal that the world looked quite different, and the interpretation of diplomatic behaviour is quite distinct, in an era when there was no conception of the balance of power.

There was, however, another dimension to the work of the British school adumbrated by Wight. The task of the theorist was not merely to use the historical method to explore the formulation and influence of ideas on practice in the states-system. It was also to assist in the process of developing new ideas. As Wight acknowledges, the absence of appropriate language precipitates a 'kind of recalcitrance of international relations to being theorized about'. As a consequence, the crucial debates about developments in the states-system, the 'stuff of international theory' according to Wight, were 'constantly bursting the bounds of the language in which we try to express it' (1966, p. 33). The only solution to this problem was, as theorists have done in the past, to develop new ideas and language to overcome these problems.

American positivists have, in the past, been very dismissive of the British school. Kaplan has even attacked Wight's work for being ahistorical. He suggested that a systems approach would help to rectify this problem (1976, p.5). Wight would certainly have rejected this charge. He argued that the committee's approach was not simply 'doing a different job from systems analysis . . . it does the same job with more judiciousness and modesty' (1966, p.32). This underestimates the contribution to systems thinking. The British have established that a system impinges upon reality only when a group of independent actors conceive of themselves as a whole. The character of the system is then dictated by the ideas formulated by its members. In recent years, however, the significance of the British school for systems thinking has been acknowledged by the Americans. Wight's work has even been characterized as 'inspired, trail-blazing' (Yost, 1979). The full significance of the British contribution, however, has yet to be realized, because the British have been reluctant to spell out in detail the nature of their approach. As a consequence, even within Britain, their work has been misunderstood and underrated (Suganami, 1983; Forsyth, 1978), because of a failure to appreciate the aims of this school. It also needs to be stressed that while Wight and his associates may have established an important research programme, the actual accomplishments are, so far, modest.

Systems Thinking Beyond the Discipline

During the last twenty-five years, the climate of opinion has changed dramatically in the United States. When Wolfe says that 'breezy optimism' has given way to 'desperate pessimism' (1977, p.322), he is perhaps overstating the case, but undoubtedly, the conviction that progress is inevitable and that science has the potential to solve all problems has waned and has given way to a more cautious and sober view. The apparently indisputable link between science and progress has been broken. The new attitude is reflected in Hayek's somber insistence that 'scientific knowledge consists in the last resort in the insight into the impossibility of certain events' (1973, p.146). Science cannot solve all problems. One obvious reason for this assessment flows from the recognition that many areas of activity are interconnected, so that one problem can be solved only by exacerbating another. Nuclear power, for instance, may help to create energy but only at the cost of increasing pollution. During the 1970s, the significance of 'inter-connectedness' was widely appreciated. It was argued more and more frequently that there was no point in trying to deal with problems in isolation. Planners who tried to single out problems were considered guilty of what Churchman labels the 'environmental fallacy' (1979, p.4).

At first sight, there appeared to be a certain rough justice about the problems created by interconnectedness, reflected in the once fashionable expression *TINSTAAFL* (there is no such thing as a free lunch). Further study demonstrated the obvious extension, however, that although the world may be interconnected, it is possible for the more powerful to ensure that someone else always pays for the lunch. During the 1960s, Third World countries began to voice this argument and to suggest that their failure to develop was primarily a product of the policies pursued by the wealthy North (Frank, 1969).

This claim had a major impact on American social scientists who recognized that in an international context the United States was in a position, when solving problems, to transfer the costs to other countries. As Aronowitz has noted, the work of many social scientists began to reflect 'the profound guilt surrounding our participation in reaping the rewards of United States domination' (1981, p.519). At the same time, there was an examination of the process by which their attention had been diverted from the role played by the United States in the world arena. Cox argues that social scientists had been subjected to an ideological hegemony, and that, as a consequence, the power base of the United States had descended 'so to speak, to the subconscious so that theorizing continues to take the power base for granted, while at the same time ignoring it' (1981b, p.61).

Most American social scientists do not accept this radical critique. They argue that they have been employing the scientific method which transcends ideology. The task of the social scientist is to develop theories to account for observed behaviour patterns. These theories are built up from abstract concepts which have no direct counterpart in reality, and the only legitimate criterion for evaluating these theories is their effectiveness in accounting for observed behaviour. Theories, therefore, are seen to be distinct from ideology. Values and goals are 'essential' components of any ideology, while theories on the other hand, are entirely neutral. These assertions constitute a reaffirmation of positivism and reflect the conviction that it is possible to study society in exactly the same way that it is posible to study the natural world.

What this defence fails to acknowledge is that there is a growing controversy about the nature of science. An emerging realist school has begun to argue that prevailing positivist theses have promoted important misconceptions about science and reality. In contrast to positivism, the realists argue that the distinction between theoretical and non-theoretical understanding is 'wholesale nonsense'. Churchland, for example, insists that there is no difference between molecules and electromagnetic waves on the one hand and apples and kitchen pots, on the other (1979, p. 1). Close inspection reveals that 'principles and assumptions constitutive of our common-sense conceptual framework can be seen to be as speculative and as artificial as any overtly theoretical system' (1979, p. 2). It does not follow, however, that realists deny the ontological status of a kitchen pot, but rather, the 'Excellence of theory emerges as the fundamental measure of all ontology' (1979, p. 2). Realists do not ascribe the ontological status of any entity on the basis of observation. Theory dictates what exists (Bhaskar, 1978). The end of a stick may appear to be bent when placed in water, but theory identifies the bend as an illusion. Science, therefore, is not concerned with providing analytical explanations of observed regularities, but rather with uncovering the mechanisms which generate the regularities. These mechanisms cannot be directly observed, but they do exist. These mechanisms, and not empirical observations, constitute reality. As scientific understanding grows, the gap between direct observations and what we know to exist increases, and realists have suggested that the development of scientific understanding creates ontological depth (Bhaskar, 1979).

Positivism and realism represent attempts by philosophers to explicate the nature of science. But while work in the natural sciences has been largely unaffected by these conjectures, the same is not true of the social sciences where the influence of positivism has been conspicuous and considerable.

Rostow's theory of economic development (1960) has often been used to illustrate the kind of problems which arise when positivist injunctions are extended to the analysis of social reality. According to Rostow, empirical observation leads to the conclusion that there are stages which states must pass through during the process of economic development. As a consequence, new states, endeavouring to promote development, must seek to follow the path pursued by the economic vanguard. Critics argue, however, that this analysis fails to recognize the real mechanisms which influence economic growth. Furthermore, they can never be understood by developing an abstract model which is disembodied from historical reality. Such a model lacks ontological significance.

These arguments came originally from Third World critics, but they have been enthusiastically taken up in the United States.

One of the most influential Americans, Wallerstein, has argued that economic development can only be understood by acknowledging the significance of the world system and has established a research framework which revolves around threee questions: how did the world system develop; how is the world system reproduced; and how can the world system be changed (1974, 1979a)? In order to answer these questions, it is admitted that the world systems approach necessitates a new way of thinking and a new logic of inquiry. Not everyone is satisfied that Wallerstein has the best approach (Trimberger, 1979), and it has been claimed that he has not yet escaped from either positivist assumptions (Aronowitz, 1981), or the individualist assumptions associated with liberalism (Brenner, 1977). Yet Wallerstein and his associates also recognize that they have not yet freed themselves from traditional modes of thought. As Hopkins has put it: 'Because we come from particular settings, we have learned to think in particular ways' (1978, p.200). But a self-conscious attempt is now being made to break the mould and establish a new logic of inquiry. Ironically, the world systems theorists have yet to see the relevance of realist ideas for their approach, a failure which perhaps reflects the continuing influence of positivism on the social sciences. Indeed, it is only comparatively recently that attempts have been made to utilize realist ideas in the social sciences (Keat and Urry, 1975; Bhaskar, 1979; Benton, 1981; Harré and Secord, 1972).

Although Wallerstein has attracted widespread interest in the broad area of the social sciences, a recent and comprehensive review of American literature on International Relations concludes that his work lies 'outside the field' (Vasquez, 1983, p.123). Vasquez justifies this claim on the grounds that neither Wallerstein nor any of the other writers who are considered to have worked within a putatively Marxist paradigm, have been published in any of the major political science journals. This raises an 'intriguing sociology-of-knowledge question' about the extent to which the American academic reward-and-punishment system discouraged International Relations specialists from using the 'Marxist paradigm as a guide'. Considering the attention given by other areas to this paradigm, Vasquez attributes the lact of interest to the fact that 'the foreign policy elite is a natural constituency for international relations scholarship' (1983, p.123–4).

This explanation is inadequate. The community of scholars in the United States is too heterogeneous to cater for a single constituency. A more plausible reason is the influence exercised by positivism. In other areas, where positivism has played an important role for a longer time, scepticism has arisen, and world systems analysis, overtly holistic and historical, has appeared as an intriguing new development. International Relations specialists, however, continue to be beguiled by positivism. yet it seems likely that soon at least some of the community will follow in the wake of other social science disciplines and develop a world systems focus.

Conclusion

In this chapter I have attempted to assess the systems approach to International Relations in the light of the Anglo-American divide. At first sight, the evidence appears to substantiate the conventional view that the approach has been studiously avoided by the British who consider that it lacks 'judiciousness and modesty' (Wight, 1966, p.32), and enthusiastically adopted by the Americans who believe it has 'penetrated into almost every nook and cranny of thought' (Easton, 1981, p.319). Closer examination reveals, however, that the British have accepted the need to adopt an holistic approach to analysis, while the Americans have, more often then not, used systems terminology merely as a linguistic device. For example, Easton has observed that the idea of a political system was developed in the 1950s as a way of avoiding the ambiguities associated with the concept of the 'state' (1981).

Although social scientists disagree about the merits of holistic explanations, holism nevertheless represents the only distinctive feature of systems thinking. In these terms, the British idealist school has certainly employed a systems approach. For them, a system only comes into existence when the constituent members of a group view themselves as part of a whole and their behaviour is conditioned by this conception. There has been no attempt to extend this line of argument, but it follows that a colony of ants does not constitute a 'system' because the ants have no conception of the whole. For the idealist, therefore, an ethologist or indeed any natural scientist has no alternative but to adopt a reductionist form of explanation.

Despite this conclusion, the American pioneers of a scientific approach to International Relations also appear to have been attracted to holistic theories. Subsequent developments reveal, however, that despite the prolific use of systems terminology, the development of holistic explanations has been very limited. It could be that the indiscriminate use of systems terminology as a cosmetic device in other areas of social science has infected the study of International Relations. A more deep-seated reason advanced in this chapter, however, is that the Americans have relied upon a positivist conception of science which transcends the distinction between reductionism and holism. Although this may appear to be an advantage, critics argue that it fails to encourage social analysts to probe below the surface manifestations of reality.

Contrary to conventional wisdom, therefore, it follows that while the British have developed a distinctive systems perspective, the reliance on positivism by the Americans has served to undermine the relevance of a systems approach for the study of International Relations. Positivism has obscured the significance of systems thinking by denying the ontological status of a system and encouraging the idea that the identification of a system is a purely intellectual activity performed by the analyst. For example, Kaplan argues that 'any set of specified variables may be considered a system'. He goes on: 'Napolean, the Columbia River and a dinosaur may be considered a system' (1957, p. 4). Recent criticism of systems thinking has focused its attack on this method of identifying a system (Spegele, 1982). Nevertheless, I have tried to show that the attack should be directed not at systems thinking, but at positivism. The criticism does not, as a consequence, weaken either an idealist or a realist approach to systems thinking. The 'incoherence' identified by Spegele is purely a product of positivism.

So far, a realist approach to systems thinking has not developed in either the British or the American schools of International Relations. Moreover, although interest in world systems analysis is growing (Hollist & Rosenau, 1981a), the realist implications of its methodology have not yet been recognized. As a consequence, the International Relations communities on both sides of the Atlantic have yet to appreciate either realism or its significance for systems thinking.

Realism is particularly crucial in the present discussion because its advocates, such as Bhaskar (1979), are aware of the importance of idealism and have tried to marry idealism with a scientific approach to social reality. Realism, therefore, should be of interest both to the British idealists and the American positivists. Any development which breaks down national divisions must be beneficial. The persistence of national approaches to the study of International Relations can only confirm the image of a parochial and ethnocentric discipline.

6

Utopianism

TREVOR TAYLOR

Utopianism can be viewed simply as one of the first waves in the development of the new subject of International Relations after the First World War, losing its credibility and significance with the rise of Nazi Germany, the onset of the Second World War and the post-1945 hostility between the US and the Soviet Union. More realistically, however, it represents one of the roots of much contemporary thinking in the discipline, and the broad argument in this chapter is that, while there was little to distinguish between British and American utopian writing in the early days of the subject, there is today a different utopian-based emphasis on world politics in the United States than in Europe. To develop this argument, it is necessary first to consider the fundamental nature of utopianism.

There is a massive body of literature, including many novels, which is characterized as utopian in political theory (Goodwin and Taylor, 1982; Manuel and Manuel, 1979; Mumford, 1959; Lasky, 1976). In general utopianism is concerned with the formulation of an ideal polity and, to a lesser extent, with how such a polity might be established. In many cases the utopia is depicted as separate from the rest of human society, a conceptual island. Indeed, minimal attention has often been paid by utopian writers to relations between political units, leading Goodwin and Taylor to observe that: 'the major area in which utopia is surprisingly silent is that of war, nationalism and international relations' (1982, p. 59). Consequently a precise conception of utopianism in International Relations must be articulated in order to define a body of literature for consideration. It is important to note at the outset that utopianism in International Relations is often not concerned specifically with the drawing–up of blueprints for some ideal world; the aim is frequently no more than to avoid imminent disaster.

In this essay, utopianism is treated as non–Marxist writing in International Relations that reflects three related assumptions. The first is that there are no major conflicts of interest between states or within human society. Utopians vary as to the reasons they offer for such harmony, but they all believe some sort of harmony exists. For Woodrow Wilson and Lowes Dickinson, for example, implementation of the principle of national self-determination should have left states without cause for major quarrels, since governments of united nations were not expected to have designs on the people or territory of others (Bourne, 1916, p. 70). Left-wing idealists in the West, who published extensively through the Gollancz New Left Book Club, rejected notions of peace based on *laissez-faire* economics, but could envisage a peace based on socialism. In contrast, there were liberals who supported the apparent order of capitalism, the concord between producer and consumer, with the former prospering by making what the latter wanted and could afford. The emphasis here was on the fact that the benefits of trade and economies of scale did not end at the border of the state, but linked together human beings everywhere. In this view, harmony is based on self-interest rather than morality. Norman Angell stressed mankind's growing awareness of complementary interests and of the value of co-operation, even when life was somewhat basic. His demonstration of the inadequacy of the simple view that man is selfish and aggressive is effective, if unsuitable for the squeamish:

> When I kill my prisoner (cannibalism was a very common characteristic of early man), it is 'human nature' to keep him for my own larder without sharing him. It is the extreme form of the use of force, the extreme form of human individualism. But putrefaction sets in before I can consume him . . . and I am left without food.
>
> But my two neighbours, each with his butchered prisoner, are in like case, and though I could quite easily defend my larder, we deem it better on the next occasion to join forces and kill one prisoner at a time. I share mine with the other two; they share theirs with me. There is no waste through putrefaction. It is the earliest form of the surrender of the use of force in favour of cooperation – the first attenuation of the tendency to act on impulse. But when the three prisoners are consumed, and no more happen to be available, it strikes us that on the whole we should have done better to make

them catch game and dig roots for us. The next prisoners that are caught are not killed . . . they are only enslaved . . . And the further the drift from force towards simple economic interest the better the result for the effort expended. (Angell, 1911, pp. 147–8)

However, for many contemporary utopians, the stress is not on global harmony as such, but on the vital shared interests of the world population. Predominantly they emphasize the common need to avoid nuclear war, revolt and chaos in the Third World and environmental catastrophe, all of which are seen as real possibilities if human behaviour is not reformed. The choice is *Disarm or Die,* as the title of one book has it.

A final view of global harmony involves the age-old belief in a natural moral order parallel to the universal physical order, both of which are discoverable by reason. T.H. Green's views at the end of the nineteenth century have been summarized thus: 'every state has the same moral objective, to enable its citizens to realise their human capacities as moral agents, and every state can achieve this without hindering any other from doing the same . . . There is a harmony of moral interests' (Nicholson, 1976, p.77; see also Savigear, 1975, p.50).

The general notion of global harmony is closely related to the second key assumption of utopianism, which asserts the existence of objective justice detectable through reason or experience The concept of justice is a philosophical minefield, but broadly speaking, in this view, morality is not something bound by culture or time but is thouht to be absolute and universal. The laws which generated justice have been seen historically as either natural or divine, or both (d'Entreves, 1970; Midgly, 1975), and their existence has been asserted regularly at least since Cicero. One significant aspect of the concept of 'absolute' justice is that it can be presented as the true, common interest of all and is therefore linked to the harmony of interest idea.

The third utopian assumption, or rather cluster of assumptions, is that people are basically rational, intelligent creatures, creating their own destiny, capable of evil and foolishness but fundamentally good. Woodrow Wilson was recognized as someone who had great faith in people and therefore in the value of public opinion. This optimism about the human capacity to reason, and then to act on the basis of that reason, was reinforced by the social and economic progress of nineteenth-century Europe. Such optimism is the vital connection between utopian prescriptions and changes in reality. Utopians entertain strong hopes of their ideas being implemented, on the grounds that rational people, once they appreciate the logic and the good behind a prescription, will put it into effect immediately. In particular, utopians believe man to be rational enough to avoid disaster, although there is considerable uncertainty about how near disaster must come before human behaviour adjusts to prevent it. This issue is discussed further below. It was on these three assumptions that utopians built their ideas, generating suggestions for the improvement of international life and in particular for the elimination of war.

The international system is characterized by diplomacy, law and warfare. Utopians sought to weaken the role of the latter and strenghten the other two. With their faith in human rationality, they placed great emphasis on the provision of new information to direct human behaviour into desired channels. Angell, in *The Great Illusion,* tried to show that neither trade, nor well-being, nor even a sense of security could be generated by the possession and use of armed force, demonstrating this by reference to the survival and prosperity of small nations. He went on to attack other widely accepted notions, arguing that human nature does not drive people towards warfare and that the warlike nations do not inherit the earth. He pointed specifically to the failure of central and south American states to achieve dominance over neighbouring countries, despite their nearly annual practice in the manly art of warfare (1911, p. 185).

Like many others before and after him, Angell believed that modern warfare was the result of miscalculation rather than clashing interests, and a related utopian theme was that the process of acquiring armaments increased the chances of such accidents. In short, arms races were seen as a cause of war, while arms acquisitions certainly did not bring security. In the period after 1919, there was a strong tendency to blame arms races particularly on the private arms manufacturers who benefited from them (Noel-Baker, 1936; Lewinsohn, 1936; Zilliacus, 1944). Noel-Baker summarized his starting-point in the following way:

> What is the fundamental purpose of an organised society today? It is that the members of that society, the individuals who compose the nation, should live their lives with full security of person, property and rights. Peace with another nation is an absolute condition of that security. Everyone is agreed, indeed, that international peace is, in the modern world, the highest and most urgent interest of every nation. Everyone is agreed that peace can only be preserved in an atmosphere of international confidence and trust. Virtually everyone

is agreed that it is the interest of every nation to maintain its armaments at the lowest level by which the safety and integrity of its territory can be preserved; and that mutual armament reductions by international agreement among all nations must promote the true happiness of them all. But it is plain that the interest of those who draw profit from making arms must be in conflict with these overriding public interests of the peoples as a whole. (1936, p.52)

For writers who saw arms races as the principal causes of war, disarmament was not only feasible but vital for reducing tension. Although they recognized the disadvantages of unilateral disarmament, it was hoped that multilateral disarmament could be negotiated once its advantages were clear. Moreover, once the world had disarmed, human rationality would preclude the tendency to rearm that political realists anticipated, since there would be wide appreciation of the improvement in welfare. Utopians also believed people would be reluctant to return to the pointless and expensive practice of arms acquisitions, which afforded only a temporary advantage and provoked others.

The concept of collective security, whose logic even Morgenthau conceded to be 'flawless' (1973, p.405), was formulated to deal with the renegade state which insisted on using force for its short-term advantage. Such states could be dealt with easily by centrally organized forces assembled for the purpose. They were not expected to be numerous since general human goodness and rationality would prevail. Moreover, most potential offenders would be deterred by the mere prospect of mass action against them. They would not threaten the basic stability of the system any more than their equivalent within states, a criminal, would threaten domestic society.

The futility of war, its origins in arms races, accidents and the machinations of other minorities within states, the desirability and feasibility of disarmament and collective security – these were the themes of much literature in the inter-war years. But utopians also sought alternatives to war as a means of promoting justice. Specifically, they sought to improve diplomacy and strengthen international law.

Two diplomatic reforms are worthy of particular note. First there was the Wilsonian commitment to 'open diplomacy', in part to prevent inter-governmental misunderstanding but also to expose negotiators and leaders to the scrutiny of their publics. Many inter-war writers were uncertain about the immediate effect of this, and Angell, for one, while generally optimistic about human nature, recognized that governments and the press could manipulate public opinion and that emotion could lead people to vote against their own interest. Despite the widespread view that democracies were inherently oriented towards peace ('peace can genuinely flourish only in the soil of representative government' (Hoover and Gibson, 1942, p.202)), others argued that public opinion would only turn against war when it was clear that the benefits of peace were as exciting and adventurous as those of war (Steed, 1936). However, this represents a diversion from the general thrust of utopian ideas which argued that governments that had to negotiate openly would need to behave reasonably if they were democratically controlled by educated populations.

The second suggestion was for an international organization to serve as a standing conference where disputing parties could meet to find a solution and from which they could appoint conciliators or mediators as necessary. It was hoped that such a conference would gain additional weight from representing world public opinion. Two interesting conceptions of global harmony pointed to the value of such a conference: first, the belief that most international conflicts arise from misunderstanding, which discussion can correct; second, the argument that, although states may have their differences, it is not worthwhile for them to be settled in the modern age by warfare. All states therefore have an interest in avoiding war. The League of Nations and, despite its failure, the establishment of the United Nations, reflected cautious official acceptance of the value of such a standing conference.

Other utopians placed their emphasis on international law as a means of assuring states of the justice that, in other times, they might have had to fight to obtain. Many observed 'the slow expansion of the power of Law, from the family to the tribe, from the tribe to the city, from the city to the nation, from the nation to the Commonwealth' (Zimmern, in Bourne, 1916, p.221). They believed that international law, generating justice, could serve as a preferred alternative to war. Irving Fisher wrote in 1923:

> History shows that, when given the alternative, man almost always manages to settle disputes by peaceful rather than by warlike methods, in short by law rather than by war. The fact that he has progressively substituted law for war proves this proposition beyond possibility of doubt . . . Over and over again, at each stage in the growth of the population, do we find this cycle: isolation, contact, quarrels, war, law, by which the peace group has been successively enlarged. (1923, p.53, 58)

Faith in international law and collective security raised the issue of
whether utopians perceived a need to introduce some kind of world
authority or government above the state. Here there was little
unanimity in utopian thinking as several factors came into play. On
the one hand, there was often an emotional readiness to accept
world government as a desirable and logical outcome of increasing
human co-operation. There was also recognition that effective
decision-making was necessary to deal with the occasional
'criminal' state which did not accept the judgement of law.
Thirdly, there was widespread recognition of the need for a global
management of interdependence, especially in economic matters.
This line of thinking led directly to the functionalist ideas of
Mitrany and others. On the other hand, many believed that it was
possible to reform state behaviour and that therefore there was no
need to abolish individual states in order to eliminate war.
Following the logic of this latter point, world government was the
world order prescription of the realist rather than the utopian.

These then were the assumptions and the main lines of thought
of traditional utopian scholars and commentators in International
Relations. It is not the main purpose of this chapter to evaluate the
utopian approach: serious criticism is available elsewhere (Carr,
1946; Bull, 1972; Herz, 1951; Clark, 1980; Suganami, 1978). What
is at issue in this essay is the literature that rests on utopian
assumptions and whether distinctive American and British schools
within utopianism can be discerned. The short answer would seem
to be no, with the major qualification being that much of the
socialist-idealist writing published by Gollancz had no parallel in the
US. Beyond this, the emphasis of individual authors varied but
does not seem to have been a function of their nationality. The
volume of literature in the utopian vein was greater in the United
States, reflecting that country's idealistic tradition as well as the size
of its book market. Carr saw the fact that the US was 'still in the
heyday of Victorian prosperity and of Victorian belief in the
comfortable Bethamite creed' as the driving force of the utopian
school (1946, pp. 26–7). But there was, nevertheless, a substantial
British contribution. Hedley Bull, seeking to highlight key utopian
works, pointed to four British authors – Zimmern, Noel-Baker,
Bailey and Mitrany – and three Americans – Shotwell, Potter and
Moon (1972).

That British and American utopian literature should be similar is
scarcely surprising. There were links of a personal nature between
Britain and the US. Angell began almost a decade of being in the

United States in his late teens, and served as an informal adviser to Woodrow Wilson in the 1916–17 period while working for the *New Republic*. Philip Noel-Baker's work on the private manufacture of armaments was financed by the Rockefeller Foundation. James Shotwell made many visits to Europe and worked at the London School of Economics for some years for the Carnegie Endowment (Josephson, 1975, pp.105–6) as did David Mitrany. Mitrany later worked at Princeton, which today is perhaps the main source of world order scholars in the US. More generally, for British and American academics, Europe was the focus of international politics and the place where political power was concentrated. Both sides of the Atlantic were looking at the same problem.

Further, if the United States was the land of pragmatic idealism, Britain had developed a liberal tradition from Bentham, Cobden and J.S. Mill, who were succeeded by a school of idealist philosophers at the start of the twentieth century (Savigear, 1975). Utopian literature in English was often published on both sides of the Atlantic and the First World War had stimulated political movements in both Britain and the US for the establishment of a league of states.

The rise of Nazi Germany, the onset of the Second World War and the emergence of the cold war, with its distinct ideological dimension, greatly reduced the impact and popularity of idealist thinking. Realism became fashionable, not just because it seemed to explain more clearly international politics of the 1930s, but also because it provided a guide and a justification for a positive American role in world politics (Spykman, 1942; Morgenthau, 1951). Yet idealism did not disappear indefinitely, and it is to its more modern manifestations that attention can now be turned.

The defining features of utopianism, the idea of objective justice, the possibility and even likelihood of progress, the acceptance of the human capacity for rational action, and notions of supreme common interests, can be found in many areas of work on International Relations, for example, in much of the literature on interdependence and world society (see Cox, 1976), and in Burton's writing on communication and conflict resolution (1969). Even some of the high priests of quantitative techniques at times display utopian tendencies. When Rummel defined his concept of a 'just peace', he advocated a mixture of freedom as well as the maximizing of those things that provided individual human satisfaction. But he had no doubt that justice existed and that people would be able to appreciate it when they experienced it (1981, p. 227). Clearly there is also much idealist influence on ideas about integration. The establishment of the UN specialized agencies represented implicit acknowledgement of Mitrany's functionalist ideas, which stressed the mass of topics on which there could be global harmony.

Additionally, after 1945, the states of Western Europe were looking for new patterns of behaviour which would end the periodic destructive warfare among them. With the rejection of federalist solutions, the consequence in intellectual terms was the emergence of neo-functionalist ideas on integration, which, while acknowledging that conflicts of interest occurred, nevertheless placed great emphasis on human rationality and progressive change (Pentland, 1973; Hodges, 1978). The neo-functionalist literature was largely produced by Americans, many of recent European descent, reflecting the general intellectual leadership that the much enlarged US academic community was beginning to exercise in International Relations.

However, the main bulk of post-war work most clearly revealing utopian assumptions did not begin to appear until the mid-1970s. This resurgence can be attributed to the enduring presence of three problems to which the realist prescription offered no long-term solution. First was the continuing danger of nuclear war and the persistence of the qualitative and quantitative arms race, which was initially concentrated on the two superpowers and their European allies but then expanded through military aid and arms transfers to other parts of the world. Despite the number of arms control agreements concluded, it was plain that most of them dealt with minor matters, and that arms control had little chance of having a major impact on the arms race. The realist-based concept of mutual deterrence offered no long-term answer since logically the deterrence system would eventually break down, if only because of an accident. Philip Noel-Baker's book *The Arms Race* (1958) represented an early effort in the nuclear age to come to terms with these issues.

The second problem which generated utopian literature was the increased awareness of the environmental damage being done to the planet by blind pursuit of industrialization and economic growth. New patterns of international co-operation were advocated by the ecological movement, so that the common human interest in the healthy survival of the planet could be realized. This second problem appeared to be of greater urgency than the first, since, in the case of nuclear weapons, if mankind continued its present pattern of behaviour, i.e. acquiring but not using such bombs, disaster would not occur. In the case of environmental damage, however, existing patterns of behaviour were seen to be leading to catastrophe. The central message of environmentalists in the face of this disaster was the insistence that there were vital links between human ethics and the physical universe. Mankind was urged to cease seeing itself as confronting nature, and to recognize itself instead as *part* of nature and needing to be in harmony with it.

The third problem was the growing gap in the wealth and quality of life between the rich states of the North and the poor states of the South. This situation was viewed from several perspectives which prompted suggestions for new modes of co-operation and behaviour. The first was the moral perspective, which saw the disparity in the human condition across the planet as massively unjust, and which demanded action to reduce it. A second, an economic point of view, looked on the developing countries as vast potential markets, which, if developed, would benefit the rich countries from the trade which would result. A third perspective emphasized the North's dependence on the South and warned that, by not sufficiently helping with development, the North was stoking up pressure for revolt and disorder among the world's poor. This would hardly be in the interests of the wealthier states, particularly if the poorer states acquired, and tried to use, nuclear weapons in order to change their position.

In the literature on the environment, an academic lead was taken by the Americans, Harold and Margaret Sprout (1965, 1971). They were followed by non-academic institutions, which enjoyed the considerable resources needed for the large-scale studies involved. European industrialization, population densities and numerous inter-state boundaries could be expected to make Europeans rather more aware than Americans of the international dimensions of environmental issues, and much attention was attracted by the two reports from the Club of Rome – *The Limits to Growth* (Meadows et al., 1972) and *Mankind at the Turning Point* (Mesarovic and Pestel, 1974). These relied heavily on the use of quantified data, models and trends to reach their conclusions, techniques with which British International Relations scholars were normally unfamiliar. There was major American participation in the Club of Rome studies: Mesarovic, for instance, was based in Cleveland, and the original *Limits to Growth* study (1972) was produced from a base at

MIT. United Nations support lay behind the Ward and Dubos classic, *Only One Earth* (1972), and Robert Allen's bluntly titled *How To Save The World* (1980).

These works fitted the traditional utopian mould of providing new information to generate reformed pattens of behaviour; they exposed sobering data about trends in population growth, resource depletion, pollution levels and other environmental issues. They sometimes lacked the optimism which may be thought to be the mark of the true idealist; consider Barbara Ward, for example, in her last book:

> We are thus, in the most fundamental sense, at a hinge of history. If we can learn from the growing evidence of destructive risk in our present policies to determine that the next phase of development shall respect and sustain and even enhance the environment, we can look to a human future. If on the contrary we have learned so little that every present trend towards pollution, decay and collapse is merely to be enhanced by its spread all round the planet, then the planet's own capacity to sustain such insults will be ineluctably exceeded. (1979, p. 266)

Yet we should be clear that utopianism does not make progress inevitable and does allow that disaster is possible. Mankind is in charge of its own future with utopians only going so far as to accept the Kantian logic, analysed by Clark (1979, p. 108), that the worse the imminent disaster and the more likely it seems, the better the chance that new modes of behaviour will be developed. Hence the emphasis from much of the peace movement on providing information both on the possibility of nuclear war and on its nature should it occur. Many governments, judging from their reluctance to be frank about the likelihood of a nuclear attack and the optimistic civil defence plans they prepare, would seem to feel this utopian reasoning has some credibility.

To meet the challenge of nuclear weapons and the arms race, peace research, an academic concept largely American in origin (but owing much to the British student of arms races, Lewis Richardson), has been adopted and adapted in Europe, attracting people who see peace, justice and harmony as both desirable and feasible (Dunn, 1978; Barnaby, 1976). It has some institutional roots in the UK, chiefly at the University of Bradford and on a smaller scale at the University of Lancaster where the Richardson Institute is based, but peace research as a concept has a broader base of support in Scandinavia where the *Journal of Peace Research* is published and the Stockholm International Peace Research Institute is located. Peace research also encompasses the Pugwash movement, movement, an international association of scientists from the East, the West and the Third World who are committed to the abolition of the arms race. Pugwash reflects scientists' sense of responsibility for the increasingly destructive capabilities of weapons and particularly for the development of nuclear arms.

Not all those concerned with disarmament associate themselves explicitly with the notion of peace research. There is obviously in Western Europe as a whole, and Britain in particular, a popular political movement for nuclear disarmament, while in the US the emphasis is on the demand for a nuclear freeze. However, in Britain the number of International Relations academics who are actively involved with nuclear disarmament is comparatively small. Particularly if a number of staff associated with the Universities of Bradford and Sussex are discounted, there remains rather a stark contrast between the UK International Relations academic community, much of which is nevertheless concerned with security politics issues, and the idealist groups outside which are arguing for disarmament, environmental protection and help for the Third World.

It could be said that the position is much the same in the US, but there at least can be found the individual writing of people like Beres (1981), G. and P. Mische (1977) and most importantly Richard Falk, who explored the relationship between the state system and threats to the global ecosystem (including nuclear war) in *This Endangered Planet* (1971). On a more institutionalized basis from what is today called the World Policy Institute in New York, there is the work of the World Order Models Project (WOMP) and its sympathizers. This project, enjoying substantial US funding from the Rockefeller Foundation and the Carnegie Endowment, was led by Saul Mendlovitz who had a background in international law and was strongly influenced by Clark and Sohn (1966). WOMP resulted in the publication of a stream of major books (Mendlovitz, 1975; Falk, 1975a; Kothari, 1974; Lagos and Godoy, 1977; Mazrui, 1976; and Galtung, 1980), two journals, *Alternatives* and the *World Policy Journal*, as well as many lesser items.

WOMP has no equivalent in Britain in terms of its radical nature, degree of institutionalization or scale, although Gordon Burt is seeking to bring together in a slightly different framework scholars who are sympathetic to WOMP ideals. Acting in the context of the Vietnam war, WOMP was conceived in the 1960s as 'a conscious political act' by a group of American academics with a commitment to reducing international violence to a minimum. They sought to control the influence of American culture on the project by recruiting academics with differing cultural perspectives from across the world. As this happened, WOMP leaders realized that they would also have to consider the problems of social injustice and poverty which loomed so much larger in the Third World than in the West (Mendlovitz, 1975). By asking its writers to provide a preferred world order along with transition strategies to build it, the WOMP leaders hoped to give their aims a practical edge; WOMP, it was claimed, was concerned only with 'relevant utopias'.

One utopian problem has always been to articulate a concept of justice which all would endorse regardless of culture. This difficulty was overcome in the WOMP project by spelling out particular values after consultation with academics from many backgrounds.

> We were able to agree that humankind faced five major problems: war, poverty, social injustice, environmental decay and alienation. We saw these as social problems because we had values – peace, economic well-being, social justice, ecological stability and positive identity – which no matter how vaguely operationalised, we knew were not being realised in the real world. (Mendlovitz, 1975, pp. xii–xiii)

A similar, implicit, conception of justice can be found in Beres (1981), who places particular emphasis on the need to change human attitudes and the possibility of doing so.

The WOMP project was part of a general trend towards treating war, the environment and Third World poverty within a single framework in recognition of the links between them. This was apparent for instance in the report of the Brandt Commission (1980), in the work of Richard Falk (1971) and Joseph Camilleri (1976). One advantage of this approach was that it offered multiple opportunities to present opportunity cost formulations, bringing home the implications of the arms race for Third World poverty. The presentation of information in this form was a fundamental feature of the annual US publication from Ruth Leger Sivard, *World Military and Social Expenditures*. Her calculations were widely reproduced and imitated, as in the Sussex University study, *Disarmament and World Development,* edited by Richard Jolly (1978).

In summary, at a time when utopian ideas have the support of a significant minority of the wider population, among American International Relations academics there is recognition of the need to assert the importance of idealism at a time when governments are apparently led on by crude realism. Utopianism has an impact on several sub-fields of International Relations where there is a strong American input. These include ideas about interdependence, integration and peace research. Most explicitly building on the utopian tradition is the growing literature on world order.

Utopian influences are in a much less predominant position in UK academic life, although one group of scholars has recently concerned itself specifically with the morality of states (Mayall, 1982). A range of factors can be adduced to account for this reluctance to accept a utopian approach. One point is that the scale of British academic effort in International Relations is much smaller than that in America, so that all the lines of investigation followed in the US cannot be matched in Britain. Certainly the large-scale funding behind research projects such as WOMP is not easily available.

But there are also factors of culture, intellectual tradition and methodology at work. Culturally, Americans are more likely to favour problem-solving than are British citizens aware that their country has been in steady decline for almost a century. In terms of intellectual tradition, Carr's criticism of utopianism still reigns supreme in Britain, where the dominant models remain either the realist perspective or the concept of international society.

The latter was advanced by Charles Manning (1975) and involved thinking of states, not as parts of a system whose anarchic nature largely determined their behaviour, but as members of a society. The term society was justified by reference to the interdependence of states and to the order supported by the practice of diplomacy and the following of legal and other rules. This order existed despite conflicts between states and the utility of power in inter-state relations. The concept of international society has been further refined particularly by James (1978, 1973), Bull (1977), Donelan (1978) and Mayall (1982).

The international society concept, like utopianism, represents a reaction against the purest forms of realism. Put briefly, it argues that things are not quite so bad as they might be (rather than the utopian view that things are not as good as they could or need to be). This is significant because it affords a perspective on international politics which respects power without having the realist weakness of recognizing little else. However, one problem with this approach is its lack of explanatory or predictive power, and the absence of clear guidance as to whether the problems noted by utopians are as grave or as soluble as they are claimed to be. In *The Anarchical Society* (Bull, 1977), where there is considerable emphasis on the continued utility of force in international politics, there is a summary dismissal of the urgency of disarmament, the problems of Third World poverty, and environmental decay. The author says of Falk and his colleagues that 'they speak of unprecedented global emergency, but what they mean by this is simply that the reality of world politics does not conform to the goals of peace and justice which they prescribe for it, which is as true of every past period of world politics as of the present' (p. 305).

Methodologically the British 'tradition', which includes the international society perspective, does not encourage its adherents to look keenly into the future. 'Prophecy', wrote James, 'is if anything, more difficult at the international level than at any other and also, in my firm view, not the academic's job' (1978, p.106). Moreover, International Relations training in the UK often does not include familiarization with the quantitative evidence on which contemporary utopians rely. This has in part contributed to the dichotomy between those with a British background who have approached utopianism from the point of view of political theory and history (Clark, Midgly, Bull and staff from the University of Leicester, for example), and their American counterparts who either have legal backgrounds and want to see international law achieve a more prominent place, or have come from the natural sciences, economics and other disciplines using quantitative methods. In the UK of the 1980s, if there is little respect paid to the meaning or consequences of any harmony of interests, there is increasing analysis of the moral dimension of state behaviour (Mayall, 1982; Linklater, 1982). Many of the objections voiced in Britain to the idea of improving the world through utopian prescriptions related not to the possibility of so doing, but to the suggested strategies for achieving change and to the anticipated ease of securing improvement. In particular it was felt that more attention should be paid to state morality.

Thinking derived from traditional utopianism on both sides of the Atlantic should not be rejected out of hand, in part because of its existing influence on the literature of International Relations, but also because of its possible future effect. International Relations, like other social sciences, exists to contribute to the amelioration of human problems as well as to generate knowledge for its own sake. Bloch's view of utopianism was that it was 'a critical weapon that made men aware of the imperfections of the present and spurred them to transform it in the light of utopian revelations' (Manuel and Manuel, 1979, p. 806). Goodwin and Taylor conclude their survey with the observation that 'underlying all forms of utopianism is the conviction that optimistic imaginative thought and action are capable of bringing about a change towards not only a new social existence, but a better one' (1982, p. 253). Camilleri begins his book thus:

> It is precisely the function of the utopian vision to challenge the existing order by establishing a sharp contrast between two models of social organization, one actual and the other potential. The ensuing tension between these two images may be said to provide the necessary impetus for action . . . the formulation of ultimate values and long-term goals is only the first step in any concrete programme of social transformation . . . strategy must provide an effective bridge between the actual and the potential. (1976, p. iii)

Surely International Relations scholars, if they are to do anything other than defend the status quo, cannot afford to lose sight of these arguments.

7
International Political Economy

ROGER TOOZE

International Relations has undergone many changes and faced many challenges in the past fifteen years, but none of these compare with the range of dilemmas, problems and opportunities now confronting the field. One of the major developments, and the source of many problems and opportunities, has been the growth, in this subject, of the study of international political economy. International political economy has developed into a significant sub-field of International Relations (and indeed might even now claim autonomy from it!). Its significance lies as much in its intellectual challenge to conventional thinking on international relations as in its substantive products of research and teaching. This chapter will review the development of international political economy, considering the various approaches evident in Britain and America. Such a review of approaches, however, will be problematic, because the process of review involves the same difficulties and dilemmas faced in the process of substantive inquiry.

The initial problem is that the philosophical traditions, the methodological and epistemological assumptions, and the political values of the reviewer inform and condition any evaluation (see, for example, Stanley Hoffmann's interesting 'reflections' on 'An American Social Science' (Hoffmann, 1977)). So the starting-point of the present analysis must be an exploration of the traditions, assumptions and values within which the reviewer works and within which international political economy has developed. Of

I am indebted to David Morrice for insight and support, and to Stephen Gill who, unknown to him, confirmed my thoughts. Steve Smith, as ever, provided the stimulus.

necessity this discussion will be synoptic. Its point is to emphasize the requisite and urgent consideration of basic problems, rather than to discuss philosophy and method for their own sakes. Indeed, one of the problems we now face is the potential 'philosophization' of theory where argument in theory becomes a 'residue of arguments in academic philosophy' (Gunnell, 1979, p.198) and increasingly divorced from the 'practice' of International Relations.

Three considerations are relevant to the task. International political economy, as a sub-field of International Relations, has developed from and within International Relations traditions, and takes its assumptions and method primarily from this discipline, rather than from (neo-classical) economics (although Frey (1984) has cogently argued the case for a neo-classically based public choice view of international political economy). In turn, the development of International Relations, and International Relations theory, although considered by many to be separate from political theory, has in fact taken place in 'correspondence' with it; 'correspondence means that . . . critical problems, theoretical developments, and methodological disputes in international relations and traditional political theory show a high degree of similarity of presentation and of shifts in orthodoxy . . .' (Maclean, 1981, p.105). Correspondence enables us to discuss international political economy in the context of political inquiry. As Maclean points out, both International Relations and politics 'have necessarily been exposed to the problems of enquiry and explanation that are general to the social sciences (*although this appears to have occurred in international relations in a more hesitant and often less explicit manner*)' (Maclean, 1981, p.106, my italics). The consequences of this 'hesitancy' and the problems of implicit assumption will be discussed later in the chapter.

Our second initial consideration relates to the status and evaluation of international political economy as knowledge. The knowledge that is produced is conditioned and directed not only by institutional, political, economic and ideological factors (see Cox, 1979) but by the prevailing consensus as to what constitutes a legitimate (or often the legitimate) form and product of academic inquiry. The existence of such a consensus (not necessarily static nor shared outside a specific academic community) which identifies the form, structure and methodology of International Relations inquiry also provides a demonstrable set of criteria against which 'new' fields, such as international political economy, are evaluated. Even if the 'new' knowledge does not claim, or desire, to fit these criteria its status and acceptability are still defined by the prevailing mode. In the US, for instance, the canons of social scientific inquiry, or, more correctly, what is regarded by the International Relations community as social scientific inquiry, constitute the defining framework for legitimate knowledge. The assumption is 'that all problems can be resolved, that the way to resolve them is to apply the scientific method – assumed to be value free, and to combine empirical investigation, hypothesis formation and testing – and that the resort to science will yield practical applications that will bring progress' (Hoffmann, 1977, p.45). The implicit acceptance of 'scientific' criteria, in what Hoffmann calls 'not merely an intellectual, but an operational paradigm' (1977, p.45), means that knowledge not conforming to 'scientific' norms is of a different and less worthy form. Each academic community produces a dominant paradigm which, in the specific sense discussed here, creates a hierarchy of knowledge. This in turn constitutes a powerful structural influence on the development of new fields of inquiry, be it 'scientific', 'normative', 'historical' or whatever. For example, the dominance of social science in the US, based on a positivist reconstruction of science, has had particular effect on what is regarded as legitimate theory:

> The positivist doctrine has, to a large extent, served the pragmatic function of an ideological weapon, to justify the autonomy of political science as an empirical enterprise (from traditional political theory) and to win the title of 'theory' from the normative concerns of so-called traditional political theory. (Gunnell, 1975, p.252)

Our final consideration concerns the nature of the basis of evaluation and comparison: the membership of the particular academic community in question. If we work within the frame of social science, particularly that denominated as logical positivist/empiricist, knowledge and theory are claimed to be universally valid in space and time (for a discussion of the consequences of this view in international political economy, see Tooze, 1981). This view of knowledge (and knowledge production) implies a world-wide community of scholars sharing the same methods and assumptions and producing value-free research and texts. More pertinent is the point that it consequently denies any fundamental distinction between, or even meaning in, the terms 'British' and 'American' when applied to approaches in international political economy. Hence, the title of this chapter and the purpose of this book as a whole would be, if not meaningless, irrelevant and misguided. The 'accident' of geography and the consequent differentiating historical experiences would merely be a temporary hurdle in the production of nomological knowledge. In this view, held by those whom Frederick Gareau calls the 'social physicists', we all are (or should be) part of a world-wide scientific community following the lead of natural science. Gareau comprehensively demonstrates that those who work within the scientific approach to International Relations 'do not constitute an international community in the sense the natural scientists do' (Gareau, 1981, p.782), and that the assumption that knowledge is structured and defined in this way is primarily an American ethnocentrism.

If, however, we work within another frame – that which is broadly represented by the British and European 'tradition' of International Relations scholarship – our view of knowledge makes the task of identifying approaches much easier but evaluating them much more problematic. This 'tradition' denies the possibility of universalist explanation in its assumption that international relations are understandable only through a detailed study of the history, values and institutions of each state. The basic unit of analysis and evaluation is national society and this produces an international relations composed of unique societies, all of which have to be understood as such. Approaches to International Relations along these lines can *only* be understood as 'British' or 'American'. There are many problems with the relativistic nature of this view, but it is one which is very widely held outside the US, and even within the American International Relations community.

Clearly, the differences between the two views make them incommensurable. Neither admits the basic assumptions of the other and neither can be properly assessed in terms acceptable to the other. This fact is equally clearly reflected in the study and institutional definition of International Relations throughout the world (see Gareau, 1981; Lyons, 1982). To the extent that some scholars in America, Britain and Scandinavia are engaged in a particular version of social scientific inquiry, there is a limited, but quite numerous, 'community' working within a moderately well-defined, if often implicit, framework which makes evaluation reasonably straightforward. But to the extent that many scholars work within a 'traditional' framework, and represent the geographically dominant mode of International Relations assessment becomes particularistic and difficult because the relativism of the traditional view precludes any legitimate transnational set of evaluative or comparative criteria. A traditional, relativist analysis of a social science based international political economy is likely to tell us much about the qualities of the different approaches and little about international political economy. This quandary cannot be resolved solely by reference to international political economy or International Relations as the fields presently stand. It can only properly be addressed through a consideration of the basis of knowledge, while bearing in mind the 'philosophization' caveat previously referred to.

Knowledge, Values and International Relations

The confrontation of two incommensurable approaches is highly characteristic of political argument. In the language of scientific knowledge it represents a clash of 'paradigms', and paradigms, of course, do more than prescribe a view of knowledge. Given the problems with the concept of 'paradigm' in science and social science (Kuhn, 1970; Lakatos and Musgrave, 1970; Barnes, 1982 (particularly Barnes' very useful bibliography)) it is best to set out a definition. John Vasquez, in a recent analysis of theory and power politics, defines paradigm as 'the fundamental assumptions scholars make about the world they are studying' which 'tell the scholar what is known about the world, what is unknown about it, how one should view the world if one wants to know the unknown and finally what is worth knowing' (Vasquez, 1983 p.5). Interestingly, Vasquez does not adequately consider the paradigmatic function of defining how knowledge is to be produced and what status is subsequently has. In this context, both approaches to International Relations discussed in this chapter are based within paradigms heavily influenced by positivism. Now, the positivist/anti-positivist debate is long and arduous, but the ideas of Kuhn and others (see Barnes, 1982) have enabled the discussion to take on new and more productive forms. The structure and implications of a positivist paradigm of social science have been dealt with elsewhere (for political theory, see Gunnell, 1975, 1979; for International Relations, see Little, 1984), and it is only necessary here to outline the considerations that are relevant to the present argument.

Positivism starts from the disjunction of fact and value, and proposes an objective, value-free account of social reality, which can be discovered through a process of rational, empirical inquiry. 'The division between "is" and "ought" is viewed as fundamental and inclusive, and it is assumed to be the basis for making a distinction between empirical and normative inquiry into politics' (Gunnell, 1975, p. 249). For empirical inquiry to produce an 'objective' view of the world, it must, under positivism, be 'value-free' and, hence, non-ideological, because ideology brings 'distortion'. 'Distortion' arises because 'facts' have a special status in positivism: '"Facts" referred to a class of phenomena which were believed to be in some manner . . . "given" in immediate experience and presented in an indefeasible observation language' (Gunnell, 1979, p. 208).

Moreover, positivist ideas about 'facts' produce a particular and instrumental view of theory. Theories are separate from 'facts', and are for making 'sense' of 'facts' in as economical a way as possible:

> The literature continually stresses that the social scientist is confronted with a 'sea of facts' which can be approached systematically only in terms of explicit analytical constructs or conceptual frameworks which, although they possess a certain arbitrary character, *are necessary as tools for description and explanation.* These frameworks . . . are to be imposed on *independent data bases,* to which they are linked by operational definitions. (Gunnell, 1979, p. 209, my italics)

Both 'traditional' and 'social scientific' approaches to International Relations share this construction of 'facts' as 'independent data bases', only differing in how they 'get at' them. That is, they disagree about the emphasis and value to be put on the role, status and construction of theory and the importance of methodology. They also differ crucially as paradigms in the Vasquez sense, in their conception of what kind of knowledge the 'sea of facts' actually constitutes, and how best it may be described.

The consequences of positivism are felt throughout the International Relations community. First, differences between paradigms become problems to be 'solved', either by the 'demolition' of one point of view by the (mainstream) other, or by a demonstration of its 'non-scientific' nature, or, more frequently than not, by evasion. The conflicts between paradigms that do develop are resolved, then, by the eventual 'triumph' of one over another or by a synthesis of alternative paradigms; each process prompts a further explanation of social reality that is much closer to the 'neutral, value-free view of the world to which all rational observers can subscribe' (Little, 1984, p. 8). Second, the emergence of a new paradigm (say, an international political economy view of International Relations) is attributed to and explained by 'real' changes in the international arena (in international political economy, the politicization of international economic relations).

As Richard Little points out, this process only reinforces the positivist belief in a 'value-free' view of the world (Little, 1984). It does so through its fact-value disjunction, and the purely instrumental role it assigns to theory.

Third, the instrumental view of theory held by positivists has clearly produced a form of acceptable and legitimate knowledge in International Relations and international political economy. From the beginning of the 1970s we can discern a growing number of works (predominant are Allison, 1971, and Keohane and Nye, 1977) based on the following structure:

Stage 1 Objective(s) of analysis is defined and the possibility of various explanations (models) for the selected problem is discussed, and key dimensions outlined.

Stage 2 Various explanations (models) are presented, briefly evaluated for their 'common-sense' appeal, and the possibilities of any combination of explanations (models) discussed.

Stage 3 The explanations (models) are tested against a presumed 'reality'.

Stage 4 Conclusions are drawn, on the basis of 'stage 3', about the adequacy of the explanations (models), either singly or in combination. This is usually followed by a consideration of 'policy implications'.

Now, while this structure represents a large and important gain in theoretical sensitivity compared to previous analytical frameworks, it does suffer from a serious, and ultimately fatal, flaw, a flaw made all the more problematic because the 'explanations' generated by this structure have high status and legitimacy in the International Relations community. The flaw is at 'stage 3' – the testing of contending explanations or models. Here, the basic, but implicit, assumption is that the language of theory (encompassed in the alternative explanations) is independent of the language of observation (facts exist in their own right and are epistemologically prior to theory). It is this assumption that both makes 'testing' possible and justifies its results. But the very basis of the 'Kuhnian' critique of positivism is that 'facts are not simply understood in terms of a theory but are actually conceptually constituted by theories' (Gunnell, 1979, p. 209). Hence, the reality against which the alternative explanations are to be tested is just as 'theoretically constituted' as the explanations used to explain it, and does not exist as the 'independent data base' assumed in these works.

Therefore any conclusions as to the relative 'utility' of explanations flowing from the application of this structure are both value laden and 'ideological' (in the positivist sense). This finding suggests a re-evaluation of the contemporary literature of International Relations which attemps exegesis in this form. It also suggests a re-examination of both 'theory' and 'ideology', for if we accept the critique of positivism articulated here our notion of knowledge, and hence of 'theory' and 'ideology', changes.

Under the 'Kuhnian' view paradigm conflict is part of the development of scientific knowledge. Crucially, for social science, in the decision between conflicting paradigms 'logic and experience alone' are insufficient:

> There is no appropriate scale available with which to weigh the merits of alternative paradigms: they are incommensurable. To favour one paradigm rather than another is in the last analysis to express preference for one form of life rather than another – a preference which cannot be rationalized by any non-circular argument. (Barnes, 1982, p.65, quoted in Little, 1984, p.9)

With paradigms of International Relations these preferences are expressed in the general form of ideologies – not ideology in the positivist sense of 'that which precludes objective analysis', but ideology as an essential component of productive analysis (see also, from different viewpoints, Maclean, 1981; Cox, 1981a). The merits of conflicting paradigms in International Relations are not, then, reducible to 'scientific' analysis in the positivist sense – to do so would be to favour the positivist paradigm above all others and this is a non-rational (ideological) preference. Moreover, the existence of competing paradigms in International Relations/international political economy is not to be judged a weakness, a failure to reach towards the goal of a single, all-embracing explanation of social reality, as the positivists would argue. Because ideological assumptions are part of our construction of reality, and give meaning to our explanations of that reality, they are an essential part of international political reality itself and cannot be 'analysed out' (for a similar argument based on the notion of 'essentially contested concepts', see Little, 1981). Any attempt to effect a reconciliation of conflicting paradigms in International Relations is to misunderstand and misrepresent the problem of explanation in this subject (Runciman (1983) has developed a particularly interesting notion of explanation that may have significant implications for International Relations).

If, as the 'Kuhnian' view suggests, knowledge has a 'conventional character', i.e. it is established on the basis of a negotiated consensus of opinion among scientists (Barnes, 1982; Little, 1984), then we should consider the process by which this occurs in International Relations. The conventional character of knowledge and what constitutes legitimate knowledge among International Relations scholars is clearly seen in a review of the literature of the past ten years, particularly as there are at least two versions (both based on logical positivism/empiricism) of what is conventional – 'social science' and 'history'. As has already been said, the prevailing mode of acceptable (conventional) knowledge has an important influence on what is produced, but the 'negotiated consensus of opinion' that defines acceptable knowledge for the International Relations community (communities?) is not a neutral or value-free 'scientific' process. All kinds of influences are present – cultural, social, economic, institutional and political (particularly 'political' in the sense of government). From the foregoing we would also expect that the process of paradigm 'definition' would be ideological, where ideologies are frameworks of interpretation. The ideological nature of the process is not always clear. Indeed, as Robert Cox emphasizes, in a different context: 'Theory is always *for* someone and *for* some purpose', and 'There is . . . no such thing as theory in itself, divorced from a standpoint in time and space. When any theory so represents itself, it is the more important to examine it as ideology, and to lay bare its concealed perspective' (Cox, 1981a, p. 128). In an earlier article, Cox (1979) analyses and illustrates the basis of the literature on the New International Economic Order, stressing the political nature of intellectual production around 'cores of orthodoxy' through the creation of (expanding) networks (intellectual production is 'now organized like the production of goods or of other services', Cox, 1979, p. 260). From the point of view argued in this chapter, it is both interesting and desirable to view the literature of International Relations/international political economy in a similar way (but with a broader series of categories), highlighting the value premises and goals which inform the eventual 'negotiated consensus of opinion'.

Approaches to International Political Economy

We are now in a reasonably well-grounded position to make some sense of the international political economy literature in Britain and America. Two general problems will be considered – the emergence and development of international political economy, and the current structure of the subject as a sub-field of International Relations. At first glance what strikes one as most apparent is the sheer volume of books, articles, reviews, notes and, importantly, courses (all under the rubric of international political economy), in the US when compared to the UK. The growth of literature in this field has been prodigious, and if the amount of intellectual production was directly related to understanding and explanation we would have few problems left! Unfortunately, the problems and issues of international political economy appear to be intractable. I would suggest that this is partly the result of the positivist influence on theories in the subject, particularly in the kinds of explanation based on positivism. It also results from an inappropriate and inadequate conceptualization of international political economy, due mainly to ideological factors. However, let us for the time being return to the literature.

If we take what would be considered on both sides of the Atlantic, despite its limitations of method and scope, as the most widely used text – Joan Spero's *The Politics of International Economic Relations* (1981) – we find a 'selected bibliography' of approximately five hundred entries, around sixty of which are British and another twenty or so non-American. The majority of British authors arc included in the section on North–South relations (multinational corporations, Trade and Aid), and only four are mentioned more than once. We could interpret this as yet another example of the American ethnocentrism noted by Gareau (1981) and Lyons (1982), and a failure to heed the 'triple distance' warnings of Stanley Hoffmann (1977). But, even though much American (and British) work is ethnocentric in its assumptions and goals and in the 'narrow' band of literature utilized, the vast majority of the 'intellectual production' of international political economy in English takes place in the US. This is not just because of the much larger (and more prolific) system of higher education in America. Stanley Hoffmann's article (1977), sets out the factors and conditions that give rise to what he calls 'An American Social Science'. We have already argued that this is in itself a narrow view, but the conditions and factors Hoffmann identifies are valid and help to explain the specific and relativistic development of International Relations in America. The same range of factors and conditions broadly hold for international political economy (although clearly not the specific historical conditions): the peculiarly American 'operational paradigm' of intellectual understanding leading to progress; the status of science and technology within American ideology; the desire of scholars to be useful and 'help promote intelligently the embattled (economic) values of (their) country' (Hoffmann, 1977, p.47); the link between the perceived need of government and the 'intellectual production' of scholars ('the literature on the politics of international economic relations . . . coincides with what could be called the post-Vietnam aversion for force, and with the surge of economic issues to the top of the diplomatic agenda . . . Once more, the priorities of research and those of policy-making blend' (Hoffmann, 1977, p.48)); and the political pre-eminence of the United States which enables its 'scholarly community' to look at global phenomena. Finally, Hoffmann identifies three institutional factors, which only exist together in the United States: the most important is the 'most direct and visible tie between the scholarly world and the world of power' (p.49); the second is the role of the network of research foundations; and the third is the flexibility and diversity of the American universities.

I have dealt at length with Hoffmann's analysis because all these factors are relevant in a changed historical situation to the development of international political economy in America and, by and large, most of these factors are missing in the UK. Even though the academic tradition of International Relations began in Britain, the cultural and ideological context, and in particular the relationship between academics and government, could not be more different. A country on the downward side of hegemony, even though it maintains strategic nuclear forces, is, of necessity, compelled to restructure its goals and redirect its research, although clearly some key individuals will not fit this pattern. We could now consider, from a relativist stance, each of Hoffmann's factors and build up a picture of international political economy in both America and Britain (not very difficult to do for Britain), but this would ignore a critical dimension of the development of this subject – the ideological dimension.

In a strict positivist sense significant changes did occur in the international arena of the late 1960s and 1970s – inflation, oil shocks, world recession, record arms budgets, and changed structures of world economy – all of which were of fundamental importance to states and the international political system, and which called for a broadening of the focus of academic International Relations away from military security. But this positivist observation does not *explain* the emergence of international political economy. The fact that both behavioural and traditional International Relations on both sides of the Atlantic were concerned with military security almost exclusively was itself an ideological product. It was ideological in two senses, related to each other by history. First, the liberal tradition formed the ideological context for International Relations, and consequently politics was separated from economics (for a critical analysis of the ideological nature of the initial, post-mercantilist separation, see Cox 1981b). Even though E.H. Carr clearly demonstrated the links between politics and economics, and urged that they be brought together, the separation was maintained and reinforced after 1944, with the result that the economic problems of the late 1960s and 1970s had to be explained in terms of 'the politicization of international economic relations'. The 'politicization' thesis was approved by the Anglo-Saxons, but was something that the French, with their centralist traditions, their strong intellectual attachment to a Marxist-based structuralism and their neo-mercantilist view of the state, could not accept. Those in Germany working within the mercantilist traditions of List (1928) were of a similar view. Within these paradigms economics, particularly international economics, had always been political. It was the growing realization of certain key individuals, in both the American and the British International Relations communities, that the existing paradigms did not reflect the reciprocal influences of politics and economics that provided the stimulus for a redefinition of the consensus of International Relations to include international political economy (see Shonfield, 1969; Strange, 1970; Cooper, 1968; Kindleberger, 1970).

The continued separation of politics and economics after 1944, particularly given Karl Polanyi's remarkable analysis which linked domestic politics and economics to international structures, can also be seen as ideological in a second sense. That is, it enabled the US government, with British support, to maintain the desired form of international economy with the minimum political and economic cost by denominating the structure of political economy in such a way that economic issues were defined as technical problems, to be solved through the application of a technical rationality. (This view was neither a conspiracy nor necessarily a conscious articulation of interest. It was, however, conducive to and supported by the expansion of direct American foreign investment.) Once the problems were defined as 'non-political' their solutions were a matter for economic experts. The late Fred

Hirsch, one of the few British writers regularly quoted by American academics in international political economy, noted, in a critique of the liberal separation of economics and politics, that: 'Economics is when I have it; politics is when you want it' (Hirsch, 1976, p.528). This is clearly the case with relations between 'rich' and 'poor' countries since 1945, but increasingly it also became the case for relations between 'rich' and 'rich', as the fragile international ideological consensus of the post-war years crumbled under the strains of political and economic change. Once the ideological overview that defined international economics as 'technical' was challenged, it was necessary for the American government (and hence for the American academic community), in Hoffmann's analysis (1977) to understand the 'politicization' process in terms of the position that America (government and economy) held in the world political economy, and the policies it should follow (see, for example, Richard Cooper's innovative study, *The Economics of Interdependence: Economic Policy in the Atlantic Community*, 1968).

In a similar vein, it is possible to argue that International Relations academics in Britain also worked in a liberal tradition that separated politics from economics. But in this case relativist considerations point to the fact that while America had ascended to a hegemonic position, Britain's leadership was in decline. It is no coincidence that the first full contemporary British study in international political economy was Susan Stange's *Sterling and British Policy: A Political Study of an International Currency in Decline* (1971), for control of the international monetary structure is crucial to hegemony. It would also be tempting to argue that the pressures and realities of the British 'decline' blew away the ideological 'blinkers' of British International Relations scholars, particularly from 1956 onwards, but this is not the case. Unfortunately, not only did academics continue to ignore ideological concerns – this disregard spread, with certain important exceptions, to government, politicians, generals, civil servants, businessmen and the public.

The field of international political economy can be seen at present to represent both historical-relativist and scientific-nomological analysis. There is an international political economy 'community' whose work is broadly within the 'scientific' paradigm (without, however, the excesses of the earlier International Relations 'ultra-behaviouralist' methodology). This paradigm is positivist and embodies an extremely instrumental view of theory and concepts. It is predominantly, but not solely American, and its 'production' is characterized by the development of a specific methodology of theory evaluation by which alternative theories or models of explanation are tested against 'reality'. The dimensions and problems of this positivist methodology have already been discussed, but its influence on the development of the academic study of international political economy has been severe. The spurious scientific status ascribed to theories produced by this method, and hence the importance attributed to the methodology, has had an enormous impact on the logical structure of countless theses and innumerable monographs. Most influential in international political economy was Robert Keohane and Joseph Nye's *Power and Interdependence* (1977). This was a highly significant book because of its substantive focus and its attempt to refine concepts, and it has become the model for many others working in this paradigm (among the latest is Cowhey and Long, 1983). In line with Hoffmann's (1977) analysis, the scientific paradigm of International Relations relates to the needs of government through the development of 'policy science' and, not unexpectedly, this has been important in American international political economy given the urgency of contemporary problems in the world political economy. However, it does seem that the further development of an 'exact' policy science applicable to the world political economy is very much a problem – a problem of uncertainty and of the unknown. Herbert Stein (1978), for instance, has argued that policies of international co-ordination cannot be implemented satisfactorily because too little is known about international 'interdependencies' and because the national (and international) policy-making process would be 'over-burdened'.

The second international political economy community is made up of the majority of International Relations-based international political economy scholars in Britain (and Europe), and a substantial number in America who work within a historical relativist paradigm. This paradigm involves a particularistic analysis which endeavours to make sense of reality by an explanation of contingent historical factors. It is characterized by the production of a narrative, drawn from an eclectic mix of factors, which is sensitive to and embodies the influences of culture, institutions and (national) ideology and traditions and is aware of moral and ethical considerations (see, for example, Shonfield, 1976). It is not normally, however, particularly aware of the role of ideology in constructing the narrative.

Much of the literature in this paradigm is directed towards immediate policy concerns and towards the establishment of viable options for government policy, or arguments against it. It is clearly ideological, but on two levels. At a 'transparent' level, policy discussion is articulated (and criticized) on the basis of certain assumptions about the goals to be achieved and the method for achieving these goals. Hence, policy analysis and prescription generally reflect 'established' positions within the US and in Britain as well. Because this literature is accepted as value-based it is subject to a value-based criticism and the consequent debate is sanitized at the level of 'transparent' and admitted ideology. It is, however, ideological at a deeper level owing to the implicit acceptance of the historical structure which sets the context for the national policy debate: in America the explicit ideology of the political economy of progress and a contingent structural role in the world economy, and in Britain an implicit ideology of a world political and economic power with the resources of a 'lapsed hegemon'.

Given the difference in the nature of British and American government–academic relationships, policy analysis and prescription is more pronounced in America than in Britain, The relatively 'stand-offish' tradition of relations between government (politicians and civil servants) and academics in Britain, notwithstanding many excellent personal relationships, together with the much less open process of policy and goal formation than in America, means that the international political economy policy debate is muted in public, and where it is not, it tends to be dominated by the economics profession, 'who seem to think of politics as the domain of another set of specialists whose job it is to find a way of putting the economists' own prescriptions into effect' (Cox, 1979, p.279). In Britain, such is the power of the liberal ideological separation of economics and politics, and such is the esteem and power of the economics profession that international political economy is very much an 'infant industry', both in academic status and acceptability and in broader institutional and public terms.

The 'historical' and the 'scientific' paradigm form the basis for most of the research and teaching of international political economy in Britain and America, but there is a third approach to the subject which is shared by a growing, but still relatively small, number of academics and which fits uneasily in either of the two dominant paradigms as they are presently articulated and developed. This is the approach, shared by many development theorists, and by those who work within and develop Wallerstein's 'world system' theory, which is a form of 'structural materialism' (on the world system view of international political economy see, particularly, Hollist and Rosenau, 1981b), This approach is positivist, and therefore scientific (but not necessarily empiricist), in the sense that it posits a reality discoverable through theoretical investigation and holds that this reality is a materially constituted holistic reality in the form of a 'world system': the 'transhistorical' structure of world political economy. The holistic form of explanation denies both the reductionism of the realist 'inter-state' system and the reductionism of the 'political' or 'economic' view of social processes. It also embraces historicism, or at least a form of historicism, in its emphasis on historical continuity. This approach is, so far, almost totally American, and constitutes an extremely challenging development in international political economy, not only in its total reconceptualization of this subject but also in its acceptance that knowledge is defined by controversy and consensus, and that this means, significantly, that the notion of 'cumulative' research is not valid (Hollist and Rosenau, 1981b). However, the 'world system' approach is still wedded to the elusive goal of a 'theoretical synthesis' that will translate the reality of international political economy – but for whom?

If we return to the two major contending paradigms we can see developments in each, partly as a result of their contention, but also as a result of internal 'improvements'. There has been a kind of 'two-way street' in the interchange between the approaches, with American scholars producing the vast bulk of the material (both 'historical' and 'scientific'), and with British scholars looking at particular problems or attempting to locate the American (mainly 'scientific') work in a historical and normative context. However, there has also been much conflict between the two and it is instructive to consider briefly just one instance of British and American paradigm contention as an indication of the dilemma we are in.

The concept of 'regime' was initially developed by Keohane and Nye (1977) and expanded in scope and domain in later publications; the 'definitive' volume is by Krasner (1982a) who edited a special issue of the journal *International Organization* on regimes. The concept of regime was postulated as an important theoretical key to understanding the problems of achieving order and control in the world political economy – scientifically legitimate, as well as neutral (or more precisely, value-free). British academics were more equivocal than the Americans about the claims made, and many were quite unwilling to accept it as a kind of 'catch-all' concept or as a value-free theory. Christopher Mason used the concept in a very specific way in his study of the North Sea. For him regimes were 'intermediate factors between the power structure of the market and the political and economic bargaining that takes place with it' (Mason, 1979, p.8), and he was unwilling to take the idea further as the Americans were then doing. In the special issue of *International Organization* Susan Strange elaborates a multi-levelled critique of the regime concept 'as a 'fad', as 'imprecise', as 'value-biased', as 'distorting', and as narrow-minded 'state centricism', arguing that consequently it leads to a status quo biased analysis of international political economy and a search for an unattainable 'general theory' of International Relations (Strange. 1982, pp.479–80). The point here is not to delve deeply into the regime debate, but merely to illustrate the ultimate problem – that debates between paradigms cannot be resolved. In this case, neither can accept the claim of the other. They literally talk past each other in the specific sense that claims and counter-claims are based on different, and differentially revealed, value positions.

A Way Forward?

The argument of this chapter would deny the possibility of 'progress' through a synthesis of the two major approaches. If it were strictly possible this would just replace two theoretically constituted views of reality with another theoretically constituted view. The paradigms are incommensurable. But does this mean no progress? The answer to this question depends, of course, on the epistemological view that is held. A supporter of the 'scientific' paradigm would see much progress possible within the 'scientific' approach and likewise for the 'historical' paradigm. Supporters of one or the other might admit they could 'learn' from each other. Clearly, for example, the British 'historical' approach could benefit from a more coherent, comprehensive and articulated conceptual basis. The problem is how can this coherence and comprehensiveness be achieved? The development of metaphorical structures (*à la* 'science') with their universalist implications, is, unfortunately, not in line with the broad philosophical basis of the 'historical' approach. Equally clearly, American 'science' could benefit from historical and normative sensitivity, but such a sensitivity would damage its claims to 'objectivity' and 'universality'. Similar considerations apply to the 'world system' approach.

It is the logic of the argument here that 'progress' can only be achieved through a recognition of the incommensurability of approaches to international political economy, acknowledging that this is in itself both necessary and desirable. It is also argued that a consideration of ideology is critical to any approach to the subject, in terms of its capacity for self-evaluation and understanding, as well as its capacity to explain. In this context John Ruggie's chapter in the special issue of *International Organization* is interesting, as he is one of the most 'sensitive' of the scholars working on ('scientific') regime theory. Ruggie argues for the 'phenomenological' dimension of regimes, particularly in the 'dimension of social purpose' (Ruggie, 1982, p.382). An emphasis on the 'intersubjective meaning' necessitated by regimes moves us squarely to ideologies as broad interpretations of the world. Most important, and last, the progress of international political economy (or International Relations for that matter) is not to be vouchsafed in the search for an 'ultimate' theory or approach, whether it be 'scientific' or 'historical'.

8

History and International Relations

CHRISTOPHER HILL

There is a good deal to be said about the intellectual differences between the study of international history and the study of international relations. The focus of this book, however, puts limits on such a discussion, and what follows is concerned only with the interplay between the two subjects in the context of the broader contrast between American and British approaches to International Relations. It pursues the question: what attitudes to history and historians are evident in the work of International Relations specialists within the two cultures, and in what ways do they use – for none can ignore it – work carried out in the service of Clio? The terms of reference are further narrowed, for the sake of manageability, to books written since 1945 and dealing with events in the twentieth century.

Despite these restrictions, confusion may still arise. For here we are talking about two distinct countries as well as two distinct disciplines within these countries. There are therefore four quite separate units of analysis, producing six dyadic relationships (see figure 1). Before my more hostile British readers put down the book and reach for their copy of Bernard Levin's collected essays, it is worth pointing out that any discussion such as this which did not distinguish clearly between the separate American and British traditions in each subject, as well as between the subjects themselves inside each country, would soon fall into lofty generalization (a sore temptation in any cross-national comparison) and an elision of the issues at stake. Accordingly, the six

The author is grateful to his colleagues at the London School of Economics, Christopher Coker and Alan Sted, for their helpful comments on this chapter.

relationships indicated in figure 1 will serve to provide the structure for our principal concern, the discussion of history's place in the development of parallel International Relations communities in Britain and the United States. We will begin by examining the transatlantic ties within each subject.

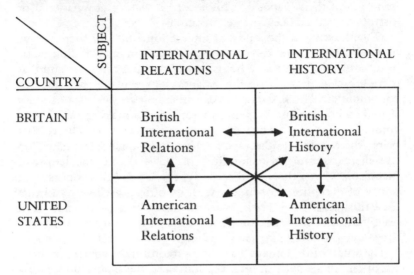

Figure 1   Two subjects in two countries, and their inter-relations

International History: A Joint Venture

'International history' subsumes what used to called 'diplomatic history', (Medlicott, 1955; Watt and Bourne, 1967, p.vi) and it is naturally the focal point for those observers of international relations who turn to the past for instruction. Although the subject now stretches to include the domestic origins of foreign policy, and economic or cultural movements as well as classical statecraft, it still quite definitely focuses on how governments have interacted, particularly during the great political events that have decided the fate of millions, such as the outbreak of the First World War or the conference at Yalta. Moreover, those working in International Relations draw readily on historical writing about events within the confines of the state such as that about nationalism in specific countries or domestic conflict over foreign policy issues. There is, therefore, every justification for concentrating on international history when discussing the views of international relations specialists on history and historians. It is also worth remembering, however, that attitudes to the study of the past are not the same as attitudes to the past itself. Disputes about how to extract evidence from history cannot conceal the fact that the record of completed experience is by definition all that anyone of an empirical turn of mind has at their disposal. This record underlies any national or disciplinary differences in interpretation.

When looking at the study of international history there can be no doubt about two facts: that the world community of diplomatic historians is dominated by British and American scholars, and that there are close ties across the Atlantic between the two research communities. The first fact owes something to the responsibility shared by London and Washington for actually making a very large amount of diplomatic history over the last century. The role of being the world's leading power has only once been taken up elsewhere (the murderous interlude of 1939–41) since the demise of Napoleon. Given that, until recently, the United States pursued a policy of exceptional openness with its official archives, and that the British have been relatively forthcoming by world standards (if not by those of efficiency or accountability), it is not surprising that they have produced extensive and high quality research.

The study of diplomacy has a long tradition, of course, in other European states such as France, Italy and Germany, and recent writing in the latter on the causes of both world wars (Fischer, 1975; Mommsen and Kettenacker, 1983) and the origins of European co-operation (Lipgens, 1982) has been of central importance to the field. None the less, the confidence associated with victory, as well as access to less mutilated archives than elsewhere in Europe, have meant that British writers like Paul Kennedy, Christopher Thorne or Donald Watt, and Americans like John Lewis Gaddis, Ernest May and Daniel Yergin, have tended to make the running as more and more of twentieth-century diplomacy has come under the magnifying glass. Helped by their common language, they tend to be familiar with each other's work and archives, and to exchange postgraduate students. Christopher Thorne's *Allies of a Kind* (1978) involved work in American primary sources in Washington and eight other cities, while Daniel Yergin's *The Shattered Peace* (1978) was based on his Cambridge (England) doctorate. Gordon Craig, seen in the United States as their most senior international historian, was actually born in Scotland; Michael Howard has been a key figure in the development of the transatlantic international affairs community;

and one of the foremost of the new generation of British diplomatic'
historians, Paul Kennedy, left the University of East Anglia for a
permanent appointment at Yale in 1983.

Perhaps the same picture could be drawn for other countries, but
the point here is simply that international history follows
Anglo-American scholarly co-operation, and is certainly not
inhibited by parochialism – although Americans have sometimes
accused themselves of being concerned only with US foreign
policy. Structural factors, including the very history of the
Anglo-American alliance, as well as language and personal ties,
encourage interchange of a high degree. It is also broadly true that
there are no fundamental differences of approach between the two
sets of researchers, although this is very far from saying that
interconnection breeds a common outlook. Even in the relatively
tranquil waters of historical argument, differences of national
tradition and political circumstance are only just below the surface.
This issue is taken up again in a later section; for now it is simply
worth noting that where the contrast goes beyond a simple
preoccupation with different national experiences in world politics
to matters of methodology, it is still confined to differing attitudes
towards experimentation with new approaches, the Americans
being far more innovative than the British. The long established
mode of writing about the history of international relations in a
broadly narrative form and making official records the centre-piece
is still predominant in both countries.

International Relations: A Faint Antagonism

Enough has already been written in this book about the tensions
between the British and American approaches to International
Relations to make only the briefest recapitualation necessary here.
However, attitudes to history are the heart of such antagonism as
exists between the two International Relations communities, and
they need to be placed in this context.

That contact is insufficient to promote consensus has been
demonstrated time without number in international relations;
indeed, the theory known as 'functionalism' has to some extent
foundered on this very rock. Certainly academic transactions
themselves do not bear out its central hypotheses. For while no one
would complain that there has been restricted intercourse –
academic travel alone would keep a small airline in business – the
meeting of minds has been partial and infrequent. In fact

International Relations is one area of study where generalities about national differences do hold. The sharp delineation between the American and British schools in this field, accentuated by the latter's internal cohesiveness, in essence derives from different interpretations of the term 'social science'. Both sides, of course, categorize International Relations as a social science, but whereas the tone of much American work is undoubtedly positivist, most British scholars define 'science' in the classical sense, as something involving a systematic but broad pursuit of knowledge along many parallel paths: analytical, legal, philosophical – and historical.

The transatlantic relationship in International Relations has therefore often been antagonistic at the intellectual level, when it has not been simply distant. It has been also always been asymmetrical. Whereas of the mainstream British International Relations figures only E.H. Carr, Joseph Frankel and Susan Strange have been widely read in the United States (unless we designate Hedley Bull and John Burton honorary Britons for the purpose of this discussion), a large proportion of the names on any booklist used in a UK university cannot help but be American. The question of history, furthermore, is bound up with both this antagonism and this asymmetry.

The British approach has always been strongly influenced by historical methods. For one thing, many of those who teach International Relations in Britain were initially trained as historians. For another, their reaction against history in favour of International Relations has been relatively mild. Very few indeed have forsworn their original training in order to embrace a wholly synchronic or comparative approach. Some indeed (admittedly a small proportion) teach and write about the new discipline in a way that is barely distinguishable from that of historical narrative. Certainly almost all would adhere to the maxim that good International Relations scholarship demands a familiarity at least with the evolution of the states–system since 1648, and preferably a detailed knowledge of the twentieth century and a number of special periods besides. Further, it is an article of faith that generalization needs to be substantiated by a wide range of historical example, and that competence in this regard is far preferable to an apparently more rigorous but ahistorical analysis of 'transactions' or 'national attributes' taken from events data and the like.

Thus the work of Martin Wight, probably the most widely admired man of his generation in British International Relations, is soaked in historical reference and allusion. Other notable figures in the development of the subject in the UK, such as Joseph Frankel, Geoffrey Goodwin, F.S. Northedge and P.A. Reynolds, have also emphasized the value of knowledge of the past as a bedrock for contemporary and theoretical analysis, and as something to be used illustratively, not as a formal data base. Their work may be thematic rather than chronological in structure, but the problems they begin with are still primarily defined in historical terms: *The Twenty Years Crisis* (Carr, 1939) and *Descent from Power* (Northedge, 1974b) are obvious examples. Even the more 'static' treatments of *The International Political System* (Northedge, 1976a) or *The Making of Foreign Policy* (Frankel, 1963) are infused with the belief that historical context is all-important, and that while the general conditions of inter-state relations may be identified, the nature of their impact in any given case is hardly predictable.

On the face of things, these beliefs should not lead to great conflict with the American school of International Relations. Many distinguished Americans have written about historically defined subjects and look with similar scepticism on behavioural approaches. The writings of Hans Morgenthau, Robert Osgood and Arnold Wolfers are hardly different in methodology from those referred to above. Yet a contrast does exist, not least in terms of mutual perceptions, and it is based on two fundamental facts. Firstly, the huge scale and heterogeneity of the International Relations industry in the United States puts the more historically inclined scholars in a minority, whereas in Britain they predominate. Nearly 900 participants were listed to attend the American International Studies Association 1984 conference in Atlanta, Georgia, compared to the average of 100 attending the British equivalent, and the American programme reveals a plethora of topics which would arouse scepticism and distate (whether justifiably is another matter) in most British faculties.

The second reason for the contrast over attitudes to history is that even those towards the traditionalist end of the American continuum use their history rather differently. The works of Graham Allison (1971), Alexander George (1980, and 1983 with Gordon Craig) and Robert Tucker (1977, 1981) find their echoes in Britain, but on the whole they are not emulated. Their distinctiveness lies in a willingness to test hypotheses, advance a general and formal argument, and delineate paradigms, thereby clearly making dialogue with the 'scientist' possible even if eschewing a strictly scientific methodology. In Britain there are very few examples of such work. The focus there, influenced in different ways by both Martin Wight and Charles Manning, has been on broader discussions of the nature of international society, its institutions and values. Long-term historical trends and enduring normative problems have been more attractive than the formulation of theories which might explain particular aspects of state behaviour, such as bureaucratic politics, coercive diplomacy and crisis mismanagement. It is noticeable, moreover, that even those American writers who stop short of this kind of limited formalism, like Stanley Hoffmann (one of the few genuinely mid–Atlantic figures) or Ernest May, are more willing to grasp the conceptual nettle than their British equivalents. For even where their interests are largely empirical and historical American academics are likely to employ ideas and images (if only such metaphors as in Campbell's *The Foreign Affairs Fudge Factory, 1971*) in any attempt to relate history to broader, semi-theoretical discussion. Where British writers concentrate on foreign policy, they tend to be highly concrete, even imitative of history. While those people who do produce concepts such as Frankel's 'role-conceptions' (1975) and Roy Jones's 'habitats' (1973), find that their images receive relatively little attention or are not picked up at all by colleagues more interested in the historical 'meat' of their books.

It is easy to overstate the contrast between British and American attitudes to history in the field of International Relations. After all, in special areas such as strategy and European integration, British writers have been willing to examine American concepts and test their utility (see Taylor, 1983). Moreover, the younger generation of British scholars is both influenced by American writing and is now increasingly the product of International Relations rather than history departments. Consequently British academics are beginning to write books which belong more to what the French see as a monopolistic 'Anglo-Saxon' community than to any distinctively British tradition (Williams, 1976; Smith, 1981; Buzan, 1983). In twenty years the contrast between British and American approaches may no longer exist as a result of this process. It can eradicate, however, neither the fact that the work of two generations has been produced along different lines, nor the temperamental split between those who see history as a resource for general explanatory statements about the world, and those who see the world itself as a historical phenomenon. This split will continue to exist long after its national manifestations have faded.

The Two Subjects Inside Britain

The differing attitudes to history taken up by International Relations specialists on the two sides of the Atlantic cannot be properly understood without seeing these specialists in the context of their domestic relationships with international historians. Obviously intellectual influences do not only come from within the discipline. They seep through from developments in every area of human enquiry, and particulary from cognate subjects like history.

Within the United Kingdom it is somewhat ironical that ties between International Relations and international history are not particulary close, given what has already been said about the historical leaning of British International Relations scholars. The British International Studies (*sic*) Association was intended to provide a forum for collaboration, but it tends to be dominated by International Relations people. There are few joint seminars parallel to Harvard's workshop on bureaucracy, or collaborative books such as Paul Lauren's *Diplomacy* (1979). Why should this be so?

Part of the answer lies in the familiar problem of territory. Leaving aside primeval forces like the selfish gene, there are practical difficulties associated with the raw materials of teaching and research. For the basic resource of the two subjects is identical: the corpus of past diplomatic exchanges, crises and political movements affecting the relative status of states. True, International Relations tends to examine contemporary events or patterns in world politics over the years, while international history prefers discrete periods rather than the long sweep of centuries, but there is a great deal of overlap. The question is how to *handle* the material. Given that the two disciplines in Britain diverge in only limited, subtle ways, there is full scope for familiarity between them. After all, International Relations has grown up partly out of the feeling that diplomatic history has not proved an adequate tool for understanding why wars occur, and most in the profession probably still harbour a sub-conscious self-satisfaction over their own intellectual bravura in daring to be theoretical. They associate historians, sometimes unfairly, with a resistance to ideas and wider horizons. There must also be a certain impatience among British International Relations academics at the historian's reliance on historical method for basic empirical knowledge – having recoiled from the behavioural alternative – and indeed over the fact that historians often teach central courses in International Relations degree courses. For, where International Relations departments teach their own history they lay themselves open to accusations of incompetence, yet few want their students to go without knowledge of this kind.

For their part, international historians look on International Relations much as the Anglican Church must have looked on the growth of Puritanism under Elizabeth I – with a mixture of bemusement and distaste. Many are deeply suspicious of its intellectual validity. Where it trespasses on their own ground, as in contemporary history, it is vilified as mere journalism which will be invalidated by the passing of time and the opening of records. Equally, broad thematic treatments are looked upon with distrust because of their apparent disdain for painstaking work in the archives. Where International Relations ploughs its own furrow by attempting to analyse and theorize about the structure of world politics, international historians may feel less certain of their ground, but in this country at least they are still extremely sceptical. Although some among them pay lip-service to the need to integrate historical and social scientific approaches (largely in the area of decision-making analysis: see Middlemas (1972), p.8; Kennedy (1981)), and others have undoubtedly found 'some of the work of International Relations theorists enormously useful in that it has provided them with a bag of intellectual tools and a vocabulary where previously they had to design their own' (Watt, 1983, p.15), very few go so far as to organize their material to make it accessible to those asking the questions generated by International Relations. (Two examples of books which, unusually, have done so, are Watt (1965), and Hinsley (1977).) In general, international historians display the attitudes of the closed shop.

Behind demarcation disputes lie the deeper issues of ethos and morale. As a new subject, International Relations has been perpetually on the defensive, struggling to get away from its earlier association with idealism, but (in the UK at least) unwilling to espouse fully a value-free approach. To some extent its practitioners have been overwhelmed by the need to be historians as well as political scientists, and unnerved by their proximity to the established traditions of diplomatic history. Whereas students of government can look back to a rich tradition of writing about the state, encompassing Aristotle, Hobbes, Rousseau, Mill and the rest, in which to ground their contrasting approach to that of history, students of international society have a much thinner canon to fall back upon. Even Thucydides was a historian. Because of its huge scope, International Relations stands out even among the social sciences in its eclecticism, inevitably borrowing concepts and data from philosophy, law, psychology, economics and government, as well as from history. It does not, therefore, easily create the sense of solid achievement which a clear and relatively narrowly defined subject can invoke. International Relations has struggled to delineate itself both in terms of scope and methodology.

International history has had the opposite problem. The last twenty years have seen a strong reaction against the 'longue durée', against the ambitions of a Toynbee and the emotion of a Wiskemann, in favour of close textual analysis of the flood of official records newly available. A book such as A.J.P. Taylor's *The Struggle for Mastery in Europe, 1848–1918* (1954) is now less likely to be written (except as a textbook) than, say, Christopher Thorne's *The Limits of Foreign Policy* (1972), a grand title concealing an excellent but very detailed study of the Manchurian crisis, 1931–3. As always, the exceptions to the rule are also important, such as D.C. Watt's analysis of European society and militarism between the wars (1975), or James Joll's *Europe Since 1870* (1973), but in general the vast amount of data to be absorbed, and the second-hand impact of positivist thinking in the social sciences, has brought diplomatic history into a phase of 'serene matter-of-factness . . . comprehension, a disinterested understanding of what is alien', as Pieter Geyl (1962, p.29) characterized the legacy of Leopold von Ranke.

British International History and American International Relations

It is ironical that in its attempt at cool objectivity British international history comes closer to the philosophy of American rather than British International Relations. The strain of critical evaluation in the latter, evident in the work of Philip Noel-Baker and Charles Manning, the first two professors in the subject at the London School of Economics, has been strongly maintained to the present day. Roy Jones's *Principles of Foreign Policy* (1979) and the two volumes produced by the International Political Theory Group (Donelan, 1978; Mayall, 1982) attest in their contrasting ways to a determination to see the history of state relations as a continuing process of interaction between ideas and ideals on the one hand, and praxis on the other. The spirit of positivism is therefore not enough, whether manifest in full-scale comparative research programmes or in historical accounts of individual events. Now it is true that one characteristic of the modern international historian is to reconstruct events rather than depend compacently on hindsight, to understand how it seemed at the time rather than to impose an anachronistic or ethnocentric judgment. Up to a point this is compatible with the tendency of some philosphically inclined academics in International Relations to believe that the *Zeitgeist* is as important to international society as it is to the culture of individual states. Yet whether the topic is Grey's Foreign Office or appeasement, Churchill or Korea, the historians' present priority (quite proper in view of the endless hot air which such subjects have attracted) is to eschew historicism and metaphysics in favour of letting the documents speak for themselves. In this they therefore echo, if only unconsciously, the value-free approach which swept American social science after the Second World War.

The convergence of the two viewpoints is not accidental, but it is abstract. On the plane of practical research there are in fact very few obvious links between British international history and American International Relations. In his acclaimed work on the Anglo-American wartime alliance in the Far East (1978), Christopher Thorne (who actually heads an International Relations department) displays some sensitivity to the work of social science. But Thorne's breadth of reference is unusual (he cites work by Almond, Brecher and Liska among many others) and even he, who argues (pp. x–xi) that 'the international historian can learn much from the political scientist or the social psychologist [and] works concerning foreign policy analysis in general', concedes that 'in *The Limits of Foreign Policy,* I have dismantled the analytical scaffolding itself before presenting the final study', by which he means that the framework of the book remains firmly chronological. We need not labour the point that British international historians have cared even less for the American brand of International Relations than for its indigenous variety. Yet it is worth noting how even those North Americans who are trained in Britain tend to lose what multi-disciplinary inclinations they have. Daniel Yergin's work with F.H. Hinsley at Cambridge produced a stimulating book that was full of ideas. But they are hardly notions taken from deterrence or balance of power theory, both of which are highly relevant to his theme. Equally, Americans and Canadians who have studied in the London School of Economics International History Department tend to be less interested in their own political science tradition than mid-Atlantic figures like Thorne or Kennedy – perhaps because they have been more exposed to it. Sidney Aster (1973) and J.T. Emmerson (1977), for example, fail to refer to a single volume of American International Relations writing between them in 800 pages of text.

British International Relations and American International History

The converse of the relationship we have just been discussing has not been particularly productive. British International Relations scholars are too few and American international historians too distracted by their own social scientists to provide many points of contact. At the same time, there does not seem to be any great interest in increasing communication. On the British side, to the extent that there is sustained interest in the history of diplomacy, this has been concentrated on the UK's own experience or been governed by the particular preoccupation of the individual researcher (for example, no one interested in the international politics of the Middle East could afford to ignore Bruce Kuniholm's *The Origins of the Cold War in the Near East: Great Power Conflict and Diplomacy in Iran, Turkey and Greece* (1980)). American writing on international history as a whole is not prominent in British International Relations circles, however, as is illustrated by the lack of impact made by its major journal *Diplomatic History*. Indeed, American foreign policy, past and present, attracts remarkably few specialists in British universities.

Such neglect is understandable. As we have seen, the International Relations specialist is hard-pressed by the very nature of the subject. In principle he or she needs to be both historian and analyst in a large field over a long period of time. Charges of unsubstantial and over-ambitious research to which the International Relations scholar is obviously vulnerable could only be overcome by narrowing the field of study, avoiding all discussion of the system as a whole, and concentrating on individual states, regions or issues. Since there are very good reasons, however, for continuing the unequal struggle to understand our dangerous and burgeoning world, those who wish to pursue research in this area must develop thick skins as well as high standards and extreme stamina. They have taken on the challenge of a multi-faceted problem and a multi-disciplinary subject, and they must rise to it.

This means that there should be no complacent pride in eclecticism and open-mindedness. Those working in International Relations like to see themselves standing on Mount Olympus, able to pick and choose from the range of specialists toiling below. They need to look at the whole picture of current developments within history and social science, because of their unique concern for time as well as space, for the evolution of international society *and* the multiple levels of analysis involved in studying man, the state, war and the wealth of nations. As a result it is easy to make large and sweeping generalizations.

If British work in International Relations has been patchy, it is also because the British community is so small. The lack of institutionalized bodies to teach the subject and a steady increase in demand from students has meant considerable sacrifices in research. It must be admitted that the 'British School' has produced only a small number of works which command the attention of their foreign colleagues. The decline of British influence on the world since 1956 has undoubtedly meant that those working on contemporary subjects turn less frequently to British authors on British problems. Even where research has a broad horizon, it is difficult to think of British equivalents to the works of Fernand Braudel (1972–3) or Immanuel Wallerstein (1974) which have had such an enormous impact outside their own circles, and which in particular aim to transcend the two subjects under discussion here (Wallerstein, 1979b).

It is perhaps unreasonable to expect impact of this magnitude. In any case mere renown is not the aim of the exercise. But in the context of this discussion of transatlantic relationships it can hardly be denied that although International Relations in Britain has made a major historical contribution to establishing the teaching of the subject in universities throughout the world, it has not in recent decades been able to compete on equal terms with the great monograph-producing machine of American academia – whatever the quality of the individual books involved. There has been neither sufficient productivity nor sufficient intellectual initiative to turn the heads of those outside the local stockade.

From the American point of view it is not as if the ethnocentrism which used to be a mark of the profession (Ernest May, 1971) ever derived from the exclusion of the British. The regard in which Michael Howard and Christopher Thorne are held in the United States illustrates how the traditionalist qualities of British International Relations make it more accessible to American international historians than the subject in its indigenous form. While the discipline remains so restricted in this country, however, with only a handful of International Relations departments and even those vulnerable to the imperialism of political science, any influence reaching across the water and across disciplinary boundaries will continue to be erratic and individual. On the other hand, American historians tend to possess as much of the national characteristics of energy, enthusiasm and inquisitiveness as anyone, and continually trawl social science everywhere for ideas, in a way which is unparalleled in Britain.

The Two Subjects inside the United States

In America, academic disciplines are remarkably sensitive to trends and developments within each other, part no doubt of a wider cultural distaste for immobility of all kinds, but also fostered consciously by numerous think-tanks and research institutes. New patterns of collaboration, after all, mean more jobs, conferences and publication opportunities. Certainly the two 'international' subjects have encouraged each other in the United States over the last decade or so. After years of being exhorted to do so, historians have begun to exploit anthropology, economics, political science and psychology. Many naturally are sceptical and prefer well-tried techniques of craftsmanship, but enough have crossed the Rubicon to transform the profession (Kammen, 1980, pp. 19–49), producing the hybrid 'social science historian' (Allan G. Bogue, 1980, pp. 245–8) who is emphatically not an historian of social science.

The debate has raged within the subject itself as to whether international history has confronted these changes constructively, or whether it has simply 'marked time' (Charles Maier, 1980, pp. 355–87). Maier highlighted parochialism (p. 378: 'American diplomatic history often remains conceptually a sub-field of the United States history'), lack of intellectual enterprise, 'of being at the cutting edge of scholarship' (p. 355), and 'the field's intransigent resistance to new techniques' (p. 357). His criticisms produced lively reactions (*Diplomatic History*, 'Symposium', 5 (4), Fall, 1981), but all disagreement was tempered by an admission of the weight which Maier's view carried, given his own influential book (1975) and the detailed documentation provided in his paper. To an outsider, the discussion testifies strongly to the robust health of international history in the United States. The range of work and awareness of other disciplines revealed in these exchanges emphasizes once more the sheer scale and energy of American university life. By comparison with Britain, and probably the other European states, diplomatic historians have already borrowed extensively from concepts of their sister-discipline. There are no illusions about what is possible with quantitative methods, but theories of decision-making, especially those relating to bureaucratic behaviour, have had considerable effect. As also in Britain (Steiner, 1969; Hinsley, 1977; Cowling, 1975), the general question of the domestic roots of foreign policy has become central to modern scholarship, although American writers are more at home with the relevant writings of political scientists and more prepared to formulate 'testable' questions which can actually be applied to particular historical cases more easily than to a long run of data. Perception and personality are other areas where US diplomatic historians have gone direct to International Relations literature for ideas or subject-matter. Figures such as Alexander George or Robert Jervis are as well known to historians as their peers (compare the bibliographies of the chapters on the British and American foreign ministries in Steiner, 1982).

For their part, the International Relations fraternity have not neglected history; although this generalization needs even more qualification than usual, for a good deal of the expansion of the subject in the United States has been a direct reaction to conventional diplomatic narrative which seemed to many an inadequate explanation of great events such as war and recession, and to hold no hope for discovering ways in which international conflict could be modulated. Quincy Wright (1942) and Lewis Richardson (posthumously, 1960b), two of the best-known writers of the new wave of the 1940s, epitomized the attempt to escape from the tyranny of circumstance and to generalize about the underlying phenomena responsible for the chaos visited on the world from 1914–45. The behaviouralist revolution followed relentlessly and produced a whole new generation of American writers on International Relations. Whereas in Britain this revolution was snuffed out before it could gain hold, in the USA there are now established career patterns in quantitative methods, comparative foreign policy, conflict studies and the like, all of which are essentially anti-historical in their approach.

This is not to say, however, that International Relations in the United States is polarized between modernists and traditionalists according to their attitude to history. Quite apart from the fact that many behaviouralists are keen to use data produced by historians where they can, and that current trends have swung back (via Marxism) towards emphasizing dynamic even historicist explanations, it remains true that there is a large nomadic population of American writers on International Relations who migrate between the mountains of formal analysis and hypothesis–generation, and the oases of historical detail. Thus the famous Harvard seminar on 'bureaucracry, politics, and policy', included major historians like Ernest May and Samuel Williamson as well as the conceptual jugglers such as Neustadt, Allison and Halperin. Thus Robert Jervis's massive book about perception and misperception (1976) is based on a painstaking assembly of all relevant historical case studies. Thus Alexander George has co-operated with Gordon Craig in a recent book now used by students from both disciplines (1983). This is not to label the non-behavioural camp as quasi-British in style, however. American non-behaviouralists differ from their British counterparts in that they often work in direct collaboration with diplomatic historians and are anxious to use history in a formal way to test the validity of theory (e.g. John Steinbruner, 1974, Richard K. Betts, 1977). British studies tend to be more departmentalized and more interested in weaving historical example and philosophical discussion into a single rich tapestry than in imitating scientific methods. History is therefore important on both sides of the Atlantic, but it is used in each country in very different ways.

Conclusions

It is common practice, not without justice, to accuse American foreign policy of being essentially ahistorical, claiming that it operates on the basis of aims and assumptions which are often anachronistic or insensitive to the peculiar origins of individual conflicts. An extension of the argument might attribute this failing to such cultural characteristics as an obsession with the present, the lack of a long American past, and facile assumptions about how to achieve change (viz.: the 'conquest of cancer'). There is some truth in all this, but our brief look at attitudes to history in the context of approaches to International Relations hardly substantiates the caricature of a behaviouralist American profession blithely consigning the work of international historians to the breaker's yard of outmoded techniques. On the contrary, in some respects International Relations in the United States tends to be closer to history than it is in Britain, where the subject is generally thought to be 'traditionalist', i.e. heavily historical.

One aspect of the central paradox may be formulated thus: whereas American political culture and the foreign policies it produces can play fast and loose with the historian's concern with particularity and context, international history itself is flourishing in the United States as never before – the Society of Historians of American Foreign Relations (SHAFR) was founded in 1967 and by 1980 had 800 members as well as its own learned journal, *Diplomatic History*. It seems likely that this is the result of anxiety among American historians themselves about the way in which history was crudely annexed for partisan political argument in the era of the Vietnam war, and, with the usual long delay, we should expect the quality of historical understanding evident in official policy-making in Washington gradually to improve. But American historians are on good terms with International Relations not just at personal and institutional levels, but in the sense that members of the two research communities actually seem to read each other's books and to benefit intellectually from exchanging ideas and facts. (A particularly representative figure is the eminent historian of the nineteenth century, Paul Schroeder. See, for example, Schroeder, 1976.) There are now substantial numbers of extant works in history that show signs of having been alerted by social science to potential explanations or methodologies, while an increasing proportion of those working in International Relations have come to distance themselves from the crass dismissal of evidence produced by historians which was associated with the behaviouralist school.

The other aspect of our basic paradox is the relationship between British political culture and international history – almost (but not entirely) the reverse of the American position. In Britain political culture is infested with historical thinking to the detriment of the government's ability to innovate. This is not just a matter of nostalgic references to a glorious past: a strong attachment to gradual change, which often means no change at all, and an immensely strong distrust of abstract thinking amounting to anti–intellectualism also permeate attitudes in Whitehall and Westminster. The corollary of this is that the historical profession is in theory highly esteemed (the prime minister still decides who shall fill the senior chair in the country, the Regius Professorship of Modern History at Oxford), although it is not quite so highly held as in the era of Winston Churchill and R.H. Tawney. The Oxbridge history schools continue to be key training-grounds for major sectors of the British élite, notably the fast streams of the civil service and journalism of all kinds, but history in the universities is in such difficulties that in 1982 a History Defence Group had to be set up. The present government stresses the importance of history in education while cutting the resources needed to produce historians (see *History Today*, 34, May 1984).

In this climate, international history clearly does not flourish, struggling as it is to establish a separate identity. The special problem of Britain's quite rapid decline in prestige in world affairs has not made it easier to justify an expansion of research into the origins of what seems like an inexorably negative record from 1945 onwards, and a now barely relevant period of great power predominance before then. International history, therefore, is now (and is likely to remain) a small pocket of excellence without particular relevance to political or even intellectual life. To the extent that those working in the field do have an impact outside their own profession, it tends to be because they are willing to open out towards other areas of study, as James Joll did towards intellectual history (1960; 1973) and Michael Howard has done towards International Relations with his writings on war and his role in stimulating strategic studies.

Such initiatives are not common. In general, as we saw earlier, students of diplomatic history in this country have been suspicious of social science and have wedded themselves to a form of professional autarky. This has been bad for international history and bad for International Relations which has been particularly unnerved by its own failure to attract the interest of historians, given the very short distance it has moved away from their subject and given the fact that this failure has not been paralleled in America. Indeed it is arguable that International Relations has not yet succeeded in marking its own intellectual territory in British universities precisely because of the ambivalence about its relationship to the study of history. Although to any outsider the intellectual gap between the two subjects seems small and easily overcome, in reality the picture is one of quite separate paths of development, close and parallel but separated by a high privet hedge, as with the Tudor maze at Hampton Court. For International Relations the consequence is an unfortunate reinforcement of the subject's intrinsic fascination with recent history, whereas study of the eighteenth and nineteenth centuries in a longer perspective could prove far more instructive for those reflecting on the nature of international politics.

For international historians the lack of interchange has had a different kind of effect. It has meant that these historians have become relatively insulated from the intellectual ferment that has affected other branches of historical study over the last twenty years. Only recently, in Donald Cameron Watt's inaugural lecture as Stevenson Professor at the London School of Economics (1983), has the profession confronted the issues of methodology and purpose raised by the growth of the social sciences and in particular by the Annalistes' attack on 'l'histoire événementielle'. (This is the case if we exclude the distinctive figure of E.H. Carr and his book, *What is History?*, published in 1961; Carr would probably not be claimed by international historians as one of their own.) Other British historians – Geoffrey Elton, Eric Hobsbawm, J.H. Plumb and Lawrence Stone – have entered into debates on the philosophy of history, but those concerned with diplomacy have rarely shown interest.

These issues cannot be gainsaid as neither historians nor social scientists write solely for themselves. As audiences, students and national interests change, so does the pressure to consider one's academic rationale. The attack on the sterility of much diplomatic history that was mounted in the United States predictably did not gain the same ground here, but its import cannot be ignored. On an individual basis changes are obviously taking place, as the interest in decision-making processes clearly demonstrates. In so far as younger people still have the opportunity to enter the profession, they tend to bring with them interests in other methods of inquiry, particularly economics. The idea that British international historians continue to be absorbed with plotting what one clerk said to another is certainly an exaggeration, but progress has been patchy towards substantive collaboration with International Relations of the kind achieved by Paul Lauren and his colleagues (1979) in the United States.

The relationship in Britain between International Relations and the international historians is therefore very different to that in America. But the differences are not irrevocably the result of national characteristics. The fundamental issues at stake are methodological, and although the increasing differential of power between the foreign policies of the two countries is bound to affect academic priorities, the scholarly communities pride themselves on a functional rather than political approach to changes in their subject. Intellectual distinction of all kinds is usually recognized and emulated in the long run, so it should come as no surprise that

International Relations in the US has once again begun to value historians highly, while international history in the UK is slowly adopting some of the more transferable paradigms from International Relations. Those mainly involved with political ideas, systems and processes cannot do without those serving Clio. Equally, those concerned with explaining historical change increasingly accept that the very nature of explanation will entail reference to debates generated elsewhere. The future is likely to see calmer general recognition of the fact that history and social science are both to be found within the same melting pot. Their common cause will be quite evident in international affairs, whose multiple complexities must drive the two subjects ever closer together on both sides of the Atlantic.

9
Transnationalism

MICHAEL CLARKE

The concept of transnationalism is difficult to place with any precision in international theory. In itself, it certainly does not constitute a theory; it is rather a term which recognizes a phenomenon or perhaps a trend in world politics, a phenomenon from which other concepts flow. The more prevalent of these are interdependence, integrationism, international regime construction and, possibly at a higher level of abstraction, systems transformation and world order theories. All these are important subjects and some aspire quite legitimately to being theories, but it would be pedantic to try to tease out distinctive British and American views on them and it would certainly not bring us any closer to an understanding of the more general concept of transnationalism. Yet the differences that arise in attitudes to transnationalism because of generality are indicative of British and American approaches to International Relations. It will therefore be more useful to discuss the theories that arise from transnationalism as a function of the broader questions that the analysis raises. We will consider transnationalism as a study, a phenomenon and as an example of the relevance of methodology to the policy process.

The Study of Transnationalism

It is a commonplace observation that transnational relations are hardly new in international politics. In the seventeenth century a certain flightiness of capital was a matter of concern to landowners who felt themselves to be the natural embodiment of the state (Hirschman, 1978, p.97). Bull points out that no modern multinational enterprise has yet had as much impact on world politics as the East India Company, which controlled both territory and armed forces (Bull, 1977, p.271). Nevertheless, it is also commonplace to observe that world politics in the later twentieth century is characterized by a high degree of transnationalism which, at the very least, raises important questions for the discipline of International Relations. There has been a vigorous debate about the strength of transnationalism, whether it is measurable in any useful sense, and how we should evaluate it in an expanding political universe. In fact, growth in the study of transnationalism is far easier to record than growth in the phenomenon itself.

The reasons for the increase in study are not hard to find. They are mostly intuitive and consequently easy to state but difficult to analyse. Transnationalism thrives in the modern world in which transport and communication have begun to play a qualitatively different role in world politics than in the past. Organizations merely operating outside state boundaries would not merit the description of transnational. Huntington (1973 p.342) would class that only as 'crossnational', and there are many other natural and human phenomena that would fall into this loose definition. Our concern is with those that are in some way deemed to be politically relevant. We ought therefore to be interested in identifying the ways in which modern communications *stimulate* organizations to function more profitably or powerfully on a global scale, without obvious reference to national boundaries. In this way transnationalism is not just a phenomenon of non-state action accompanying international relations (which has always existed) but a pervasive and politically salient phenomenon likely to develop under the conditions created by modern communications.

A more specific reason for the growth of the study lies in the *pax Americana* that followed the Second World War. Essential global stability and economic expansion afforded a political climate in which transnational organizations could flourish. Gilpin (1971, pp.63-7) narrows this further and points to two 'most crucial relationships' – that between the United States and West Germany, and that between the United States and Japan, – which provided the political prerequisite for transnational economic activity after 1945. Interest in the phenomenon was stimulated not only by a recognition of these political conditions but also by an acknowledgement that transnationalism had become both part cause and part effect of a dynamic *pax Americana*. Not only does transnationalism affect states, states affect transnationalism. Then again, transnational organizations have their own quite separate interactions which form part of the international fabric (Alger, 1977). Anyone who tried to make sense of the post-war order, therefore, could not help but be impressed by the degree to which this phenomenon was an intrinsic part of that order. 'Transnationalism', says Huntington (1973, p.344), 'is the American mode of expansion. It has meant "freedom to operate" rather than "power to control".' It is, in short, a concomitant of the most central fact of the post Second World War era.

A final condition for the growth in the study of transnationalism was methodological. Recognition of favourable technical and political circumstances, established the salience of the phenomenon. But there was also a methodological root to the study since transnational organizations have more specific functions than states, a narrower index of power (financial assets, membership, dispersion etc.), and a clearer criterion of growth. The susceptibility of transnational phenomena to measurement suggested that greater rigour would be possible than was normally the case in studying state-centric affairs. While the existence of transnationalism was a matter of importance, the *concept* of transnationalism was cause for excitement since it promised the scientific study of something that could become the most significant dimension of world politics. It was no accident that interest in this phenomena coincided with the growth of quantification and behaviouralism as methodological innovations in the discipline: 'scientism', as Parkinson calls it (1977, p.185). If the precise calculation of personal and organizational behaviour seemed like a useful hammer for the student of international politics, transnationalism seemed like the ideal type of nail.

Describing the conditions in which the study of transnationalism arose is not just a matter of intellectual history. It also tells us that transnationalism as a concept is very much an American creation. It flowed from the manifestation of American power; it was in part a rationalization of broad US policy, and it appealed to an American academic *penchant* for quantification as a step towards greater scientific rigour. It has not of course remained exclusively American either as a phenomenon or a study, but it is hard to imagine how it could have arisen without both a political and academic *pax Americana*. For the same reasons the elaboration of the concept and the implications which flow from it have changed as the original conditions have changed. After twenty years of observing a communications revolution, it is not clear whether the trend is unequivocally towards transnationalism or internationalism in world politics. In itself communication strengthens parochialism as much as it attacks it, and communications theory has not developed in the international integrative directions predicted by Deutsch in his earlier works of the mid-1950s (Tooze, 1978, pp. 222–6). The *pax Americana* is now clearly characterized by a high degree of regional and functional fragmentation. This, arguably, may stimulate certain types of transnationalism, but at the very least it is also a development which has encouraged states to be defensive and which has created a less permissive environment for the operation of transnational bodies. Partly for the same reasons, the discipline of International Relations is now notable for a good deal of methodological pluralism; there is a recognition that beyond a certain degree of raw statistical data the evaluation of the political effects of transnationalism is as much a matter of intuition as computation.

Given this history, it is not surprising that transnationalism has been difficult to place within the range of international theory. Its fortunes are bound up with those in the American academic community who are seeking to make sense of America's role in the world. This was expressed neatly by Rosenau in 1976 who reviewed the state of international studies in the light of transnationalism and wondered why there was not more puzzlement – in the sense of a greater willingness to specify new hypotheses about the way the contemporary system operated. Rosenau's 'genuine puzzles' were very much a reflection of an American academic community which saw a new phase of US power as *ipso facto* a new phase of world politics (Rosenau 1976c, 1976d). Thus Northedge (1976b) could criticize Rosenau's puzzles about transnationalism as 'the American illusion', transnationalism being more a reflection of the discovery of an idea than a significant trend in world politics.

The Phenomenon of Transnationalism

It would be too contrived to try to point to particular Anglo–American differences in the manifestations of transnationalism. In any concept which owes so much to the United States, it is inevitable that interpretations will be derivative and imitative of US interpretations in both academic communities. Further, in a concept which is as broad as this, any number of particular ideas will be drawn from it to buttress the interests of different academic schools. Some interesting differences in emphasis emerge over particular issues, however, but it is important to view them in a broader perspective in order to discern the key divergence between British and American approaches to the methodology of transnationalism and its relevance to policy-making.

The phenomenon of transnationalism is, in itself, hard to pin down. We must first face the question of whether transnationalism is more important in world politics than ever before. The answer to this question rather depends on how the terms are defined, how transnationalism is measured or is measurable, and what assumptions we make about the national components of world politics. There is, for example, a straight contradiction between the assumptions made by the doyens of transnationalism, Keohane and Nye (1971), that transnational relationships do play an increasing role, or the assertion of Rosecrance and Stein (1973, p. 21) that 'The horizontal interaction of transnational processes is higher than at any point since World War 1', and the doubts expressed by Bull (1977) on this score. According to Bull, it is just as likely that the state-system has 'extended its tentacles over world politics' (p. 279) to intrude into areas of non-state activity that have only recently become politicized. Thus, what appears to be an increase in transnational activity may actually be no more than an increase in the number of states and the scope of their activities, which merely illuminates transnationalism in a political context. According to this view, there is stark disagreement between American transnationalists and avowed traditionalists who follow in the footsteps of Charles Manning and Martin Wight. In reality, no great conflict exists. Wolfram Hanrieder, for example, has expressed views close to those of Bull in suggesting that the state is in the process of 'domesticating' international politics (1978) a process in which he recognizes the growth both of transnational forces and the power of the state. Ultimately, since what one sees in transnationalism depends upon prior assumptions about definitions and methodology, the question whether transnationalism is more important today than ever before must remain a matter of contention, and it would be fruitless to contrast assertions as if they were bodies of evidence.

Let us, however, at least make the assumption that transnational phenomena (however they arise) are politically significant and do have some impact on international relations. The debate over the extent of their significance and impact can be analysed more clearly under two general headings: effects on the structure of the international system, and effects on the processes therein.

Structural Effects

The implications of transnationalism on international structure can be defined by asking two major questions. Firstly, what is the role of the state in a transnational world and how shall we define an international actor? Secondly, how far does transnationalism depend upon an essential political stability between those actors?

On the first issue, the debate has challenged the pre-eminence of the state in the international system. In a general sense, the 'global village' perspective which emphasizes the behaviour of individuals in a shrinking world of modern technology, has adopted transnationalism as the mechanism by which states are by-passed and eventually ignored. Transnationalism is the engine of, to quote Inkeles, 'the emerging social structure of the world' (1975). A major, untypical, British contribution along the same lines has been the work of John Burton in his *World Society* (1972). In his study of transnational, Rosenau (1980c) sees government relations as being crucially affected by the activities of private individuals reacting to the dynamics of modern technology and communications. They have their own goals and this represents 'a transformation, even a breakdown, of the nation state system' (pp. 1–2). A derivative strand of this perspective is that which focuses on demographic and ecological dimensions of the world. The most salient structures of world politics, in this view, are those of the global environment. Individual actions and transnational contacts are the raw material of an 'eco-system' or 'eco-politics' with which the state is unable to cope. In 1971 Richard Falk identified four dimensions of 'planetary danger', namely the 'war system', 'population pressure', 'resources' and 'environmental over-load'. They constituted a 'mismanaged environment' that grew inevitably from 'a defective set of political institutions' (Falk, 1971, p. 98). This was a beguiling approach but ultimately not an influential one. The realization that the international system could well be depicted as a system of global transactions does not, in itself, produce a better explanation as to why anything within it happens as it does.

More specifically, the pre-eminence of the state seems to have been threatened by the growth of economic actors playing an international role alongside it (and sometimes in opposition to it).

The growth of the multinational corporation and the role played by banking and financial institutions in the management of international economic relations have for a long time questioned the competence of the state, and they mount a more serious challenge to it than conceptions of a vaguely defined 'globalism'. This emerged as a more prevalent aspect of transnationalism partly because it was a more tangible manifestation and partly because of the evident ability of financial institutions and multinational corporations to cross national boundaries in a highly consequential way. The focus on this was also consistent with the growth in formal international organizations charged with financial responsibilities. If one could assume that economic relations were a major determinant of other facets of world politics, then, clearly, the state was now sharing the political arena to an unprecedented degree with international governmental and non-governmental bodies which all operated transnationally.

There is a vast literature on the multinational corporation and many different answers to the question of whether it has usurped some or all of the authority of the state. It is not part of our present purpose to try to review this literature, but Raymond Vernon – among the most influential of those to pose the original question – in his article '*Sovereignty at Bay* ten years after' (1981) puts the issue in perspective most eloquently. The fear of the multinational corporation as a usurper of the state rose and then fell in the 1970s. In his book, *Storm Over the Multinationals* (1977), Vernon had recorded that the relationships between states and multinational corporations were highly complex and subject to enormous variation. By the late 1970s both the state and other bodies had in fact reasserted themselves over the corporation. By 1981 the question did not even seem particularly interesting. Vernon writes that while multinational corporations 'taken as a class continue to account for a considerable share – even an increasing share – of the economies of most countries, individual multinationals have nothing like the bargaining position they sometimes held in the past' (p. 527). The real question is now more subtle: 'How do the sovereign states propose to deal with the fact that so many of their enterprises are conduits through which other sovereigns exert their influence?' (p. 528–9). On this most sensitive aspect of transnationalism the trends are contradictory. The original question – is the multinational corporation usurping the state? – is not resolved so much as integrated into a more subtle calculation concerning the way corporations interact with certain *types* of states to produce politico-economic structures that are advantageous to some political leaderships and to some corporate managers.

The same is true of the growth of international financial institutions. While their role visibly increased as the Bretton Woods economic system went through its final crises, and while in the absence of purposeful state action in the early 1970s they seemed to play a major part in economic management both at domestic and international levels, their development has not been consistent. The IMF's role has been widened but it now takes account of more governments in its decision-making to reflect the shifting balance of economic power between them (Ruggie, 1982, pp. 409–10). The GATT (General Agreement on Tariffs and Trade) is just as much subject to bilateral governmental negotiations as it always had been (Curzon and Curzon, 1976, chapter 3). Moreover, as Krasner points out (1981, pp. 326–8), the major regional development banks – in his analysis, the Inter-American, Asian and African – are crucially subject to the influence of major states, both formally and informally.

If nothing else, therefore, the last decade has offered enough conflicting evidence on the role and function of the state to keep a legion of analysts busy. And within this debate over empirical evidence it is certainly possible to discern different nuances between an American community who looked for a new role for the state, and a British approach which saw modernization and the decline of American hegemony as merely a new set of problems for the state. The influential work of the American Edward Morse in 1970 examined the effect of 'modernization' on the conduct of foreign policy (Morse, 1970). In 1976 Morse was concerned with the effects of the same strands of modernization on the international system which was more interdependent and transnational in nature (Morse, 1976b, p. 14). He is clearly not in the 'withering away of the state' camp, but he was overtly absorbed with looking at the fundamental effects of modernization on the role and behaviour of the state: 'the general influences that have transformed foreign policies are ubiquitous . . . these changes are likely to be dispersed throughout the international system far ahead of other aspects of modernity' (Morse, 1970, p. 392). This rather distinguishes him from mainstream British foreign policy analysts, such as Wallace, who are also much concerned with the effects of modern conditions on foreign policy. In his analyses of the forces acting upon foreign policy Wallace has long since maintained that the shape and style of governmental activity in Western Europe has changed considerably

(Wallace, 1975, pp.268-74). Nevertheless the states of Western Europe respond in their own most appropriate ways to pressure. Foreign policy may indeed, to use his own characterization, be less 'foreign', but it is not a matter of system (even foreign policy system) transformation. The conditions in which West European, and particularly British, foreign policy operates has undoubtedly changed, but Wallace is continually struck by the persistence of centralized foreign policy-making in one form or another, and by the individuality with which states react to their own problems. Perhaps his level of analysis is simply more specific than Morse, or perhaps he resists analyses which tend towards determinism (Wallace, 1978; 1980). The European Community has become more than an international regime, in many respects it is an impressive organization, but even here Wallace is sure that the essential processes of members' foreign policies dictate the degree of transformation – even further adaptation – that may be possible for the Community (Wallace, 1983b, pp.431-2).

A similar difference in emphasis between British and American views can be discerned in looking at another structural manifestation of transnationalism. Whether or not the state's role is fundamentally altered by the forces of modernization, it is generally agreed that it does share the political arena with a nunber of other types of actor. The resulting conglomeration of rules, norms and institutions is frequently defined as a regime, and the study of regimes has become an object of much interest in international politics. The concept of regime suggests a way to rationalize a mix of authority structures and a range of geographical and functional variations. Keohane and Nye (1977) popularized the concept in a major study on the workings of complex interdependence and since then a great deal of material, principally American, has been devoted to it. Keohane and Nye looked at the outcome of situations in which governments had to co-exist both with the power of inter-governmental organizations and international non-governmental organizations. In defining the complex regimes which resulted they were keen to challenge the assumption of the state as a unitary actor and the role of force and military security as first-order priorities. They were more interested in bargaining and coalition management as a dominant mode of international behaviour. In a similar vein, Oran Young has spent much time discussing how we might define the actors in the international system. His concern is not merely pedantic, for Young analyses a 'mixed-actor' system and asks whether it is essentially stable or whether it tends towards structural instability (Young, 1972; Yalem, 1978). His conclusion rather supports the thrust of Keohane and Nye's argument, that while a mixed-actor system can certainly be mishandled, it can in fact be regarded as essentially stable where a division of labour is recognized between actors and necessary tasks are performed without raising basic questions of authority. In 1980, Young defined regimes as social institutions around which the expectations of various actors converged (Young, 1980). This may seem a rather loose definition, but it captures the essence of the organic nature of the concept, and similar definitions have been offered by Haas (1980) and Krasner (1982b, p.186). Probably the most influential expression of American views on international regimes was contained in a special issue of *International Organization* (Krasner, 1982a). Here, an eminent collection of writers examined a number of facets of the problem.

Against this, British concern with international regimes is harder to define. Krasner (1982b, p.186) quotes one of Hedley Bull's more philosophical passages (Bull, 1977, p.54), declaring that Bull all but explicitly agrees to the existence of regimes. As an international scholar whose work sits firmly within the British tradition on these matters, one suspects that Bull would not support this claim, or that if he did, he would not be referring to quite the intellectual construction that Krasner and his other contributors have in mind. British academics see less significance in the notion of regimes than their American colleagues. The neatest example of this is provided within the *International Organization* collection itself. Susan Strange (1982) offers a personal critique of regime analysis. She criticizes it – perhaps almost too sharply to point the contrasts – believing that as a passing fad it is quite overestimated, that it is imprecise even if it is carefully formulated (like the 'global village' it cannot rise above the status of metaphor), and that in practice it is simply not accurate because it is both too static and oddly state-centric. She is concerned that political economy should be studied within a framework that is not restricting in ways for which she attacks the regime concept (pp.493-6). She is very typical in the general thrust of her argument which finds regimes to be more apparent than real.

For British academics, the influence of transnational force has been most marked in relation to the European Community. For as the integration process has slowed in the 1970s, so the politics of Europe have increasingly been described in terms similar to those used to describe a developed regime. In the European Community there is a drive to establish more and more institutions and deliberative bodies, and there are clearly some genuinely integrated policy areas. But the focus on coalition-building, on parallel rather than convergent policies, and on the dynamics of patchy and selective co-operation, brings the student of European integration rather close to the concerns of the student of regime construction. There is still a difference between them however, which is partly one of focus and partly one of expectation. The focus on the Community is more specific and concerned not with how an 'international order' might arise or change, but how a particular inter-governmental organization has failed to achieve its early objectives and the degree to which it is a prey to other world forces. Whereas regime analysts view regimes as a synthesis of prevailing world forces (Keohane (1982) sees a growing structural demand for certain types of regime), modern integration theorists do not now proclaim such determinism in the process and certainly regard the European Community as more effectively specific, and more limited, than a general organic arrangement known as a regime (Wallace, 1983a). As far as structural issues are concerned there is a marked difference in emphasis between the *International Organization* collection and, say, the essays in Wallace, Wallace and Webb (1983), though they are frequently dealing with the same political developments.

The theoretical bias of integration studies reflects the second major concern in considering structural implications, a concern which is also a more perennial interest in the British approach to transnationalism. If we accept that the role of the state has to be expressed more subtly and that states have not disintegrated in the face of transnational phenomena, then it becomes important to ask what political structures and conditions are conducive to the growth and existence of transnationalism. Here, we may suspect, Hedley Bull feels rather more comfortable. What is it, it is asked, in the response of states that gives various transnational phenomena access to domestic society, and either permits or prevents domestic institutions operating freely outside it? This is not just a sterile argument over whether the state acts as an effective gatekeeper between national and international society, but rather a structural argument about the pressures and inducements that bear on the motives for state behaviour. Reynolds (1979), for instance, tries to define a framework within which to analyse the conditions in which state/non-state actor relationships will produce certain kinds of international results. He is careful to emphasize that the lack of a state-determined outcome does not necessarily mean that events have been determined by the power of non-state actors: 'It may be that outcomes will in general be increasingly indeterminable' (p. 94). In other words, British studies assume transnationalism to be less of a determinant in world politics and more of a dependent factor which arises from the political structures prevailing at the time. For an American community that has sought to explain the decline of a *pax Americana*, transnationalism has seemed to be an independent phenomenon working against it: for a British community that is less surprised by the demise of the old order, transnationalism varies according to the permissiveness of political structures as they evolve – in this case from a bipolar to a multipolar structure.

More specifically, Susan Strange (1976) considers transnationalism as it is expressed in its most tangible form, through international economic relations. She wholeheartedly agrees with Gilpin (1976), who notably disagrees with some of the key assumptions made by Keohane and Nye, that 'international economic relations are always political' and that 'one cannot really distinguish between wealth . . . and power as national goals' (Strange, 1976, p. 337). She is not state-centric in her approach; indeed, she asserts that 'the half-integrated world economy of today is much more likely the economy and society of pre-industrial mediaeval Europe . . . than the age of the supreme nation-state' (p. 341). Her approach is contained in a characteristic British plea for a more authentic political-economy approach to transnationalism: authentic in that it recognizes the inseparability of structures of political authority and international economic relationships.

Thus, consciously or not, governments do affect the workings of the international market, and *some* governments in their own domestic regulations will have deep effects on the behaviour of other governments and transnational actors. This is true of the United States, from its interest rate policy to its Food and Drug Administration regulations on permitted additives. A reassertion of the principles of international political economy, therefore, would see transnationalism as a direct function of the relationship between political and economic forces as they evolve over time. Transnationalism should not be regarded as one of the 'new forces' in world politics, nor necessarily as something which attacks the fabric of a state-centric world (though that fabric may be changing for other reasons), nor as a force creating the politics of the 'global village'. Rather it is a variable symptom of a politico-economic international system in the process of change.

Process Effects

Similar differences in emphasis can be discerned when we turn to the possible effects of the phenomenon of transnationalism on patterns of international behaviour. In this instance the implications of transnationalism revolve primarily around arguments about interdependence, for the notion of interdependence represents a recognition of the complexities of modern world politics. It tries to describe a condition of behaviour where transnational processes cross foreign and domestic boundaries, creating links between domestic interests in separate states which are perceived by both as being costly to break. A vast amount of literature has been produced upon this subject since it encompasses both the perceptions of state and non-state actors' interests, and the complex patterns of behaviour in which they have to engage (Keohane and Nye, 1977; Morse, 1976a; Scott, 1977; Alker, 1977; Rosecrance and Stein, 1973). The idea of interdependence, therefore, has major implications for the assumptions we make about power, foreign policy and bargaining behaviour in world politics (Holsti, 1980, pp. 26–7; Cooper, 1972; Morse, 1972).

Keohane and Nye (1977) begin their analysis of interdependence from the realization that power is exercised in a highly complex environment. At what point, we are led to ask, does the exercise of power become so contingent upon other actors and interconnected issues that it is effectively not a manipulation of a 'power relationship', but an attempt to manage an interdependent structure in some favourable way without producing serious ruptures within it? Inevitably this question has an effect on our characterization of foreign policy. Morse (1976a), for instance, stresses the way in which reacting to interdependence promotes certain characteristic types of foreign policy output. At a more specific level foreign policy outputs in a condition of interdependence are concerned with the particular 'linkage' between issues, and the ever increasing need for foreign policies to find ways of maintaining their political and economic structures of exchange and management. This leads to a need to identify the types of bargaining behaviour that are required to achieve this. If foreign policy is more a question of 'steering' and 'management' then 'goal-setting' and 'statecraft', then special sorts of bargains have to be struck and coalitions must be built. Puchala (1972), for example, wrote an early and influential piece which stressed that the behaviour of the highly interdependent states of the European Community in relation to the integration process could not be characterized as 'federalism', 'nationalism', 'functionalism' or even as 'power politics'; rather, it was necessary to move towards a 'new conceptualisation' of international bargaining behaviour which he termed the manipulation of a 'Concordance System'.

Now all these issues are contestable and have been matters of contention within the general rubric of discussions on interdependence (Goldmann and Sjöstedt, 1979). For our purposes it is interesting that these debates turn around certain central issues which illuminate different British and American perspectives. Is interdependence a new theory, or simply a metaphor which serves as a useful image of contemporary world politics? Keohane and Nye, though cautious in their choice of words, certainly see interdependence as something capable of generating hypotheses and testing further otherwise untestable hypotheses about puzzling aspects of inter-state relations. They deliberately set it against the major assumptions of the realist school in order to establish the theoretical credentials of the concept itself (Keohane and Nye, 1977, pp. 23–4), and they are at pains to demonstrate the greater salience of different types of issues in international relations. Most theorists of interdependence have looked to economic and social rather than military-security issues for their evidence. This has only enhanced the contrast with power politics realism, and hence the appearance of a new emergent 'theory' of world politics.

Against this, Reynolds and McKinlay (1979) reflect British attitudes and maintain that interdepenence is too wide-spread and complex a phenomenon to disentangle single causes and consequences; it is no more than 'a summary desription of the current state of the international system' (See Reynolds, 1979, p. 91). As a solid traditionalist, James Cable (1983) sees interdependence from the British point of view as simply a phrase to signify a condition – perhaps even a deliberate choice – of dependence (p. 366). For Cable, the continuum running from independence to dependence is no less explanatory than it ever was. More fundamentally, it is frequently pointed out that interdependence does not have to be seen as an alternative to realism and 'power politics'. Keohane and Nye, it is claimed, may well have overdrawn and misrepresented the nature of realism to produce an artifical contrast (Michalak, 1979, pp. 145–9). Goodwin has taken up this last point in more than one context. 'Realists have some reason for being scornful of the rhetoric of interdependence' he says (1978, p. 295): the task should not be to establish alternative constructions of international processes but rather 'to make the realist approach more realistic' (1979, p. 253). In this, Goodwin expresses succinctly a suspicion that many British writers seem to have. Few British scholars are unreconstituted realists.

Similarly, in the field of European Community studies where one would expect the greatest attention to be paid to interdependence, there is a general consensus among British scholars that while that particular phenomenon poses genuinely international problems, it does not offer correspondingly international solutions. In a condition of interdependence where the degree of control that anyone has over the outcome is very restricted and where inter-governmental action is the best hope but not the likeliest prospect, governments tend to resort to national measures, not because they are the best, but more because they are the only measures over which a government has some control. Thus Webb (1983, p. 35) observes that: 'The European Community constitutes an almost purpose-built laboratory for examining the impact of transnational actors and relations on policy processes.' Indeed, interdependence approaches do offer an alternative to a series of neo-functionalist assumptions, which look increasingly questionable in the light of the history of the European Community in the last fifteen years. But Webb is also very clear that what she calls a 'transnational-interdependence approach' does not provide a suitable model for an examination of actual Community activity (pp. 36–7). Rather the European Community, she says, must prove to national governments and publics that it can deliver the goods as a policy-making machine. The interdependence approach is simply not sufficient to explain how different policy outcomes arise (p. 38). Helen Wallace offers evidence for this in the same volume. She points out that national governments, operating in the much more complex conditions in the European Community, often have to strike 'compromise agreements at home before they go into Community negotiations' (Wallace, H., 1983 p. 77). But such complexity is as likely to make national governments defensive as it is to make them amenable to integrated policies (pp. 69–71).

In the case studies that follow the chapters by Webb and Wallace in the same book, one is struck by the extent to which the contributors' explanations owe more to the assumptions of realism than to any other specific alternative. Transnationalism and interdependence express the context in which difficult national government policies have to be made. But transnational phenomena do not play much of a role, for example, in policy-making for the Community's regional fund, since the bargaining between national governments has left so little scope for non-governmental groups to operate (pp. 97–8). The same is true with regard to competition policy (p. 231), and again in relation to industrial policy (p. 279). In the face of transnational problems, and in a condition that they would all be happy to class as interdependent, all these writers (Wallace, Allen and Hodges) see policy-making – in this case the bargaining process at the Community level – as being jealously guarded by governments. This is despite the fact that the competence and effectiveness of the member governments is often very low when facing such problems. These are not encouraging conclusions for the more ideologically minded interdependence theorists.

Finally, a difference in emphasis may be discerned in the degree of relevance British writers accord to the notion of interdependence. Whereas it has been fashionable to claim that the world of the 1970s displays interdependence on a global scale (in resources, economic management or increasingly regional security arrangements), it is noticeable that some writers go out of their way to stress the limits of interdependence in explaining the foreign policies of states outside the developed world. When examining Third World foreign policies it may seem more useful to borrow assumptions from the realist. Mere complexity is not in itself interdependence, and the existence of interdependence does not prevent many states from undertaking unilateral actions which are extremely damaging to their domestic interests (Hill, 1979).

All this is only to outline differences in emphasis on the questions that the phenomenon of transnationalism raises. The divisions are not neat and tidy and they do not in themselves indicate two schools of thought on the issue. They do, however, point to a more important underlying divergence in British and American approaches since it is clear that all the emphases we have identified can be traced back to different methodological assumptions.

The Methodology of Transnationalism

Methodology arises both from one s view of the world and one's view of the discipline of International Relations. In this respect, there is a marked difference between the two academic communities and consequently between the two policy-making communities. To express it crudely, we could say that the real difference between British and American approaches is not in the study of transnationalism itself, but in the judgement of what is at stake in that study. The difference is more conceptual than empirical and it involves three related methodological issues.

Firstly, it is clear that most American scholars attack the question of transnationalism with the assumption that they are investigating a possible paradigm shift. Ronald Yalem (1978) surveyed some of the literature of the 1970s and cast the argument explicitly in terms of competing paradigms. He quotes Leurdijk (1974) extensively as typifying the rejection of an 'international politics paradigm' which 'runs counter to reality' (Yalem, 1978, p. 243). Rather, 'interactions are initiated not by governments but by non-governmental actors' (Leurdijk, 1974, p. 58). In other words, the reality of international politics now demands nothing less than a new paradigm to encompass it. Not all writers would assert this so glibly, though Rosenau in a number of works has argued the necessity for a paradigm shift on similar grounds. In the late 1960s Rosenau appealed for an explicit theory of 'linkage' which took account of transnational phenomena (Rosenau, 1969b; 1980a, pp. 372–3). By the late 1970s theory-building was inadequate since: 'a process of paradigm deterioration, I believe, is under way in the study of world affairs' (Rosenau, 1979, p. 130). The task is to 'construct the outlines of a world in which the course of events is sustained by processes rather than actors' (p. 135). In 1980 he introduced his analysis of transnationalism and interdependence by stating that 'the study of transnational relations encompasses the study of international relations' (Rosenau, 1980c, p. 2). Certainly Rosenau best expresses the characteristic American search for a comprehensive paradigm of world politics. In the late 1960s transnationalism seemed to attack the basis of the state system: this required a new paradigm of international relations. Since the late 1970s it has become clear that transnational trends are contradictory: now that very contradiction requires a new paradigm to explain how economic, technological and social factors can work in opposite ways at once. The assumption that transnationalism involves a paradigm shift goes deeper, however, than Rosenau's 'puzzlement' at the differing trends in world politics.

It is not only that transnational phenomena are in themselves intellectually challenging. There is now greater understanding in the American academic community about what exactly it is that is being challenged. The realist formulation of world politics was elevated to the status of a paradigm. To challenge it has therefore required the development of a new paradigm. Krasner (1982c) notes how writers on transnational regimes arise from the realist school. They started with a more consensual image of the world, and nothing less than a new paradigm could displace realism from its theoretical pre-eminence. 'When paradigms crumble, they crumble very quickly' says Rosenau (1979, p.130), making the assumption that there *was* a paradigm to be attacked. A variation on this point arises from the decline of the *pax Americana*. The diffusion of American power was not accompanied by inexorable world disorder. Clearly, some other forces supporting world order were operating in lieu of hegemonic US power. For the structural realists who had previously placed undue faith in the concept of power 'management' the very survival of a form of world order seemed to undermine the assumptions that had surrounded their analysis of hegemonic power (Krasner, 1982c, pp.499–500). Transnationalism, as we have seen, grew partly out of the analysis of changing American power in the 1970s. British writers tend to suspect that just as assertive realism was a rationalization of hegemonic power, so a paradigm shift to transnationalism is an attempt to rationalize a puzzling decline in that power. This, say British writers, is to mistake American power for power itself and throw out the baby with the bathwater.

Smith (1980, p.243), for example, in offering a critique of Rosenau, denies that there is a real paradigm – in the Kuhnian sense – from which to depart. Goodwin (1979) and Northedge (1976b) are both clear that realism, if it can be considered a paradigm, is a very wide one and not subject to particular limits. This point had been well made by Burton et al. (1974) who pointed out that undermining the billiard-ball model of international politics did not mean undermining the general approach of which that had been a part. Similarly, Taylor (1978, pp.135-8) traces the pitfalls of 'power politics' very carefully but still concludes that the evolutionary nature of the approach is a testimony to its impressive, if imprecise, ubiquity. In a British academic community that was always less committed to the study of International Relations as a science, there has seemed less need to recognize competition between paradigms, and less need for comparative and cumulative data collection or for so intense a debate over those phenomena which are deemed most relevant to the discipline. The lack of a paradigm from which to shift, and a faith in the ability of a realist 'approach' to accommodate changed conditions, stem very much from the broadly traditionalist attitude to the subject identified in the so-called 'great debate' on the study of International Relations (Knorr and Rosenau, 1969).

The second methodological issue concerns the search for a general theory of international politics, and in particular for a theory of systems transformation which would contribute substantially to such theory. Keohane (1982), for instance, interprets the growth of regimes as a function of systems transformation: 'several assertions of structural theories appear problematic' he says. 'In particular, it is less clear that hegemony is a necessary condition for stable international regimes under all circumstances' (p. 354). In this view regimes are therefore both cause and effect of systems transformation and Keohane proposes 'two major research' hypotheses on this basis. In another analysis Keohane (1980) outlines a differentiated 'structural model' as an alternative to a 'hegemonic stability theory' and states that without a structural model as a starting-point the analysis of international economic regimes would be merely descriptive (p. 156). Keohane is commendably specific about the forces that produce economic regime change. Similarly, Katzenstein (1975) has attempted to assess with some precision the degree of structural change occasioned by conditions of interdependence. In his study of regimes Haas (1982) identifies the problem to be tackled in a series of structural questions and declares that 'we study regimes because they mirror the evolving capacity of man to redefine and perhaps to solve common problems.' At a more general level Rosenau (1979, p. 133) recognizes the possibility that the interest in systems transformation, in the guise of transnationalism, interdependence and regime constructions, may be an American over-reaction to marginal changes. But he still asserts that the analysis of system transformation is 'the central question'; indeed European reluctance to confront this as a genuine question (in some of his other works 'a puzzle') is in itself evidence of a prevailing paradigm from which to depart. This is not to say that the American approach assumes systems transformation to be an automatic consequence of transnationalism. Holsti (1980) is at pains to point out that even in a highly transnational world this cannot be taken for granted (p. 49). But whatever the answers on both sides of the Atlantic, the question is posed more persistently and more acutely by American scholars.

A belief in the importance of systems transformation carries with it a greater belief in the elaboration of a general systems theory. As Smith (1983, p.565) points out, there is a penchant in American academia for the pursuit of generally applicable theory; a stronger faith in scientific methods which can compare cases across time and place. Rosenau's studies, particularly that on aspects of transnationalism, constantly work at the need to construct general theories, to link up 'islands of cumulation' in what is 'a flegling science' (1980b, p.241). Zinnes (1980, pp.18–19) spells it out more precisely. There are two rationales in the literature of systems transformation: it is, as an empirical event, a matter of some importance; more fundamentally, systems transformation is a macro approach to system processes, a way of theorizing about cause and effect relationships and a device to make us specify what Zinnes calls 'the research question'.

It is on precisely these grounds that Strange (1982, p.493) takes issue with the American proponents of regime analysis for at the back of their efforts lurks a continuing belief in 'that El Dorado of social science, a general theory capable of universal application to all times and places and all issues'. This, one suspects, is the true source of British and American differences over transnationalism. The argument is not over the interest, or even importance of transnational phenomena, but over the importance of our study of it. Since both British and American scholars now acknowledge that transnational trends operate in several directions, it is impossible to deduce their significance as empirical facts. Our assertions of importance, therefore, are more reflections of our certainty about what we are looking for rather than our uncertainty about what is there.

The third methodological issue revolves around the value judgements that have underpinned many attempts to analyse transnationalism. It may be inaccurate to characterize transnationalism as the 'new utopianism' of international politics, though in some of the earlier formulations of transnational analysis it was scarcely less than this. (Some of the work of Deutsch (1968; 1978) provides a good example.) Nevertheless, even more cautious analyses often retain a large normative element. There is what Goodwin (1978, p.293) has described as a reformist analysis of interdependence and transnationalism. Occasionally it surfaces in visions of the 'global village' referred to earlier (Young, 1972). In its more prevalent form it emerges as a new liberalism among analysts. In lieu of the *pax Americana* there is a concern to analyse mechanisms in order to maintain international order during a period of fundamental change. Krasner linked the changes of the 1970s 'to the most fundamental concern of social theory: how is order established, maintained and destroyed?' (Strange, 1982, p. 487). The concern is with order rather than equality, justice or toleration. British academics would not differ in seeing this as the natural bias of the status quo, but they would question the assumption that order *needs to be* maintained by some transnational authority structure. For most British scholars this both underestimates the capacity of a plurality of states to maintain essential order when hegemonic power declines (Bull, 1977), and overestimates the ability of transnational regimes to fill the gap (Strange, 1982, pp. 486–7). Regimes are far more transitory than they seem and international order may not be such a fragile blossom as those who support the paradigm shift assume.

Yet the decline of American power which we have referred to almost as a shorthand term has always been recognized as an uneven process; 'loss of control is not uniform for all types of state objectives' (Keohane and Nye, 1971, p. 393). Security issues still represent important areas of state-centred control. The areas of economic and social policy which seemed to be far less controllable and which have formed most of the raw material for interdependence and regime analyses have thus appeared more interesting because they represent different means of exercising power and upholding international order. In other words, the very fact that transnational phenomena apply to non–military activities, *in opposition* to the retention of military means of exercising power, increases the appeal of transnationalism to the liberal conscience. This certainly has loud echoes in the bulk of the earlier literature on integration, both British and American. The attractions of this, however, are much less for British writers in the 1980s, for integration theory has more modest aspirations now than at any time since 1945 (Wallace, 1983b, p. 430) and is less applicable as a general theory of integration outside Europe (Hodges, 1978, p. 253).

Methodology and Policy

The link between academic methodology and public policy are often extremely tenuous. In the case of transnationalism, however, they are of more than passing interest and are themselves a commentary on British and American perspectives. They are relevant in so far as ideas and actions exist in a dialectic relationship and, as Haas points out, the vocabulary and cognitive grasp we have of transnational phenomena not only matter, but will be in a constant state of evolution (1982). In the United States, this dialectical process is less indirect than in Britain. Further, there is a great deal of interchange between academics and policy-makers. For this and for other reasons there is a much higher degree of consensus in the academic/policy community. This does not manifest itself in common views so much as in a general agreement over the intellectual agenda for foreign policy. To be sure, there are any number of different opinions available to the American policy-maker on every issue, but there is also a remarkable weight of attention which transfers itself quickly and efficiently both to immediate issues and emerging trends once they have arisen as cases in the foreign policy machine. A good example of this is the case of the Reagan administration's interest in space-based ballistic missile defence. President Reagan made his 'star wars' speech in March 1983. This speech did not represent a carefully planned presidential initiative; it was purely speculative. Certainly, the technical and political issues surrounding this kind of defence had not changed noticeably for some time. The political disincentives were great, the technical and economic problems huge and the matter had effectively rested on those conclusions since the late-1960s. Within six months of the President's speech, however, not only was space-based ballistic missile defence firmly on the political agenda with the commitment of exploratory funding, but it was also on the academic agenda. Immediately, there were sharply divergent views on the subject but the political and technical credibility of the whole concept was effectively reincarnated when, in truth, a year earlier it had been the argument of a previous era (Carter and Schwartz, 1984).

A good example of a more long-term trend being elevated by the weight of attention is transnationalism itself. In so far as it is possible to define an American 'world view' since 1945 it has clearly always been much more geo-political than that of the Europeans. This is reinforced by interaction with the academic community: there is, to a British observer, a strangely mechanistic application of balance of power principles to diverse areas and issues. The vocabulary of 'leverage' does not fit in easily with British perspectives on foreign policy.

It was no accident, therefore, that maximum attention was given to transnational phenomena and particularly to interdependence at a time when US policy-makers found themselves frustrated in so many different areas. We have pointed earlier to the interest in transnationalism as a source of hypotheses to explain a general decline in American power. This was made even more acute, however, by the particular problems of US policy during the administrations of Presidents Ford and Carter. As American policy became almost immobile between 1973 and 1979, the majority of the seminal works on interdependence and complexity began to appear. In reviewing American foreign policy in the 1970s Oye (1979) overtly moulded his analysis around Keohane and Nye's *Power and Interdependence* (1979, p. 3n.). He concludes gloomily that the 'constraints and contradictions' of 'President Carter's policy were 'largely environmental in origin' and in the absence of major policy changes 'the situation will persist and confound future administrations' (p. 29). Other noted transnational analysts – Keohane, Krasner, Haas, Lieber – also contributed their policy analyses to this volume, and are of a similar mind. The argument, however, does not rest on mere coincidence. For even in a situation of highly complex interdependence major powers are still powerful. They have the ability to determine largely *what* in the tangle of interdependent issues will be politicized and in *what forum* it will be represented. As Strange points out (1976, p. 338) this occurs both in the overt sense that the United States can direct its attention deliberately to certain issues – like East-West trade within Europe – and less consciously by adopting domestic regulations and standards which have an enormous effect on many transnational operations – as is the case in the American banking and financial system (de Cecco, 1976, p. 382). The major powers can also determine the appropriate political forums for discussion. Krasner (1979, pp. 143-4) records how the US and its allies have determined that the discussions over a new international economic order should be conducted through established channels of international organization. The less developed countries have therefore been forced to concentrate their demands for a new order on the question of control of those organizations. In other words, though a superpower may not be able to manage successfully its complex transnational relations with other actors, it can determine the subject and the level of its attempts to do so. Further, its power to ignore items that might otherwise be on the agenda will be a crucial determinant of which transnational processes are politicized.

The views of the academic and policy communites in the United States, therefore, are of more than indirect relevance to discussions of transnationalism, not just because the communities are in a position to influence each other, but because the very vocabulary and perceptions of transnationalism held by the Americans have a crucial effect on what and how certain issues are politicized for everyone else. Indeed, following the deep uncertainty of the 1970s, US foreign policy has attempted to be more assertive in the 1980s in ways that have affected, for good or bad, most other important states in the world.

Throughout these perceptual fluctuations it is apparent that the American academic/policy community has searched constantly for fixed intellectual points. US hegemony was itself a fixed reference point for the management of foreign policy. When this was seen to be inadequate the Nixon administration tried to intellectualize a 'pentagonal' or 'polar-pentagonal' world view which suggested a realist management structure for a network of regional balances of power. When this image proved too simplistic the Ford and Carter administrations intellectualized interdependence into a structural phenomenon that would, they hoped, become susceptible to management. In 1980 for example, Cyrus Vance stressed the pervasive nature of interdependence as a policy constraint. Lord Carrington (1980, p.11) and Francis Pym (1982, p.3), however, both see interdependence in more instrumental terms.

Finally after 1980, when it became clear that transnational processes might well reduce the power of states (particularly superpowers) without diminishing their assertiveness and without necessarily replacing their control functions with anything else, the Reagan administration – almost in sheer exasperation – fell heavily back onto geopolitical images of foreign policy. On October 21 1983 Joseph Nye produced an opinion piece in the *New York Times* which stated that America's first priority in Europe was to maintain the cohesion alliance. The second priority was to avoid war. Most Europeans would put these in exactly the reverse order (MacGwire, 1983), but for Nye, an American analyst who has devoted much of his attention to transnationalism, this was consistent with a globalist conception of the balance of power.

The search for fixed intellectual points goes on in circumstances where transnational phenomena, whether they are increasing or diminishing, are nevertheless dynamic. Analysts and practitioners of British foreign policy respect the reality of multilateralism. No major aspect of British policy makes practical sense except as part of a multilateral framework. For British policy-makers the condition of interdependence imposes great uncertainty and tends to lead analysts to concentrate on the form of multilateral action as much as the substance. This becomes in some cases an end in itself. Barber (1980), for instance, stresses the need for flexible but open-ended thinking about Britain's foreign policy future. He specifically warns against an assumption that regimes are deeply rooted (p.108) and is concerned that all the intangible aspects of foreign policy – the art of it – should be considered when assessing Britain's 'role' in world politics.

For American analysts and practitioners, however, the search is more for a method of 'managing interdependence'. If transnational processes and the condition of interdependence frustrated the realism of state action, then a state/international organization/non-governmental organization construct might be envisaged which would provide both a systemic reference point and be in effect a steering mechanism for handling the major issues in US foreign policy. It is interesting that in the mid-1970s the US Council on Foreign Relations made a major research effort to study 'the management of interdependence'. The British Royal Institute of International Affairs, on the other hand, looking at the same phenomena undertook a study of 'issue linkage' between Atlantic governments. Precisely because America is somewhat the one-eyed man in the land of the blind its attempts to 'manage interdependence' have taken the form of what Wallace (1975) calls 'grand-design foreign policy'. The problem with this, as he points out, is that a genuine 'management' of interdependence requires delicate and continuous handling 'which can only be damaged by too frequent changes in the outline of overall assumptions and priorities within which it operates' (p.177). 'Managing interdependence', then, is a process of politicizing and then trading off, various aspects of transnationalism. On that basis it may, so to speak, be too serious a business to be left to the politicians.

10
International Organization

DAVID ARMSTRONG

International organizations are not just subjects for academic inquiry, they have been a continuing concern of governments. Hence an investigation into British and American approaches would be incomplete without an examination of the contrasting official attitudes of the two countries to complement a survey of the differing perspectives of the two academic communities.

From League of Nations to United Nations: The Official View

The Covenant of the League of Nations was, to a great extent, an Anglo-American document and represents a sometimes awkward compromise between two conceptions of the League: one derived from President Woodrow Wilson, the other inspired essentially by the British Foreign Office. Neither official view owed much to the popular societies that were advocating a League of Nations although the main American society, the League to Enforce Peace, contained many influential figures, so that Wilson made at least a show of paying close attention to its activities, in private dismissing such bodies as 'woolgatherers' (Armstrong, 1982, p.7). Similarly, one of the most important British drafts of a possible covenant, the Phillimore Report, acknowledged some of the general principles being advanced by Britain's League enthusiasts, but rejected their specific proposals as 'impracticable' (Miller 1928, vol.1, p.4).

Many of the fundamental differences between the Wilsonian view of the League and the prevailing British conception were foreshadowed in two speeches made within three days of each other by Wilson and Britain's Prime Minister, David Lloyd

George. In the first, delivered on 5 January 1918, Lloyd George declared: 'we must seek by the creation of some international organization to limit the burden of armaments and diminish the possibility of war' (Bendiner, 1975 p.25). Wilson's contribution was his famous 'Fourteen Points' speech of 8 January 1918 the last point of which called for 'a general association of nations . . . formed under specific covenants for the purpose of affording mutual guarantees of political independence and territorial integrity to great and small states alike'. Lloyd George, of course, had little time for the League either as an abstract ideal or as concrete reality so his statement was based on far less previous reflection and still less genuine commitment than Wilson's, whose ideas about guarantees of independence and territorial integrity went back some years (see Armstrong, 1982, pp.6–10). But even allowing for the fact that the reference to an international organization in Lloyd George's speech was something of a casual afterthought (whereas for Wilson the League lay at the heart of his conception of the post-war order), the differences in outlook on this matter revealed by these brief statements remain profound. 'Some international organization' could encompass a wide range of post-war systems, including a great power concert, whereas 'a general association of nations' clearly meant something very different. The contrast between the two men's view of the purposes of the proposed organization were even more fundamental, with Lloyd George envisaging limited arms control and crisis management functions while Wilson called for far-reaching collective guarantees.

When the Anglo–American discussions on the League entered the stage of detailed planning in January 1919 more specific differences emerged, in four distinct areas in particular. The first arose out of Wilson's call for guarantees of independence and territorial integrity. The British preferred a looser, less formal commitment, and one which did not appear to underwrite in its entirety the existing territorial distribution at the moment of signing the covenant. This reflected a more basic difference in approach. The British were inclined to deal with international situations as they occurred with a view to hammering out a compromise settlement; they adopted a traditional give–and–take diplomacy requiring a flexibility that was not available in the new order which effectively froze the status quo of 1919. Wilson, on the other hand, was anxious to lay down basic principles which would be enshrined in the League of Nations and which would predetermine the outcome of any conflict (if they did not actually prevent it).

The three additional differences between Wilson and the British were over less important aspects of the League but still highlighted fundamentally opposed conceptions of international organization. The British wanted decision-making in the League to be centred in a great power council, and in general tended to envisage the League as an institutionalized great power concert with smaller states excluded from any significant role. Wilson, in contrast, wanted the League Council to be a more 'representative' body. Similarly, Wilson advocated extensive and unique powers for the League in administering the former enemy colonies, a notion that was opposed by Britain both because Britain and the Dominions wanted some of these colonies for themselves, and because the idea that an international organization might enjoy quasi-sovereign powers was anathema to the British Foreign Office (Armstrong, 1982, p.10). Finally, the two states had differing views on the League's responsibilities in the area of international law. Wilson initially called for a rather complicated system of compulsory arbitration but eventually accepted the alternative suggestion of Britain's Lord Cecil for a permanent Court of International Justice which was not to enjoy powers of compulsory jurisdiction (Miller, 1928, vol.1, p.63; vol.2, pp.106–16).

The compromise draft covenant – the 'Hurst-Miller draft' – which was eventually agreed for presentation to the other delegates at the Paris Peace Conference pleased neither Wilson nor Lloyd George. Both men made last minute attempts to have it discarded, in Wilson's case for a covenant that more truly reflected his idealistic aspirations, while Lloyd George took the opposite position, arguing that the covenant was already far too ambitious and should be abandoned in favour of a return to the British idea of an institutionalized great power concert (Armstrong, 1982, p.18).

Not all Americans shared Wilson's idealistic view, nor all the British Lloyd George's cynicism. But even American opponents of the League exaggerated its potential significance in world politics – this was one reason for the Senate's eventual rejection of it – whereas British enthusiasts (at governmental levels at least) had fewer illusions about the League's ability to play more than a marginal role in ameliorating major conflicts between the great powers. The tendency among American officials to hold unrealistic expectations (or fears) about a project of this kind was repeated when the United Nations was created, although on this occasion the UN was seen less in idealistic terms as ushering in a new era in international relations than from the *realpolitik* standpoint of it being a potential weapon for American diplomacy. As early as April 1946 the State Department was arguing that the UN Charter 'affords the best and most unassailable means through which the US can implement its opposition to Soviet physical expansion. It not only offers the basis upon which the greatest degrees of popular support can be obtained in the US but it will also ensure the support and even assistance of other members of the United Nations' (Foreign Relations of the United States (FRUS), 1946, vol.1, pp.1167–71). This was not the only American opinion of the UN: Roosevelt had seen it as a means of continuing the wartime alliance; his Secretary of State, Cordell Hull, advocated a multi-purpose organization with the UN undertaking various economic and social roles as well as a central collective security function. (Weiler and Simons, 1967, pp.39–43). But as Soviet-American relations deteriorated the idea of the UN (with its pro-American majority) as a crucial arm of American diplomacy grew in importance.

British officials played a much smaller part both in the drafting of the Charter and the subsequent running of the UN than they had with the League. Britain's overwhelming interest was to ensure that there was no repetition of America's inter-war isolation and this, together with Britain's weaker circumstances, meant accepting a dominant American role in the creation of the UN. Moreover, Roosevelt and Churchill were closer on this question than their predecessors had been in 1919.

Even so there were some important differences in emphasis. The British were anxious that the UN should provide a forum within which the traditional diplomatic processes could take place whereas they believed the Americans were inclined to look for ways of supplanting traditional diplomacy (Goodwin, 1957, p.20). Moreover, Churchill's primary concern was with obtaining effective American guarantees of security in Europe. An organization with worldwide responsibilities might fail to concentrate American attention sufficiently on European affairs, so Churchill at first advocated a number of regional collective security organizations to operate under the auspices of a Supreme Council that would consist mainly of the three wartime allies (Goodwin, 1957, pp.5–8). Britain also disagreed with the American view that the economic and social functions of the UN should be carried out by a separate body that would not be dominated by the great powers (Luard, 1982, p.26). Finally, Churchill was deeply suspicious of American proposals for extending the policy of international trusteeship for former enemy colonies (which had originated with the League of Nations' mandates system) by giving the UN a more general responsibility for the well-being of people living in all colonial territories.

Churchill's fears on this last subject were to be confirmed during the next five years when American support for decolonization and for the idea that states should be accountable to the UN in their colonial policies became a serious point of contention between London and Washington. In Anglo-American discussions on this matter the following points of principle emerged, all of which go to the heart of the larger issue of the differences between the two countries over international organizations:

1 The British felt that the UN trusteeship system 'was contrary to the principle that responsibility should not be divorced from authority, which was necessary for good administration'.
2 They did not accept the notion of accountability to 'world opinion'.
3 In an era of increasing self-government the British argued that it would be more appropriate for London's administration of the colonies to be replaced by local control than by a system of international supervision.
4 Where international administration had a part to play it was in technical matters where experts would discuss such problems as illiteracy, malnutrition or soil conservation. The UN committee that handled colonial matters was, in Britain's view, a body of political representatives that lacked competence to deal with these questions 'in a practical or constructive manner'. In such a body, the affairs of colonies were judged 'not, as they should be in relation to general standards of achievement but against hypothetical standards of perfection in an atmosphere of political prejudice and suspicion'.
5 Criticism of Britain's colonial policies in specific cases played 'straight into the hands of extremists and communists' because it could be portrayed as legitimizing their activities (FRUS, 1950, vol.2, pp.442–4).

The American response to these British arguments was consistent in upholding the principle of international accountability and the notion that there existed such a thing as 'world public opinion' which should be respected. In addition, Washington tended to stand for a more liberal view of the powers of various

UN bodies, notably the General Assembly and the Secretariat (Luard, 1982, p. 58).

As the pro-Western majority in the General Assembly started to evaporate, criticism of the UN began to be heard on both sides of the Atlantic. In a notable speech in 1961 Britain's Foreign Secretary, Lord Home, referred to a 'crisis of confidence in the United Nations' and drew attention to what he saw as the General Assembly's habit of passing resolutions that 'can only be described as reckless and careless of peace' (Boyd, 1962, p. 12). At that time the official American position as enunciated by President Kennedy was still one of strong support for the UN. But ten years of persistent attack by the General Assembly on American policies and support for resolutions that were seen in Washington as hostile to important American interests led President Nixon in 1972 to adopt a stand much closer to that of Lord Home. Declaring that 'a pervasive skepticism concerning the UN is widespread', he announced his intention to reduce the level of America's contribution to the UN budget from 31.5 percent to 25 percent (Hiscocks, 1973, p. 313). If anything, the extent of American disillusionment with the UN was such that Washington's attitude to the UN became much harsher than Britain's, as evidenced by its withdrawal for a period from the ILO (International Labour Organization) and its threatened withdrawal from UNESCO.

Academic Approaches in Britain and the United States

Until relatively recently British and American thought on international organization might in broad terms have been said to be proceeding along parallel rather than divergent paths. There were, it is true, some slight differences: American utopianists tended to be even wilder and woollier than their British counterparts, while at the other end of the spectrum the American opponents of specific organizations were often harsher and more uncompromising. These marginal differences reflected both the influence of the traditional British distaste for intemperate enthusiasms (or antagonisms) and the fact that there were far more Americans than Britons writing about international organization making a wider range of opinions inevitable. But the overwhelming majority of analysts in both countries fell into one of four categories which for convenience may be labelled 'idealist', 'realist', 'empiricist' and 'legalist'.

Two of these terms will need no introduction to students of

International Relations. The antithesis between the utopian view of the League of Nations which saw it as a major force against war if not an embryo world government, and the realist critique which depicted the League as merely another arena where states could pursue their contending interests, was apparent long before E.H. Carr expressed it in these terms in 1939. 'Empiricist' indicates someone who, while advocating neither realism nor idealism with regard to international organizations, none the less thinks them worthy objects of study simply because they exist and play a part on the world stage. Finally, the legal approach to international organizations places these bodies in the context of the development of international law. As such they are seen to perform several functions. They are themselves the embodiment of international law: an attempt by states to give substance to their endeavours to regulate various aspects of their relations. They may be allocated the task of enforcing one or more areas of international law. Further, in certain respects they may also act as a source of law or play a part in the codification or development of law.

During the last twenty years the study of international organizations has developed in ways that have made these distinctions less valid. The old idealist–realist dichotomy has gradually lost its force as, on the one hand, earlier optimism about the United Nations gave way to disillusionment and cynicism and, on the other, realism came to be seen as providing a less than adequate framework for appreciating the full complexity of international relations in the twentieth century. Empiricists are still to be found and indeed empirical studies of specific organizations and of such phenomena as international bureaucracies or UN peace-keeping have grown increasingly sophisticated. Much the same can be said of the legalists. But the considerable changes in the theoretical and conceptual frameworks employed to appraise international relations as a whole have produced a significant divergence between British and American perspectives on international organization.

The differences between the two communities should not be exaggerated: most of the more impressive (or sometimes simply the superficially more exciting) theoretical developments have taken place in the United States and many British scholars have not been slow to adopt these for their own purposes. However, to the extent that there is a distinctly British approach, this tends to take a socio–legal form with international institutions being placed in the larger contexts of an international 'society' with its own rules and structures or in the context of a quest for international order. American writings, by contrast, encompass a wider and more complex range of viewpoints. The idealists have become less simplistic in their outlook and are now advocates of world order models (see Trevor Taylor's chapter in this book). The realists have divided into two separate groups. Some have moved in the direction of much greater theoretical rigour allied to an emphasis on more precise measurement of the phenomena being studied. The aim is still to see the world as it really is, but it is now appreciated that the old model of states as sole actors on the international stage doggedly pursuing national interests is less appropriate to a world containing increasing numbers of transnational structures and processes. This shift away from the state-centric model has affected many areas of International Relations but in the case of international organization it has led to a different approach to the study of international integration and to seeing international organizations as centres of transnational activity and even as actors in their own right. The second line of development from earlier realist thinking in the USA has moved towards a contemptuous dismissal of many international organizations, especially those in the United Nations, as irrelevant and anti-American.

Although there has been a steady flow of British books on international organizations since 1945, these have, in the main, been either descriptive or historical accounts of particular institutions or if they have adopted a theoretical perspective they have tended to follow the lead of the principal American theorists. Where a distinctive British approach has emerged it has placed less emphasis on organizations as separate phenomena, seeing them instead as merely a part of the general pursuit of order in international society. From this standpoint their role may seem, at best, marginal, as is most clear in the work of Hedley Bull (an Australian but more 'British' than the British in this context):

> to find the basic causes of such order as exists in world politics, one must look not to the League of Nations, the United Nations and such bodies, but to institutions of international society that arose before these international organizations were established and would continue to operate (albeit in a different mode) even if these organizations did not exist. (1977, p.xiv)

He identifies these 'basic institutions' as the balance of power, international law, diplomacy, the role of the great powers and war. Other 'British' academics are less dismissive of international organizations and believe that they have changed the conduct of international relations in important respects (James, 1976). Nevertheless, they still always see these organizations within a larger social context and as subordinate parts of international society.

The British perspective on international organizations derives its inspiration less from recent theoretical advances than from historical experience and the insights of various 'classical' thinkers of the past. At times the disdain for modern scholarship reaches somewhat eccentric extremes, as in a recent study of confederation which amasses an array of thinkers from Aristotle to Ernst Rudolf Huber but somehow contrives to omit the names of Karl Deutsch and Ernst Haas (Forsyth, 1981). Although others may pay more attention to contemporary analysts, there is an enduring fascination with much earlier figures, especially Hobbes, Kant, Rousseau, Grotius and Vattel (all five appear, for example, in Bull (1977); Mayall (1982); Vincent (1974); Wight (1977)). The ritual incantation of the great names of the past finds its echo in the British school's approach to historical illustration: ancient Greece, China's warring states, fifteenth-century Italy and the Concert of Europe may all be employed to shed light on the present; the intricacies of current relations among Latin American, Middle Eastern or African states tend to be ignored. Similarly, knowledge of languages such as German, French and Italian is most acceptable, but Russian, it seems, has little to offer.

The focus on the concept of international society has led the school to adopt a socio-legal approach to International Relations that draws heavily upon historical experience and philosophical speculation. Its most fundamental questions revolve around the problem of achieving order in a sociey without government, legislature or sanctions against law-breakers. Its sociological interests express themselves in questions like the following. In what sense, if any, is there a community among states? Does it possess a shared ideology or value system or a common culture? Does it function hierarchically? What are its underlying institutions? From a legal perspective, the school seeks answers not only to basic questions about the nature and origins of international law and the meaning of sovereignty, but to such matters as the sources of legitimacy in international society and the extent to which rules, principles and agreements exist which lack the status of law but which none the less play a crucial part in regulating the relations of states. International organizations are clearly relevant to all these issues but, as already suggested, for some their role is only peripheral.

The British school attempts to answer these important questions with elegance and erudition. But the overwhelming impression it creates – even for one who shares some of its predispositions – is one of stagnation. The problem is not so much with the questions posed by the school as with its overly conservative and traditional approach to answering them. Precision is always to be avoided, as is any systematic attempt to assemble evidence to support or refute particular propositions. Methodology is a dirty word. Contemporary writings are inadmissible unless they emanate from fellow members of the school. Indeed the world of today, with all its rich complexity, should be eschewed if at all possible. It is hardly surprising that international organizations are not a central concern: most are of too recent a lineage to be of interest to these lofty minds. Besides, with their mass of publicly available documentation and multitude of resolutions these bodies are dangerously open to some newfangled scientific perspective on International Relations which might require the school to learn mathematics or statistics or some other nonsense in entering this field.

It is tempting to charge American writers with the reverse of the British offence and say that they have adopted the right approach to the wrong questions. This, however, is unacceptable for two reasons: no question can be ruled out of place in an academic enquiry, and, as already suggested, American writings on international organization have been too diverse to be appraised as a single entity.

International organizations are central to several American theoretical approaches to the study of International Relations. One of these approaches, transnationalism, has already been discussed (chapter 9) but it is worth noting briefly some of the ways in which transnationalist ideas relate to international organization. The leading American writers on transnationalism claim that:

> in a world of multiple issues imperfectly linked, in which coalitions are formed transnationally and transgovernmentally, the potential role of international institutions in political bargaining is greatly increased. In particular, they help set the international agenda, and act as catalysts for coalition formation and as arenas for political initiatives and linkage by weak states. (Keohane and Nye, 1977, p.35)

They note in particular the role of international organizations in enabling 'sub-units of governments to turn potential or tacit coalitions into explicit coalitions characterised by direct communication among the partners'. The organizations achieve this by providing 'physical proximity, an agenda of issues on which interaction is to take place and an aura of legitimacy' (Keohane and Nye, 1974, p.51). Transnationalism is seen as having even more relevance to the broader process of international organization (of which formal institutions are only a part) in which specific functional areas of activity acquire 'international regimes', that is to say sets of rules, norms and structures that provide some degree of international management and/or regulation. Finally, transnational world politics may allow international secretariats to play an important part in various decision-making processes, thus enabling international organizations to function as independent 'actors'. These theoretical generalizations have been accompanied by numerous studies of individual organizations.

The principal achievement of the transnationalists has been to demonstrate something of the complexity of world politics, especially using issues that do not impinge directly upon security. In the particular case of international organizations, transnationalism has taken us away from a narrow focus on institutions in terms of 'their accomplishment of their explicit goals through the explicit mechanisms established for this purpose' (Alger, 1961, p.29). Instead of seeing world politics simply as a struggle for power among states operating within a single international system, transnationalism presents us with a range of international systems involving a wide variety of actors and issues and a multitude of important roles for international organizations. But transnationalism, too, has its flaws. At times it comes close to denying the state any behavioural validity as a unitary actor because the state is seen as a 'legal fiction', while simultaneously it accords validity to various non-governmental entities whose status is not merely derived from law but from law promulgated by one or more of these 'legal fictions'. Similarly, there is something paradoxical about works which, on the one hand, dismiss notions of the state as a purposive being, but, on the other, sketch out recommendations for United States foreign policy.

In the particular case of international organizations, Keohane and Nye argue that these should be seen 'less as institutions than as clusters of intergovernmental and transgovernmental networks associated with the formal institutions' (1977, p.240). As such they facilitate contact between various technical elites and promote the formation of transnational coalitions on specific issues, as well as achieving the results mentioned earlier. There is sufficient evidence to support these assertions but three principal criticisms may be made of the specific transnationalist thesis on international organization. First it can be argued that others (including British writers such as Cosgrove and Twitchett (1970)) have made much the same points as the transnationalists but without the jargon – although they have also worked, perhaps, without the systematic approach and the attention to evidence. Secondly, all that Nye, Keohane and others have to say about international organization may well be true, but how important is it? While what goes on in the world's many international institutions is not without significance, it can hardly be claimed to have more than marginal influence upon the fundamental issues of war and peace or the global distribution of wealth. Thirdly, the state – especially the powerful state – retains a veto over the work of international organizations which it is not afraid to use: ten years of negotiations at the third United Nations Law of the Sea Conference, which saw some of the most interesting and sophisticated examples of transnationalism at work, could be set aside by the unilateral action of one American president.

Similar criticisms can be made of the other major American contribution to theory that has had important implications for international organization – integration theory. This has attracted a wide range of approaches: neo-functionalism, federalism, transactionalism and numerous variations on these themes, with the most noted names out of many in this field being those of Deutsch (1957) Haas (1964; 1970; 1976) Lindberg (1963; 1970) and Nye (1970; 1972).

Whereas transnationalism essentially provided a different perspective on world politics rather than a complete theory, integrationists aspired to propositions that not only explained but predicted events. The aspiration to theory inevitably made them vulnerable as world politics failed to unfold in the expected manner, particularly in the principal laboratory, the European Community. The integrationists' first response to this set-back was to seek to refine their theories. Later, as reality continued to disprove their assertions they were more ready to acknowledge the inadequacy and even the obsolescence of their ideas (Haas, 1976; Lindberg and Scheingold, 1970).

The chief error of the regionalists was probably to have

employed the term 'integration' in the first place, thus nailing their colours to an a priori assumption that developments in the EEC and other regions were part of a discernible process that was working towards clearly defined ends. This emphasis derived from a belief that the intentions of the Treaty of Rome would continue to guide the members of the EEC. The readiness of Haas and the others to believe this would be so may be seen as evidence of a basic split in British and American thought. American political writing sometimes seems to reflect a deep-seated constitutionalism: a belief that form or structure will determine content or practice. When this is added to the US success in achieving integration, it is easy to understand why Americans might be predisposed both to see integration as an ideal goal and to believe that the right kind of organizational structure might help to achieve it. Britain, on the other hand, has a long tradition of suspecting any but the most limited attempts to effect European integration and also a pragmatic and *ad hoc* rather than constitutionalist approach to political development. However, it remains the case that relations – both transnational and inter-governmental – among the members of the EEC have a number of unusual if not unique features and that American analysts have provided more insights into the workings of the complex EEC system than their British counterparts, even though the more ambitious objective of a general theory of integration is as far away as ever.

Conclusion

Although such distinctions are always to some extent artificial, the preceding discussion suggests that there are a number of discernible differences in British and American approaches to international organization at both academic and political levels. In general terms these may be summarized as follows:

1 The Americans tend to invest international organizations with greater importance than the British.
2 Americans tend to look forward to a future that will be changed in significant respects from the present and to allocate to international organizations a major role in this process of change. British statesmen and academics look to the past with a view either to building institutions on what are seen as the workable aspects of previous experience or to find reasons to doubt the prospects of international organizations ever playing a more substantial role in world affairs.

3 The American perspective is strongly influenced by an underlying idealism, although among academics at least this is often concealed beneath the 'scientific' appearance of much of their work. In Britain 'piecemeal social reform' tends to be the most that is ever expected or desired – or indeed believed possible.

4 There is far greater and more explicit stress on methodology among American academics.

Clearly these differences stem from more profound differences in experience, tradition and ultimately from the different ideologies of the two countries. This adds to the difficulty of an objective assessment of the relative merits of the two approaches since any American or British writer is inevitably affected by one or other system of belief. However, the two-pronged nature of the discussion in this chapter enables us to conclude with a compromise. There may have been occasions when one could have wished that American statesmen had been less intent upon eradicating sin from the world and more willing to base their new world orders upon the solid foundation of past experience. Yet equally, one seeks in vain among British academics for that sense of adventure and discovery that distinguishes the best of their American counterparts.

11

From Atlanticism to Trilateralism: The Case of the Trilateral Commission

STEPHEN GILL

Most of the essays in this volume have focused on the different American and British approaches to the study of International Relations. This chapter concentrates on the Trilateral Commission, an organization which seeks to combine the theory and practice of international relations by fusing perspectives from a series of countries or 'trilateral' nations: the USA, Canada, Japan and the major Western European countries, notably France, West Germany, Britain and Italy. Consequently I will attempt to outline its concerns in a trilateral framework which stretches from Western Europe to North America and to Japan. In order to illustrate the importance of the Trilateral Commission I intend to sketch a series of general issues and propositions connected with the Commission, its relationship to institutions with similar aims, and then to concentrate on its political policies and the nature of its research activities. I hope to illustrate that the Commision provides an extremely important forum for the exchange of national and international views and for the discussion of foreign policy in a broad multilateral context.

The Trilateral Commission was set up in 1972 to cope with the divisions and tensions between the major capitalist powers in the era which followed the so-called *pax Americana*, as well as to provide a forum for analysis and for bringing together the different but commensurable academic traditions in the study of International Relations. At the heart of its concern lay the idea that the crises and conflicts of the 1930s had sacrificed a large part of the gains that had been made from economic interdependence. By pursuing autarkic and nationalistic policies the major powers had prepared the way for war: the nearer countries came to 'economic war' the nearer they would be to a 'killing war'. This diagnosis of the causes of the Second World War was the conventional Anglo-Saxon wisdom of the post-war era. It stressed the fact that peace and prosperity required an open, interdependent world and encompassed the belief that it would be unwise to adopt a punitive approach towards the defeated countries – notably Japan and Germany – as this might well sow the seeds of a nationalist backlash. This view of the causes of war and the problems of maintaining prosperity underlay the creation after the Second World War of multilateral economic institutions such as the IMF.

The peculiar conjuncture of 1945 allowed a widely held Anglo-Saxon vision of the world and its problems to emerge and form the conceptual basis for the largely US-dominated post-war order. However, it should be stressed that this was a particularly 'freakish' historical situation. The USA and the UK were culturally very close, and despite their differences they were firm allies. They had closely interlocking academic traditions particularly in the field of economics, and to a lesser extent in politics. This made collaboration on post-war issues unusually easy for them.

Seen from this perspective, the Trilateral Commission's role can be interpreted as the provision of a forum which could help to create a new 'common vision' of how the world works, what its key problems are, why these problems exist, and how they might be collectively approached by the trilateral powers. It also, of course, enables the development of a trilateral elite solidarity. It explicitly 'sets the scene' for the agreement about proposals to cope with the problems as well as setting up an 'educational' and consciousness-raising forum for those less central to the analysis and consideration of key issues but whose personal influence and affiliations could potentially contribute to the wider propagation of the Commission's perspectives. The Trilateral Commission is, of course, only one private council in which this process takes place – other major 'private' institutions with similar aims are the Atlantic Institute, Bilderberg and the Anglo-American Ditchley Foundation. At the governmental level the Organization for Economic Co-operation and Development (OECD) is in some senses a counterpart to the Commission, as are, on a much smaller scale, the annual economic summit meetings among the 'big seven' capitalist powers (these summits embody the trilateral idea in their membership). These of course are only the elite bodies in a vast series of international governmental, political, cultural and economic interactions and exchanges which form the substance of the relations between the trilateral countries. These relations are still 'thickest' across the Atlantic, are 'thickening' between the USA and Japan, and are still 'thin' between Europe and Japan.

The idea for the Trilateral Commission was mooted in a Bilderberg meeting, and indeed Bilderberg is the Atlantic expression of the concepts which underlie the *raison d'être* of the Commission. Bilderberg, created in 1954, was rooted in the cold war politics of the early 1950s as well as in the Anglo–Saxon post-war Atlanticist vision. It was, and still is, a series of top secret annual meetings at the highest level between political, military, economic and cultural leaders from North America and Western Europe. As in the Commission, the meetings are off the record, private, and attendance is by invitation only: there is no permanent membership, although a steering committee has always existed to organize meetings and invite individuals to present papers and/or attend. As has been said, the role of Bilderberg, like that of the Trilateral Commission was rooted in the post-war Atlanticist vision. It was founded to help foster a common perception and analysis of problems. Most of the continental European states – notably Germany and France – had more nationalist, mercantilist and *dirigiste* traditions which in fundamental ways were antithetical to the Anglo–Saxon vision of an open liberal post-war order. Nevertheless, Bilderberg was a powerful enough body to persuade the continental Western Europeans to move towards European political unity and to accept the institutional order set up at the end of the war. For, by 1954, the 'freakish conjuncture' of 1945 was gradually eroding with the post-war recovery of Germany and France and to a lesser extent of Italy, Belgium and the Netherlands. If the trend in institutions and ideas established in 1945 was to be maintained it was necessary to 'win over' continental Europeans to the liberal, Anglo–Saxon view of the world in order to form the basis for a workable consensus.

Seen from this perspective, the need for the Trilateral Commission was created by the emergence of Japan as an economic superpower in the 1960s and early 1970s, and by specific historical strains in the relations between the major capitalist powers at the start of the 1970s. It superseded Bilderberg which remained in the Atlanticist mould. If Bilderberg's goal is argued to be the containment of Franco-German rivalry, the setting up of the Trilateral Commission can be seen as an attempt to overcome Japan's fear of the outside world and the racism directed towards her by the USA and Europe. The Commission embodies – on a private level – a tripartite steering mechanism, a more or less organized relationship among the US, the EEC and Japan in order to manage their interdependence. This requires more than simply adopting common rules. It requires conscious co-ordination of macroeconomic and other policies, the restructuring of institutions and the creation of new institutions (like the Commission itself and like Hakone). More fundamentally it requires a common conception of the essential characteristics of the international system if the countries involved are to control the system efficiently.

Underpinning the aims of the Commission is the search for a workable short-term and long-term policy consensus among the establishments and governments of the trilateral regions in the spheres of international politics, security and economy, as well as in substantial aspects of domestic policy. In order to accomplish this the Commission employs theorists and practitioners in the fields of political science, economics, International Relations, diplomacy, politics, the media and law. Most of those called upon in this way are at (or near) the apex of their professions and often hold key institutional positions in prestigious universities, think-tanks, multinational corporations, banks and law. This does not of course guarantee agreement or consensus, though it does imply an extremely well-informed discussion of perspectives, problems and policies. The Commission's theorists are almost all members of liberal or conservative capitalist elites, and many have been associated with the 'realist' and 'transnational' schools of International Relations.

The development of the transnational school of theorists, whose focus is more on the international political economy, has been primarily associated with the United States particularly in the late 1960s and 1970s as the United States became increasingly conscious of the costs as well as the benefits of international interdependence. Much of this upsurge in 'transnational' academic literature has found its way into US journals such as *International Organization, International Studies Quarterly* and *World Politics*. British theorists on the other hand have tended to be more 'classical' in their orientation, using the disciplines of history and philosophy in a relativist framework to stress the specificity and uniqueness of national development and institutions in a 'realist' framework. The 'British school' of foreign policy analysis has been inclined to eschew general systems of explanation and logical empiricist theories which seek to generate predictions about change in the international system.

The US perspectives, embodying interdisciplinary approaches from liberal political economy and functionalism have developed rapidly in the 1970s – the period in which the Trilateral Commission was created – as the relative decline of post-war US power became more manifest, and (as has been said) as the costs of US global involvement became more obvious. Consequently, British 'classical' approaches to the study of International Relations are under-represented in the Commission, although conversely, the key centres of power in terms of the conduct and shape of British foreign policy are well covered. The British theorists who are members of the Trilateral Commission are similar to their predominantly Ivy League university and 'think-tank' US counterparts.

Most of the Commission's authors carry out the majority of their work in applied policy areas, and apply interdisciplinary methods in an instrumentalist/pragmatic discourse which attempts to determine the nature and terms of foreign policy debates. They, together with their European and Japanese colleagues, therefore start from similar applied orientations, similar class backgrounds, and work from compatible discourses, albeit from different regional perspectives. Authors of the Commission's reports are instructed to follow Jean Monnet's adage and 'put the problem on the other side of the table' and attempt to solve it from a trilateral, rather than a national or bilateral perspective. They are to search out incrementalist changes in policy or to suggest innovations which might be acceptable in the broad trilateral framework. The Commission's output thus often has a managerialist and in some limited senses reformist orientation, seeking to summarize an opinion which incorporates what Falk has called 'the geoeconomics of the multinational corporation' and what former US Secretary of State, Cyrus Vance, and former US National Security Advisor, Zbigniew Brzezinski, have called 'world order politics'.

The Trilateral Commission's publications are in almost all cases a response to 'crises' of or threats to world capitalism. Initially their concern was with the international economic and to a lesser extent political aspect of the threat, and with attempts to produce a smooth 'management of interdependence' (Camps, 1974). In the mid-1970s the focus shifted to an examination of the domestic 'problems' of the 'governability' and viability of liberal democracy as a political form in the advanced capitalist countries (Crozier et al., 1975). Thereafter a more fundamental change in perspective took place. Falk argues that this move increasingly came to represent an endorsement of the new militarism promoted by the US Committee on the Present Danger and the CIA team 'B' assessments, a militarism also seen in the shift to the right in US electoral politics which eventually culminated in the election of President Reagan. This has led to a relative abandonment of economic co-ordination and 'the management of interdependence' because the consensus underpinning this orientation broke down during the Carter administration (staffed at the top level by many ex-members of the Trilateral Commission). In 1977 the three chairmen of the Commission were able to note:

> intensive debate between the members of the Commission has helped to increase understanding between the three regions, and often even to reach some form of consensus about the policy recommendations formulated by the three authors of a report . . . This consensus was possible because of some convictions shared by all members – particularly the conviction that the cooperation of all three regions is essential to assure the smooth management of interdependence. (Berthoin et al., 1977, p. vii–viii)

In 1981, however, after the Soviet invasion of Afghanistan the three chairmen reported on 'an increased willingness to think in 'trilateral' terms when discussing security challenges, particularly those in and around the Middle East' (Berthoin et al., 1981, p. vii).

Later attempts have been made to integrate economic, political and strategic concerns into what can be described as an 'ultra-imperialist' framework of the sharing of responsibilities' – an effort to outline the criteria for a debate on a new political division of labour congenial to the transnational class formation represented by the Trilateral Commission (see Ushiba et al., 1983; Cox, 1979). It is the function of the Commission not only to produce elite consensus on the outlines of policy in the short and longer terms, but also to put limits on the scope of reasonable discussion, behaviour and policy within the competitive framework of US political life via its control over the general political climate and the 'boundaries of the reasonable'. However, part of the US power structure (notably the south and west and the new wealth of the sunbelt) is not properly incorporated into the Commission's forum

(Falk, 1980). At the core of this split within the US establishment is the contrast between the Reagan administration's neo-mercantilist, territorial and productivity orientation with its concern to build up maximum productivity and resource security within the domestic economy, and the international capitalism of the Trilateral Commission embodied in the banking and transnational corporations of the Rockefeller empire. The latter tends to be preoccupied with an image of a 'businessman's peace', a preference for a world order where the role of the state is relegated to keeping domestic order and where economic efficiency is not eroded by social movements redefining goals (Falk, 1980).

More crucially, however, in the USA in the 1980s a 'hyperconsensus' has emerged on the need to reverse the deterioration in the US world position primarily through military means. This reorientation operates in concert with the increasingly neo-mercantilist foreign economic policies noted above. In the trilateral context it requires the imposition of US political will on recalcitrant situations and countries in the alliance. To an extent the Trilateral Commission has embraced this view, although Europeans in particular are not enamoured of the Reagan administration's perspective on the Soviet Union, nor of its view of detente as a 'one-way street'.

As a result of the 'hyperconsensus' numerous US Commission members have been publicly mute on many of the issues raised within the forum; this perhaps indicates the depth of the transatlantic crisis as the views of US globalism and the liberal establishment are increasingly eclipsed by resurgent right wing and militarist tendencies in the USA. Thus the risk of a 'decoupling' of US and European perspectives remains possible, at least in the long-term, if US attitudes continue to diverge from mainstream European thought (Falk, 1982; Rosenau and Holsti, 1983). Members of the Commission are alarmed at this prospect, and the Commission's most recent publications outline ways to contain some of these unilateralist and militarist tendencies in US politics by coupling US politico-security policies more firmly with those of Western Europe and Japan; they also sketch an alternative division of labour within the alliance to maintain trilateral domination of world order. An unfortunate side-effect of these moves, however, may be to transfer the emphasis of the resugent militarism and new cold war politics from the US to Europe and Japan.

These are some of the important problems faced by the Trilateral Commission. I now propose to examine the processes by which the

Commission has attempted to deal with these issues, and to discuss the origins, nature and implications of these processes.

The Trilateral Commission describes itself as:

> a non-governmental, policy-oriented discussion group composed of about 300 distinguished citizens from Western Europe, North America and Japan, drawn from a variety of backgrounds. Its purpose is to encourage mutual understanding and closer cooperation among these three regions, through analysis of major common problems and consideration of policy proposals for addressing them. (Trilateral Commission, 1973)

The 'historical roots' of the Commission are attributed to 'serious strains' in relations between Japan, North America and Europe in the early 1970s. These strains had, by 1982, affected international relations throughout the world and the work of the Commission, as evidenced in its reports and meetings, has adjusted accordingly. The Commission's initial long-term objective was no less than 'the renovation of the international system' based on an ongoing 'process of creation' in which 'prolonged negotiations' were to be initiated. Its role was to nurture 'habits and practices of working together among the trilateral regions, and to help set the context for these necessary efforts' (Trilateral Commission, 1982, p.40).

As we have seen, many theorists who participate in the Commission's activities are related to the liberal 'transnational relations' school of International Relations though none can be described as adhering solely to this approach. From the point of view of Samuel P. Huntington's work on transnational organizations (Huntington, 1973), the Commission might be said to perform a specific political function: it enables the representatives of national political coalitions and interests (largely liberal and conservative and to a lesser extent social democratic) together with the leaders of transnational and international organizations and theorists in cognate disciplines, to debate the issues of 'access' and 'accord' from a shared interest in more liberal trade. This takes place in a unique international institution which to an extent downgrades the importance of government and national sovereignty. Its organizational form is looser and more flexible than most other international and transnational bodies, with a small secretariat and minimal bureaucratic support. Central to its activities are the search for consensus and the creation of ongoing processes of problem-solving and mutual interaction among the elites within the three trilateral regions.

The Trilateral Commission is also a consciousness-raising

organization. This objective is accomplished in debates, in the corridors of hotels at meetings, in seminars and through the distribution of papers, publications and memoranda to members and 'opinion leaders' in the wider international society. Seen from a Marxist perspective, the Commission's search for co-operative political relations among the world's major capitalist powers is an attempt to create an ultra-imperialist alliance which will prolong the life of the capitalist mode of production, and produce a unified capitalist political front *vis-à-vis* the two major axes of conflict in the international system, the East–West conflict and the increasingly important North–South conflict. If such an alliance can hold together during the post-war period's most prolonged economic crisis, then, in a negative sense the Commission's work and other 'trilateral' efforts will have been successful in preventing economic disputes (trade wars, differences on protectionism, international monetary problems) from spilling over into political rivalry. The political significance of the Trilateral Commission is in the following sense two-fold and has both short-term and long-term dimensions. On the one hand it is concerned with the immediate problems of alliance cohesion and crisis management and with avoiding misunderstandings or a breakdown in communications during times of stress or strain (the negative sense of 'keeping the alliance together'). On the other hand it is engaged in a positive process of trilateral alliance-building as it debates and considers the long-term development of strategy to optimize the collective political and economic interests of the trilateral alliance; it is also involved in recruiting from among the elite within alliance countries current and future leaders who will continue to support policies based on trilateral perspectives (Makins, 1979).

The Trilateral Commission was the brain-child of four Americans: banker and businessman, David Rockefeller, and academics Zbigniew Brzezinksi, Henry Owen and Robert Bowie. Rockefeller had made several speeches in 1972 to the Chase Manhattan Bank International Financial Forums and to the Bilderberg meeting in Knokke, Belgium calling for a private commission on peace and prosperity drawn from the trilateral regions. Bowie as head of the Harvard Center for International Affairs had instituted a series of Japanese and European fellowships and exchanges at the Center. Owen as Director of Foreign Policy Studies at the Brookings Institution had organized a series of tripartite (i.e. trilateral) seminars for economists in Washington DC in the late 1960s and early 1970s. Brzezinski in his book *Between*

Two Ages had called for a 'community of the developed nations' to meet the challenges of the 'technetronic era' in the coming decades (Brzezinski, 1970). On Rockefeller's initiative these and other forces were brought together and a meeting was held at Rockefeller's Pocantico Hills estate in the Hudson Valley late in 1972 to discuss the prospects for such an organization (Rockefeller, 1979). Funds to set up the Commission were obtained mainly from David Rockefeller and the Ford Foundation and, after further consultations with Takeshi Watanabe (Head of the Asian Development Bank) and the Japanese planning group formed at the Pocantico Hills meeting, an informal advisory council was established, and the Trilateral Commission itself was created by spring 1973. For the first executive committee Gerard Smith (a Rockefeller in-law and the US negotiator for SALT I) was appointed North American Chairman, Max Kohnstamm European Chairman, and Watanabe Japanese Chairman (Trilateral Commission, 1973).

Plenary meetings of the full membership of the Trilateral Commission are now held every year in rotation among the regions, usually in four-star hotels and protected by tight security. The Commission is a non-permanent organization which renews itself every three years (a 'triennium') if the membership favours continuation: this device is said to keep staff members active and alert as well as continually forcing them to re-examine both the purposes and usefulness of the Commission's activities. It is, moreover, a requirement made by funding agencies such as the Ford Foundation (Rockefeller, 1979). Proponents of the principle of the Trilateral Commission also argue that the meetings develop a sense of collegiality and mutual confidence among the members of this prestigious collection of establishmentarians, allowing a group of people to emerge who can increasingly 'work together on issues that we would have found too sensitive before'. This becomes more possible under the Commission's rules concerning private discussion and non-attributable commentary (Brzezinski, 1982), which enable lines of exchange to be kept open within this forum even when communications are solidified or even severed between the trilateral governments.

The nature of this council has led to an accusation from Third World countries that it is a 'rich man's club' (in addition to questions of wealth there are indeed very few women members). Also, 'first world' countries like Australia and New Zealand are concerned at their exclusion from the debates. Further, the election of President

Carter and his appointment of numerous ex-Commission members to key positions within his administration has prompted, not unexpectedly, numerous 'conspiracy' theories about the Commission in the USA and elsewhere. Many of these argue that the Commission has achieved a takeover of the US government and accuse David Rockefeller of orchestrating the *coup d'état!* Indeed the importance of the far right in US domestic politics in the 1970s enabled Ronald Reagan to exploit George Bush's former membership of the Trilateral Commission during the Republican primary elections. None the less, Reagan accepted Bush afterwards as his running mate for the Presidency and as President chose as his Secretaries of State and Defense two former Commission members (Haig and Weinberger).

There can be said to be two types of members of the Trilateral Commission. The first are the 'established patriarchs' who are key politicians, top bankers and corporate heads, senior academics (policy specialists) and influential lawyers. The second kind are the 'up and coming' people who may potentially rise to the top during the coming decades, hence providing a continuing body of people imbued with the 'trilateral idea' and avoiding a trilateral 'leadership crisis' in the future. Geographically, the membership has been extended to include all the European Community countries except Greece, and also to Spain and Portugal who are not community members. Membership numbers are in rough proportion to a country's gross national product, although Japan is paradoxically accorded 'regional' status and is proportionately over-represented with the USA under-represented in these terms.

The US delegation is very powerful politically and includes notable figures such as David Rockefeller, Henry Kissinger, Zbigniew Brzezinski, David Packard, Alexander Haig, Lane Kirkland (AFL-CIO), Robert S. McNamara, Elliot L. Richardson, Robert V. Roosa, Helmut Sonnenfeldt, Andrew Young and Harold Brown. Former members now in the US federal government include Paul Volcker (Chairman of the Board of Governors, Federal Reserve System), George Bush, Caspar Weinberger, Arthur Burns (US Ambassador to West Germany) and Bill Brock (US Special Trade Representative).

The British group has tended to be heavily representative of merchant and commercial banking, of multinational corporations and of a 'Foreign Office' orientation to policy. Virtually all its current and former members were educated at Oxford or Cambridge. Of the ex-diplomats who have been members most have either strong connections with Japan or with the USA. Until the fall of the Labour government in 1979 no senior Labour politicians had played any part in the Trilateral Commission – now Denis Healey (Deputy Leader of the Labour Party and former Labour Foreign Secretary) and David Owen (Leader of the SDP) are full members. The Rio Tinto Zinc Corporation has three representatives. Former Conservative Prime Minister and ex-member of the Brandt Commission, Edward Heath is also involved, but before he became a member the only important Conservative representative was Lord Carrington, who joined briefly prior to becoming Foreign Secretary in 1979.

Most of the UK's contributions to the Commission's publications and debates have been economically and policy-oriented and have come principally from ex-diplomats, graduates from Oxbridge, the RIIA (Royal Institute of International Affairs) and Sussex University (this may be due to contacts made by Francois Duchene who has been a professor at Sussex since leaving the IISS (International Institute for Strategic Studies)). Moreover, British academic contributions have rather declined over the last few years. One reason for this is that for most of the Commission's operations reference to the work of British academics is simply not necessary. The majority of British academics in International Relations therefore play little or no role in policy debates and those who do tend to cluster in the institutions from which the Commission recruits members of the diplomatic corps and Oxbridge. This if the Commission is seeking to co-opt and influence those who are amenable to its perspectives, it need look no further than Oxbridge, the RIIA, the Foreign Office, the LSE (London School of Economics) and the PSI (Policy Studies Institute).

The same is roughly true for the USA, although here there is much more diversity and competition for a place in the making of foreign policy. The most represented institutions are Harvard, Brookings, Columbia, the Council on Foreign Relations and Yale, while ex-diplomats and former politicians are also well covered. All the centres of research used by the Trilateral Commission tend to stress applied, interdisciplinary empirical work, often fitting this work into a neo-classical functionalist perspective (the Harvard Center for International Affairs is a good example). There is therefore a degree of commensurability between the institutions and orientations of the academic contributions from the USA and the UK.

This 'core' of institutional capacities is fairly well developed in the UK and particularly strong in the USA, as is the process of generating interdisciplinary consensual reports by committees of experts from academia, business, government and the media. British International Relations theorists, however, due to their 'classical' tendencies are almost entirely separated from the concerns of applied policy and the institutions which embody them. An analogous law-oriented tradition is also found in Japan, although strenuous efforts have been made to encourage a more policy-oriented academic International Relations community there. Moreover, many of the institutions incorporated into the Commission's research efforts have strong links with the foreign ministries of their own countries (for example, the CFR has often been described as a shadow State Department, and its members have frequently manned the top positions in the US foreign policy apparatus), so some limited influence on governments exists as a result of these associations.

Let us now look at the techniques by which the Trilateral Commission attempts to reconcile different theoretical and geographical perspectives in its research activity. These techniques also contribute to consciousness-raising and to the construction of a consensus within the Commission.

The primary responsibility for the choice of subjects for research rests with a small programme advisory board of international specialists from different disciplines, which proposes topics to the executive committee and the chairmen and sets up the priorities for research. Key figures on the board during the first triennium (1973–76) were Zbigniew Brzezinski, Francois Duchene, Robert Bowie and Henry Owen. Later Bruce MacLaury (President of the Brookings Institution) and Kinhide Mushakoji (Vice-Rector of the United Nations University in Tokyo) became heavily involved in these affairs.

The technical role of the programme advisory board is to construct an overall plan for the research of the Trilateral Commission into the problem of 'the renovation of the international system' in the political context of trilateral and global relations. The academic approaches to this task are essentially liberal, reformist and piecemeal, seeking to chart a 'middle way between the rock of conservatism and the whirlpool of revolution' in order to move towards a 'more equitable global system' whose basis is not radical redistribution (which is seen as a negative-sum game), but an 'expansion of the global economic pie' (a positive-sum game) which is believed to be 'the most hopeful means of improving the economic position of the poorer nations' (Makins, 1975). The achievement of this end rests upon the liberal democracies taking charge of the trilateral world, as well as on their effectively managing East–West relations. The problems are long-term and require a reconciliation of the divergent approaches in the trilateral countries, 'for example between the market-oriented philosophy which has characterized US policy and the more interventionist, dirigiste approach of some Western European governments and political parties'; they also demand 'the more effective mobilization of the resources and policies of the trilateral regions' (Makins, 1975).

These concerns inform the choice of areas for research as well as the discourses employed from modern liberal political economy and international politics. Once topics have been agreed upon a 'task force' of ten to twenty specialists is selected, and three or more authors or 'rapporteurs' are chosen from each of the trilateral regions. These authors have final responsibility for the text. The reports take between eighteen and twenty-four months to prepare and involve often extensive consultation with specialists who are not necessarily Commission members, or from countries not represented in the Commission.

In the period 1973–6 eight economic task force reports were produced. These dealt with threats to the changing liberal political and economic order: with the international monetary system, North–South economic relations, world trade, energy (two reports here), world commodity markets and oceans management and the Law of the Sea conference. Four political task force reports were also published, three of which were international and which analysed problems connected with international consultation and co-operation, and the prospect of reform for international institutions. A fourth political task force produced a controversial study on the primarily domestic problems of governability and liberal-democratic politics within the trilateral countries; this report, *The Crisis of Democracy,* is the Commission's only book-length study to date (Crozier et al., 1975). Thereafter in the 1977–80 period reports dealt with East–West relations (two reports), energy, international financial stability (this report was unpublished), rice production in South East Asia and the more domestic topics of industrial policy and labour–capital relations (Triangle Papers 13–17). The most important article of this period was the ambitious Triangle Paper 14, 'Towards a Renovated

International System', which draws on the work of earlier task forces and offers procedural guidelines and criteria for policy in a Popperian, incrementalist and functionalist framework.

The following period (1979–83) saw reports on labour markets and unemployment (unpublished), North–South trade in manufactured goods, the Middle East, the global diffusion of economic power, East–West trade, security and arms control, Third World development and the debt crisis (Triangle Papers 18–27). The crucial work here was paper 25 'Sharing International Responsibilities Among the Trilateral Countries' which is in effect an attempt to outline the basis of a new international division of political, economic and military responsibilities among the trilateral countries and to sketch the agenda for trilateral relations in the 1980s (Ushiba et al., 1983). Finally, 1984 will see the publication of a new report – paper 28 – on 'The Political Implications of the Continuing Economic Crisis', a title which has a surprisingly Orwellian ring to it, given the broad sweep and ambitious aims of the Trilateral Commission's stated objectives.

The majority of the reports are supplemented by a synopsis of the Commission members' discussion at plenary meetings. The most extensive of these was for the 'Crisis of Democracy' report which was severely criticized by a number of Commission members and by the special consultant Ralf Dahrendorf for its pessimistic and authoritarian stance, and its implication that democratic processes should be restricted and international participation curtailed (see Crozier et al., 1975, especially pp. 188–95). Reports are also reviewed in the quarterly *Trialogue* (with supplementary articles following each study), in addition to news about the Commission's activities and notes on plenary meetings. The reports and *Trialogue* are distributed free to 'opinion leaders' and the Commission members, and are available upon subscription to the wider public.

Virtually all the reports embody what Cox calls the the 'establishment' perspective on international order, which he further identifies as monopolistic liberalism. The Trilateral Commission is the most important forum organizing this network of political, business and academic forces who use the 'hegemonic discourse' to legitimate and interpret the existing structure of power in the world economy. Cox contrasts its perspective with what he refers to as a 'social democratic variant' of the establishment view, which also accepts the rationality of neo-classical economics but which is ultimately more humane, putting greater stress on the needs of the poor. It constitutes 'a more generous view of the adjustments that can be made without fundamentally altering the existing hegemony'. Cox associates the social democratic view with the Brandt Commission, the Club of Rome and the Institute of Development Studies at Sussex University. He sees that social democratic theorists are also members of the Trilateral Commission and that several faculty members of the Sussex Institute have been consulted in the preparation of certain reports for the Commission. Thus there can be no absolute separation of these two approaches.

Cox views the Commission's fourteenth report as a classic illustration of the functionalist political route towards rebuilding an international economic order. The idea of an inner core consisting of countries with the biggest stake in a particular issue area is introduced in this report and is repeated in the later 'Sharing Global Reponsibilities' study. The image is of concentric circles of participation with the trilateral countries at the centre, and generally the USA, Japan and West Germany at its core. This is seen as a more efficient mode of decision-making, with the task of ensuring overall consistency of policies falling to the trilateral nations. Cox, moreover, points out that this political position falls far short of many Third World demands which tend to reject the Commission's 'piecemeal functionalism' and neo-Popperian stance towards policy planning and implementation.

Apart from the social democratic variant, Cox identifies a range of Third World perspectives (some of which share the epistemological orientation of the Commission), two variants of neo-mercantilism (left-wing and right-wing) and a historical materialist perspective. Of these, the most politically significant is right-wing neo-mercantilism because of its historical and in some cases contemporary strength in the USA in an era of recession. It comprises neo-conservatives who write for *Commentary* magazine, as well as significant portions of the Republican Party, US labour organizations and 'national' capital seeking protection from the effects of international competition. The idea of state power is central to this point of view and economic power is seen as an instrument for attaining political goals. In the early 1970s the Nixon administration displayed tendencies towards this position with more unilateral foreign economic policies exemplified by the so-called 'Nixon shocks' of August 1971; the most important of these were the imposition of a 10 percent import surcharge and the suspension of the convertability of the US dollar. On the political front, the 'opening' with China after Kissinger's secret diplomacy shook Japanese politics to its foundations and helped topple the Sato government. These moves which antagonized the US allies in Europe and Japan were part of the larger 'pentagonal design' – an image which sees world power organized into competing economic blocs.

As the US economic recession has continued, however, the voices of the right-wing neo-mercantilists have become much more audible, and certain elements of the Reagan administration and much of the US Congress support its stance particularly on the issues of 'fair trade', 'reciprocity' and on the politicization of aid and assistance programmes to Third World countries. This and other movements and the political constellations they represent are working to undermine the hegemonic rationality and the legitimacy of the institutional arrangements favoured in the Trilateral Commission's publications on the world economy. Current economic conditions underpin these developments with slow growth, increasing unemployment and the problem of inflation all pressing the nation-state both to intervene in the domestic economy and to manage foreign economic policies from a neo-mercantilist perspective. These trends are becoming noticeable in the Reagan administration, despite the President's largely consistent support for liberal trade policies. Pressures within the administration and in Congress are expressed increasingly in nationalist terms. Moreover, many of the largest blue-chip multinational companies in the USA have begun to call on the US government to arrest the long-term decline in the US manufacturing industry, arguing, among other things, that the US must 'strengthen' its international trade policies, lower the US dollar exchange rate to make US industry more internationally competitive, and act to preserve the US lead in high technology industries.

Let us now consider the mechanics of the construction of task force reports by examining the Commission's report on 'Sharing International Responsibilities Among the Trilateral Countries'. This was written by Nobuhiko Ushiba (former Japanese ambassador to the USA and adviser to the Minister of Foreign Affairs), Graham Allison (Dean of the Kennedy School of Government, Harvard University), and Thierry de Montbrial (Director of the French Institute for International Relations (IFRI), and former Chief of Analysis and Planning Staff in the French Ministry of Foreign Affairs (1973–7)). Ushiba is essentially a diplomat, Allison a political scientist and de Montbrial an economist. The rapporteurs were aided by six special consultants: Peter Dobell (Director, Parliamentary Center for Foreign Affairs and Foreign Trade, Canada); Masashi Nishihara (Professor of International Relations, National Defence Academy, Tokyo, Japan); Tadashi Yamamoto (the Japanese director of the Trilateral Commission); Charles Heck (North American director of the Trilateral Commission); Charles Morrison (visiting scholar, Japan Center for International Exchange, Tokyo); Paul Zigman (assistant to Dean Allison at Harvard). There were thirty-four other consultants, fifteen of whom were attached to Harvard University (with no less than seven of these working on Harvard's programme of US–Japanese relations). In disciplinary terms the consultants comprise eleven political scientists (in the fields of International Relations, government and public policy), three economists, a historian, a sociologist, a journalist and a lawyer. There were six Commission staff members involved as consultants, and seventeen American consultants, seven Japanese, four French, three Germans, two Italians and a solitary Briton, Elizabeth Sherwood of of Balliol College, Oxford.

Many British International Relations theorists are peripheral to the focus and orientation of most of the Commission's reports. The vast majority of the Commission's task forces are heavily economically and/or domestically biased. Given the initial reluctance of the Japanese membership to be associated with overt discussion of security matters in the early years of the Commission this is not surprising – the turning-point seems to have come around 1978/79 when the Japanese leadership began to get more involved in security debates. Moreover, the incrementalist, functionalist policy-orientation of the task force reports is not entirely commensurable with all aspects of the hegemonic discourse in British International Relations: the power-realist approach. Where it seems the British theorists might have an important role to play, for example, in report 27 'Trilateral Security', they are not significantly represented as consultants, although Christopher Makins (Fellow of All Souls, Oxford and an ex-diplomat) is an associate author. For this report only six Britons were consulted (including Denis Healey, who was the founder of IISS). Of the six only two could be considered academics: David Boulton of the Royal United Services Institute and Air Marshall Sir Neil Cameron, presently teaching at King's College, University of London. A perhaps more plausible explanation of the neglect of

British International Relations specialists might therefore be that Britain – in the context of sharing responsibilities – already devotes a greater proportion of its gross national product to defence then all other trilateral countries (with the exception of the USA).

The situation with Japan, however, is very different. One of the key elements in current US policy toward Japan is the attempt to force a sizeable and, if possible, fairly swift increase in Japanese defence expenditures – this would release the USA from some of its South East Asian engagements and might slow down Japanese penetration of US markets. This seems to be the central purpose of report 25. However, the USA cannot simply impose this policy on Japan, and the Japanese government has been very successful during the 1970s in resisting US pressure to expand their military expenditure too fast. Japan's 'peace' constitution (which forbids training an army for other than defence purposes and outlaws nuclear weapons) together with solid public opinion against 'rearmament' mean that only by developing a strong countervailing body of opinion can the USA hope to win over Japanese political parties, public opinion, business and government to co-operate with their aims. This perhaps explains why in report 25 so many Japanese are involved as consultants, and so few Britons. There is simply not the same need to incorporate the British in a process which is largely related to reallocating military burdens within the alliance and developing a usable consensus which will influence the Japanese stance. Moreover, the larger numbers of Japanese engaged in applied security studies may be extremely significant in the longer term *vis-à-vis* the construction of common trilateral concepts and perspectives on the issue of collective defence.

It has been stressed several times in this book that approaches in Britain to the study of International Relations have been mainly classicist, with philosophy and history the core disciplinary base. The situation in Japan is very similar, with a lack of policy-orientated work and with relationships between the government and the disciplines of political science and International Relations still weak. Japanese International Relations specialists continue to be relatively parochial in their outlook and tend to write almost exclusively for a Japanese audience; there is a large gap between 'theorists' and 'empiricists', as well as a continuing indifference to the contribution of research to policy. Although, as has been said, there has been a slow shift towards a more policy-oriented International Relations community, work in this field is still mainly characterized by its affinities with the European (and British) rather than the American approaches (Kamura, 1981). Kamura's study identifies a corps of security theorists equipped with 'solid empirical-analytical methodology' which has grown considerably since 1978, the first post-war year when security and defence debates were no longer 'taboo' in Japan. Some of these theorists have been incorporated as consultants in several of the Commission's studies, and in particular in report 27 on security and in paper 25 on 'Sharing Global Responsibilities'. Therefore these theorists not only contribute to the Commission's preparations they also can help to propogate the Commission's ideas in the search for a new domestic consensus on Japan's defence role. It might be suggested that the Trilateral Commission particularly through its relationship with the powerful Japan Center for International Exchange (Tadashi Yamamoto is Japanese director of both), has helped to finance and cultivate this embryonic policy-oriented group of International Relations intellectuals in Japan. On the other hand, there is very little evidence for such a change in the British International Relations community as a result of the Commission's efforts, although a Japanese Studies Centre has been created at Sheffield University.

The first meeting of authors and consultants for report 25 'Sharing Global Responsibilities' took place between 28 and 30 March 1981 and the final draft was completed for publication in November 1982. During this period meetings had taken place in Washington DC, New York City (three separate two-day meetings), Paris (two meetings), Tokyo (two meetings). Overall it can be stated that the process of putting together the report – just 102 pages long – was extremely labour intensive and time-consuming. However, it should also be noted that participation in preparing such a paper itself gives credibility and legitimacy to the Trilateral Commission as an institution, as well as incorporating a large number of theoreticians and practitioners into the Commission's activities and deliberations. This, as I have noted, is particularly important for Japan.

The general focus of the report continues a series of studies carried out under the Commission's auspices concerning the division of labour between the trilateral allies. These studies were completed in 1972–4, 1974–6 and 1975–7 (Duchene et al., 1974; Bergsten et al., 1976; Cooper et al., 1977). Underlying the work is the belief that forces ouside the trilateral regions threaten the international political and economic order of the 1980s more severely than at any time since the Second World War; that any disruption of this order would have catastrophic consequences for the trilateral countries and the rest of the world; and that the trilateral countries – because their stakes are so high and their capacities so great – have a special responsibility to preserve the status quo (Ushiba et al., 1983). Underpinning the study are normative commitments to the liberty of the individual, representative government, the market economy, 'an international order that encourages efficiency and equity through specialization and trade', and 'an international political order based on national self-determination and evolution' (Ushiba et al., 1983). The report argues that international conditions are not currently favourable to the achievement of these objectives, and emphasizes that they can only be attained if collective capacities are optimized in an overall strategy.

Four principal areas of threat are identified: the problem of neutralism and alliance cohesion, the challenge of Soviet military power, the plight of the the poorer nations and East–West confrontations in the Third World and the Middle East; a fourth threat is to the trilateral countries' domestic political capacity and ability to govern. The authors outline four concepts which clarify the issues connected with sharing responsibilities 'the positive-sum game' of international trade; the Ricardian notion of comparative advantage; the concept of public goods; and the 'free rider' problem. The dominant message is the necessity for leadership groups in the trilateral regions to agree on basic concepts and to mobilize collective resources under agreed criteria.

The authors of the report also analyse the different attitudes and political trends evident among the trilateral countries. Japan comes out worst in these assessments: it is most susceptible to the accusation that it takes a 'free ride' in the security and development areas, and to the charge that it has not yet assumed full global responsibilities concomitant with its massive economic power. The Japanese feel vulnerable to these attacks and are worried more about economic than military threats. They feel they are scapegoats for the economic woes of the 'sick man of Europe' and are also anxious about protectionist trends in the US. They are concerned about the possibly reckless US policy in the Middle East and fear that President Reagan has unnecessarily aggravated East–West tensions. To placate the US and Europe, Japan has since developed the concept of 'comprehensive security' in which economic contributions play a central role. However, it appears that the

Japanese establishment is also increasingly prepared to agree to modest rearmament and a stronger regional military stance because of mounting US pressures on it to succumb to 'burden sharing'. This is being started on a piecemeal, step-by-step basis. The authors stress that there is still a large gap between Japan's international efforts and her inherent capacities and that she is not yet doing enough to overcome the 'free rider' argument.

The authors discuss US post-war policy pointing out America's paternalism towards its allies and the disproportionate burden it carried to maintain international order after the war. Irrespective of the motivation for this conduct the authors state that it is now clear that the USA refuses to 'pick up the tab' in the same way. Its attitude is becoming more narrowly self-interested as a result of a number of significant changes in US domestic politics notably institutions, demographic shifts among both the masses and the elite, and an increased consciousness of the outside world which is also linked to the 'experience of failure' in foreign policy. The net result is a sense of US decline and a more reassertive neo-mercantilist stance. Despite this reaffirmation, US domestic economic policies are constrained by the fragmentation of the US state's institutions and its decreasing autonomy in international terms – the 'end of American exceptionalism' to use Daniel Bell's phrase (Bell, 1975). While Japan becomes moderately more globalist, the USA retreats from globalism to nationalism and unilateralism and American theorists begin again to view the world through strategic lenses as they did in the 1950s and early 1960s. Detente becomes a 'foreign' word and arms control ceases to be the centre-piece of America's Soviet strategy. Two elite views emerge: the Reagan administration perceives threats primarily in terms of their Soviet dimensions; the alternative view tends to see threats more as 'variegated challenges' in which the USSR plays an important but 'rarely decisive' role.

Looking at Europe the authors contrast the promise of a European union and the slow laborious progress towards that end over the last ten years. National rivalry is played down in their account of the causes for this delay, which are seen as primarily economic – the crisis of the 1970s and 1980s being held chiefly responsible. Europe's economic ills have allowed less room for manoeuvre in the international sphere and increased vulnerability to world economic conditions: a vulnerability now far greater than the USA's or Japan's. The authors also note a 'lack of political leadership or coordination' at precisely the moment when the web of interdependence has become more tightly woven. This is viewed as the central contradiction in European politics. The report seems to recommend a tightening of political discipline and governability on a European scale in order to meet the external challenges – the central theme of the *Crisis of Democracy*. The authors lament the lack of a European consciousness, yet, although they discuss the peace movement in a different context, they do not review its potential importance at the level of European consciousness perhaps because of its democratic content. This 'consciousness gap' has meant that the enlargement of the European Community has paradoxically made it more difficult to progress towards a politically unified Europe.

The authors also emphasize the different views of the Soviet threat held by the USA and Europe since the intervention in Afghanistan in 1979 and list differences over nuclear weapons, East–West trade and interpretations of the general nature of the Soviet Union in the 1980s as evidence of this. Europeans rely considerably on developing trade with Eastern Europe particularly when their economies are in crisis, and this results in a tendency to placate the Soviet Union least they jeopardize their own interests. The USA, on the other hand, which runs much smaller risks in East–West trade is more likely to be confrontationist and unilaterally to impose its positions on the European countries, as in the case of the Siberian gas pipeline sanctions. More generally, Europeans are inclined to argue that the Soviet system is in difficulties while Americans stress the increasing Soviet military threat. The two positions are very far apart. On economic policies, which are said to harm European and Third World economies Reagan's military Keynesianism and the spiralling budget deficits which shoulder its costs alarm many Europeans, as does the increasing US repudiation of multilateral aid bodies and the tendency to see the Soviet Union's hand behind crises and instabilities throughout the Third World. The sum total of these political and economic differences leads to a danger of 'decoupling' between Europe and the United States.

European views on Japan are similar to those held in the USA, except that they are founded, according to the authors, on a more fundamental ignorance. Japan's economic penetration of Europe is feared and there is also concern that strengthening US-Japanese economic ties will mean declining US interest in Europe. Japan is not generally seen as a 'natural ally'. However, no concern is expressed at the possible resurgence of Japanese militarism. More worrying it seems, to France and Britain in particular, is that the growth of the arms industry in Japan (though it might enhance trilateral security overall) could mean a loss of overseas arms markets as inevitably the Japanese would compete successfully in them. This flank of trilateralism contains very little sense of mutual solidarity except among a select few.

The picture painted of the state of trilateral relations is thus one of strain, stress and diverging perceptions of threat and interest. The authors do not attempt to prescribe formulas for sharing responsibility but seek to point out the threats to the aims and interests of the trilateral countries, and give guidelines for modifications to the political division of labour in the areas of international economic management, the Soviet threat and North–South relations. They argue vigorously for a defence of the liberal trading system, and recommend a strengthening of GATT (General Agreement on Tariffs and Trade) (including services, investments and intra-firm trading); institutions like the GATT and OECD (Organization for Economic Co-operation and Development) should also be more active in monitoring trade. They repeat earlier calls from the Commission for more frequent consultation and (where possible) co-ordination in the field of macroeconomic policy. These positions clearly reflect the consensus of the liberal establishments and multinational capital.

The authors also demand a 'major Japanese initiative' – Japan should take 'unilateral steps to open its market' to head off protectionist pressures in the US Congress and the European Community. The issue of the 'conceptual basis' for interpreting East–West relations leads the authors to prescribe world strategic summits to hammer out differences and to optimize the alliance's military stance. Military policy itself should continue to 'couple' Europe and the US in 'the strategic, political and psychological sense', increase NATO's conventional capacities, complicate Soviet calculations through the enhancement of individual nations' self-defence forces, and develop co-ordinated trilateral approaches to political and security issues in the Middle East. They underline the need for a common conceptual framework built from regular staff-level consultations and focused in annual strategic summits. To cope with potential challenges from the South, the report argues that demands for a New International Economic Order should be taken seriously and steps should increasingly be taken to integrate particularly newly industrializing Third World countries into the international political and economic order. Third World countries should become more and more involved in international economic institutions such as GATT, the IMF and the World Bank. The trilateral countries should open their markets to Third World imports and substantially increase the flow of aid – the UK, Japan and USA are singled out for criticism on this last issue. On the political front the model of the Contact Group on Namibia is cited as reason for more involvement with 'indigenous groups' to produce solutions to Third World political conflicts where trilateral countries have vital interests. The proliferation of nuclear weapons should be avoided although the report argues for the 'peaceful diffusion' of nuclear technologies to the Third World.

This report's wide-ranging subject-matter makes it almost a summation of previous reports and efforts by the Commission, as well as a means of outlining the future agenda for discussions on trilateral relations over the next ten years. The Commission's activities, along with those of groups like Bilderberg, the Atlantic Institute and Hakone, are all part of the same enterprise – a fact which prompted merger attempts between the Institute, the Commission and Bilderberg in the late 1970s. These efforts failed for a number of institutional and political reasons, the most important of which was Japan's desire to retain its relative autonomy and co-equal status in the Commission's unique forum. However, it may be noted that the primary achievements of the Trilateral Commission – from its own point of view – are in the realm of long-term projects and consciousness raising: setting the agenda to be considered by the privileged elites of the transnational corporations and other interests represented on the Commission as well as helping Japan to become integrated into the core of a US-dominated alliance system.

In conclusion, however, it is worth discussing some of the ongoing problems faced by the proponents of trilateralism. Firstly, at the tactical level, the general bias against social-democratic or socialist interests and, conversely, right-wing neo-mercantilists particularly in the USA may mean that the long-term aim of cultivating a sufficiently broad domestic consensus to support trilateral initiatives may not be realized. The Trilateral Commission as it is presently constituted may thus be more 'clubby' but potentially less effective in the longer term. This is true in the case of Japan despite the unbroken post-war rule of the Liberal-Democratic Party. Japan has a sizeable socialist party, and a major shift in Japan's security policies will require a very broad domestic consensus indeed: pressure from the USA is not in itself sufficient to bring about the required changes. The same is true with regard to Europe and the USA. In Europe there is still little sign of a broad-based consensus in favour of trilateralism, although it would appear that support is strong among the elite in several countries. Unless significant domestic interests and a range of political perspectives can be incorporated into the Commission it seems unlikely therefore that the long-term goal of associating Japan and Europe as 'partners' in the public consciousness will ever be achieved. On the other hand, the Commission faces the difficult question as to how far it can dilute the strong agreement on basic structural principles and values its largely establishment constituencies already hold.

From a more general perspective, it is clear that the lack of European political unity or integration is probably the major structural and political problem for trilateralism together with the historically minimal political links with Japan. There seems little medium-term prospect of a unified Europe while its separate national economies limp along in a semi-arthritic condition, and it seems clear that trade and economic tensions will persist and intensify as Japan's economic strength increases in relative terms. These 'rivalries' and political tensions are compounded, notably in Europe, by the relative failure of governments to cope with the economic difficulties of restructuring: unemployment levels are now much greater than in the USA or Japan, and are astonishingly high by historical standards. This gives rise to different problems of 'governability' and legitimation which may prove in the longer term impossible to surmount, despite the neo-liberal rhetoric in Britain and to a lesser extent in West Germany. All these economic and political problems are related to the continuing salient feature of European politics: nationalism. Virtually every European country has been impelled to adopt an *ad hoc* protectionist and mercantilist stance towards other nations out of necessity and for short-term purposes of economic welfare. The structural condition which underpins all these economic problems it the uneven development of the European economies *vis-à-vis* each other, and of Europe as a whole *vis-à-vis* the USA and Japan. This uneven economic development is reflected in the USA's increasing interest in the Pacific Basin, the penetration of the Chinese economy and the thickening of relations with Japan – these trends are also related to the 'power shift' within the USA to the sunbelt and to the West Coast, exemplified by the presidencies of Nixon, Reagan and to a lesser extent Carter. It is easy to overestimate the role of isolationism in the USA today but this new movement may have some impact on the deployment of US military forces overseas and is used by US leaders as a potential threat when persuading the trilateral allies to 'share burdens' – in this sense the Commission's approach is more reasonable, less intimidatory but none the less stressing the same US demands.

Thus the notion of 'decoupling' must be taken seriously. US domestic criticisms of Europe are misplaced to the extent that the USA has continuing and significant interests in Europe. For example, the USA has enormous investments in the European economy, a massive bilateral trade surplus, and has benefited over the last few years – as a result of high US interest rates and a strengthening dollar – from an enormous capital influx, much of which is European in origin. On the other hand, the political conflicts between Europe and America are dramatized by problems in the energy politics of the Middle East. Europe, despite being split in 1973, is essentially pro-Arab because of its extreme dependence on Middle Eastern oil producers, whereas the USA, because of its powerful domestic Jewish lobby and historic links with Israeli development, has a double-edged set of interests. Because of its almost total dependence on US policy in the area the Europeans looked askance during the Iranian revolution, and uneasily followed the USA into a more hostile political posture towards the USSR after the intervention in Afghanistan. They also agreed to increase military contributions to NATO and, at the behest of Chancellor Schmidt of West Germany, to deploy Cruise and Pershing II missiles in Europe in 1983 – a move that was a major catalyst in the development of the European peace movements. These Middle Eastern uncertainties lie behind the European willingness to do business with the Soviet Union over the supply of gas from Siberia (and thus risk dependence on the Soviets). France and Germany took their decision to go ahead with the pipeline in a quest for diversified sources of energy, as well as a means of mediating the tendencies towards East–West polarization which had been building up in the USA's policies since 1977–8.

The conclusion this analysis points to, of course, is that the permanent interests, uneven economic development and competition among the three trilateral regions will present perennial problems for co-operation and may, in fact, make co-ordination of policies virtually impossible (except in a very loose, informal sense). However, the theorists of the Trilateral Commission do not appear to neglect the real basis of these problems, nor to underestimate their significance. Nevertheless the Commission's forum is useful in that it provides at least the possibility of communication in times of stress or strain and may thus help to ease international political tensions. It cannot in itself, however, produce the conditions for a fully developed trilateral alliance, which requires a firm and extensive set of interactions as well as, from a European perspective, a wide domestic consensus on the necessity for a closer set of arrangements with the Japanese. Moreover, as the Commission has acknowledged, the trilateral concept itself may become obsolete as new centres of power develop and the so-called newly industrializing countries of the Third World (such as Saudi Arabia, Brazil and Indonesia) emerge to the front rank of powers so that the 'firstness' of the trilateral powers is challenged from below, as well as from the Soviet bloc.

Bibliography

Adomeit, H., Boardman, R. (eds) (1979) *Foreign Policy Making in Communist Countries*. Farnborough, Saxon House.

Alger, C.F. (1961) 'Non-resolution Consequences of the United Nations and their Effect on International Conflict'. *Journal of Conflict Resolution*, 5 (2), pp.118–145.

Alger, C.F. (1977) '"Foreign" Policies of US Publics'. *International Studies Quarterly*, 21 (2), pp.277–93.

Alker, H. (1977) 'A Methodology for Design Research on Interdependence Alternatives'. *International Organization*, 31 (1), pp.29–63.

Allen, R. (1980) *How to Save the World*. London, Kogan Page.

Allison, G. (1971) *Essence of Decision*. Boston, Little Brown.

Angell, N. (1911) *The Great Illusion*. London, Heinemann.

Angell, N. (1951) *After All*. London, Hamish Hamilton.

Armstrong, D. (1982) *The Rise of the International Organisation*. London, Macmillan.

Aron, R. (1966) *Peace and War*. London, Weidenfeld and Nicolson.

Aronowitz, A. (1981) 'A Methodological Critique of Immanuel Wallerstein; The Modern World System'. *Theory and Society*, 10 (4), pp.503–20.

Aster, S. (1973) *1939*. London, Deutsch.

Axelrod, R., (1976) *Structure of Decision*. Princeton, N.J., Princeton University Press.

Azrael, J., Lowenthal, R., Nakagawa, T. (1978) *An Overview of East–West Relations*. New York, Trilateral Commission.

Bailey, S.H. (1938) *International Studies in Modern Education*. London, Oxford University Press.

Ball, G. (1975) *Global Companies: The Political Economy of World Business*. Englewood Cliffs, N.J., American Assembly/Prentice-Hall.

Barber, J. (1980) 'Britain's Place in the World'. *British Journal of International Studies*, 6 (2), pp.93–110.

Barnaby, F. (1976) 'Twenty Years of Peace Research'. *New Scientist,* 11 November, pp.320–22.

Barnes, B. (1982) *T.S. Kuhn and Social Science.* London, Macmillan.

Baylis, J. (ed.) (1983) *Alternative Approaches to British Defence Policy.* London, Macmillan.

Bebbington, D. (1979) *Patterns in History.* Leicester, Intervariety Press.

Beigie, C.E., Hager, W., Sekiguchi, S. (1976) *Seeking a New Accommodation in World Commodity Markets.* New York, Trilateral Commission.

Bell, D. (1975) 'The End of American Exceptionalism'. *The Public Interest,* 41 (fall), pp.193–224.

Bendiner, E. (1975) *A Time for Angels.* London, Weidenfeld and Nicolson.

Benton, T. (1981) 'Realism and Social Science'. *Radical Philosophy,* 27, pp.13–21.

Beres, L.R. (1981) *People, States and World Order.* Itasca, Ill., Peacock.

Bergsten, C.F., Berthoin, G., Mushakoji, K. (1976) *The Reform of International Institutions.* New York, Trilateral Commission.

Berridge, G. (1980) 'The Political Theory and Institutional History of States Systems'. *British Journal of International Studies,* 6 (1), pp.82–92.

Berridge, G. (1981) 'International Relations'. *Teaching Politics,* 10 (1) pp.78–84.

Bertalanffy, L. von (1971) *General Systems Theory.* London, Allen Lane.

Berthoin, G., Smith, G.C. Watanabe., T. (1977) *Triangle Papers,* 1–12. New York, Trilateral Commission.

Berthoin, G. (1980) Interview with S. Gill. London, 28 January 1980.

Berthoin, G., Rockefeller, D., Watanabe, T. (1981) *Triangle Papers,* 15–19. New York, Trilateral Commission.

Betts, R.K. (1977) *Soldiers, Statesmen and Cold War Crises.* Cambridge, Mass., Harvard University Press.

Bhaskar, R. (1978) *A Realist Theory of Science.* Brighton, Harvester.

Bhaskar, R. (1979) *The Possibility of Naturalism.* Brighton, Harvester.

Blackett, P.M.S. (1948) *The Military and Political Consequences of Atomic Energy.* London, Turnstile Press.

Blackett, P.M.S. (1962) *Studies of War–Nuclear and Conventional.* London, Oliver and Boyd.

Blau, P. (1964) *Exchange and Power in Social Life.* New York, John Wiley.

Bogue, A.G. (1980) 'The New Political History in the 1970s'. In M. Kammen (ed.) *The Past Before Us: Contemporary Historical Writing in the United States,* Ithaca, Cornell University Press, pp.231–52.

Bond, B. (1977) *Liddle Hart: A Study of His Military Thought.* London, Cassell.

Boulding, K.E. (1962) *Conflict and Defense: A General Theory.* New York, Harper and Row.

Bourne, R.S. (ed.) (1916) *Towards An Enduring Peace: A Symposium of Peace Proposals and Programs, 1914–1916.* New York, American Association for International Conciliation.

Boyd, A. (1962) *United Nations: Piety, Myth and Truth*. Harmondsworth, Penguin Books.

Brailsford, N. (1928) *Olives of Endless Age*. New York, Harper and Row.

Brandt Commission (1980) *North–South: A Programme for Survival. Report of the Commission on International Development Issues*. London, Pan.

Braudel, F. (1972–3) *The Mediterranean and the Mediterranean World in the Age of Philip II* (2 vols), translated by Sian Reynolds. London, Collins.

Brenner, R. (1977) 'The Origins of Capitalist Development: A Critique of Neo-Smithian Marxists', *New Left Review*, 104, pp.25–92.

Brodie, B. (ed.) (1946) *The Absolute Weapon*. New York, Harcourt Brace.

Brodie, B. (1966) *Escalation and the Nuclear Option*. Princeton, N.J., Princeton University Press.

Brookings Institution (1975) *The World Economy in Transition: A Tripartite Report by Seventeen Economists from the European Community, Japan and North America*. Washington DC, Brookings Institution.

Bryce, J. (1922) *International Relations*. New York, Macmillan.

Brzezinski, Z. (1970) *Between Two Ages: America's Role in the Technetronic Era*. New York, Viking Press.

Brzezinski, Z. (1982) 'Building a Wider World Order? Averting a Global Breakdown?'. *Trialogue*, 29, spring 1982.

Bull, H. (1968) 'Strategic Studies and its Critics'. *World Politics*, 20 (4) pp.593–605.

Bull, H. (1972) 'The Theory of International Politics, 1919–1969'. In B. Porter (ed.) *The Aberystwyth Papers: International Politics 1919–1969*, London, Oxford University Press, pp.30–5.

Bull, H. (1977) *The Anarchical Society: A Study of Order in World Politics*. London, Macmillan.

Burton, J. (1965) *International Relations: A General Theory*, Cambridge, Cambridge University Press.

Burton, J. (1968) *Systems, States, Diplomacy and Rules*. Cambridge, Cambridge University Press.

Burton, J. (1969) *Conflict and Communication*. London, Macmillan.

Burton, J. (1972) *World Society*, Cambridge, Cambridge University Press.

Burton, J., Groom, A., Mitchell, C., De Reuck, A. (1974) *The Study of World Society: A London Perspective*. Occasional Paper, no. 11, International Studies Association.

Butterfield, H. (1931) *The Whig Interpretation of History*. London, Bell.

Butterfield, H. (1966) 'The Balance of Power'. In H. Butterfield and M. Wight (eds), *Diplomatic Investigations*, London, Allen & Unwin.

Butterfield, H., Wight, M. (eds) (1966) *Diplomatic Investigations: Essays in the Theory of International Politics*. London, Allen & Unwin.

Buzan, B. (1983) *People, States and Fear: The National Security Problem in International Relations*. Brighton, Wheatsheaf.

Buzzard, Rear-Admiral, Sir Anthony (1956) 'Massive Retaliation and Graduated Deterrence'. *World Politics*, 8 (2), pp.228–37.

Cable, J. (1981) 'The Useful Art of International Relations'. *International Affairs*, 57 (2), pp.301–14.

Cable, J. (1983) 'Interdependence: A Drug of Addiction?' *International Affairs*, 59 (3), pp.365–79.

Camilleri, J. (1976) *Civilization in Crisis: Human Prospects in a Changing World*. Cambridge, Cambridge University Press.

Campbell, J.C., de Carmoy, G., Kondo, S. (1974) *Energy: A Strategy for International Action*. New York, Trilateral Commission.

Campbell, J.F. (1971) *The Foreign Affairs Fudge Factory*. New York, Basic Books.

Camps, M. (1974) *The Management of Interdependence: A Preliminary Review*. New York, Council on Foreign Relations.

Camps, M., Hirono, P., Laursen, K. (1982) *'Trilateralism' and the International Economy of the 1980s: Three Essays*. New York, Trilateral Commission.

Carr, E.H. (1939) *The Twenty Years Crisis, 1919–1939*. London, Macmillan.

Carr, E.H. (1946) *The Twenty Years Crisis, 1919–1939* (2nd edn). London, Macmillan.

Carr, E.H. (1961) *What is History?* London, Macmillan.

Carrington, Rt. Hon. Lord (1980) *Interdependence and Revolution: The West in the World Today*. London, David Davis Memorial Institute.

Carter, A., Schwartz, D. (eds) (1984) *Ballistic Missile Defense*. Washington DC, Brookings.

Carver, Field Marshall Lord (1982) *A Policy for Peace*. London, Faber and Faber.

Churchland, P.M. (1979) *Scientific Realism and the Plasticity of Mind*. Cambridge, Cambridge University Press.

Churchman, C.W. (1979) *The Systems Approach and its Enemies*. New York, Basic Books.

Clapham, C. (ed.) (1977) *Foreign Policy Making in Developing States*. Farnborough, Saxon House.

Clark, G., Sohn, L.B. (1966) *World Peace Through World Law* (1st edn, 1956). Harvard, Harvard University Press.

Clark, I. (1979) 'World Order Reform and Utopian Thought: A Contemporary Watershed'. *Review of Politics*, 41 (1), pp.96–120.

Clark, I. (1980) *Reform and Resistance in the International Order*. Cambridge, Cambridge University Press.

Colombo, U., Johnson, D.G., Shishido, T. (1978) *Expanding Food in Developing Countries: Rice Production in South and South-East Asia*. New York, Trilateral Commission.

Cooper, R. (1968) *The Economics of Interdependence: Economic Policy in the Atlantic Community*. New York, McGraw-Hill.

Cooper, R. (1972) 'Economic Interdependence and Foreign Policy in the Seventies'. *World Politics*, 24 (2), pp.159–81.

Cooper, R., Kaiser, K., Kosaka, K. (1977) *Towards a Renovated International System*. New York, Trilateral Commission.

Cooper, R., Kaji, M., Segre, C. (1973) *Towards a Renovated World Monetary System*. New York, Trilateral Commission.

Cosgrove, C.A., Twitchett, K.A. (eds) (1970) *The New International Actors: The UN and the EEC*. London, Macmillan.

Cowhey, P.F., Long, E. (1983) 'Testing Theories of Regime Change, Hegemonic Decline or Surplus Capacity'. *International Organization*, 37 (2), pp.156–88.

Cowling, M. (1975) *The Impact of Hitler: British Politics and British Policy, 1933–40*. Cambridge, Cambridge University Press.

Cox, R.W. (1976) 'On Thinking About Future World Order'. *World Politics*, 28 (1), pp.175–96.

Cox, R.W. (1979) 'Ideologies and the New International Economic Order: Reflections on Some Recent Literature'. *International Organization*, 33 (2), pp.257–302.

Cox, R.W. (1981a) 'Social Forces, States and World Orders: Beyond International Relations Theory'. *Millennium: Journal of International Studies*, 10 (2), pp.126–55.

Cox, R.W. (1981b) 'In Search of International Political Economy'. *New Political Science*, 5/6, pp.59–77.

Crick, B. (1959) *The American Science of Politics*. London, Routledge and Kegan Paul.

Crozier, M., Huntingdon, S.P., Watanuki, J. (1975) *The Crisis of Democracy*. New York, Trilateral Commission.

Curzon, G., Curzon, V. (1976) 'The Management of Trade Relations in the GATT'. In A. Shonfield (ed.) *International Economic Relations of the Western World, 1959–1971*, 1, London, Oxford University Press/Royal Institute of International Affairs.

Dando, M., Rogers, P. (1984) *The Death of Deterrence*. London, Campaign for Nuclear Disarmament.

de Cecco, M. (1976) 'International Financial Markets and U.S. Domestic Policy Since 1945'. *International Affairs*, 52 (3), pp.381–99.

d'Entreves, A.P. (1970) *Natural Law* (2nd edn). London, Hutchinson.

Deutsch, K.W. (1953) *Nationalism and Social Communication*. Cambridge, Mass., MIT Press.

Deutsch, K.W. (1968) *The Analysis of International Relations*. Englewood Cliffs, N.J., Prentice-Hall.

Deutsch, K.W. (1978) *The Analysis of International Relations* (2nd edn). Englewood Cliffs, N.J., Prentice-Hall.

Deutsch, K.W., Burrell, S.A., Kann, R.A., Lee, M., Lichterman, M., Lindgren, R.E., Loewenheim, F.L., Van Wagenen, R.W. (1957) *Political Community and the North Atlantic Area*. Princeton, N.J., Princeton University Press.

di Paliano, G.C., Trezise, P.H., Ushiba, N. (1974) *Directions for World Trade in the Nineteen-Seventies*. New York, Trilateral Commission.

Diplomatic History, 5 (4) (1981) 'Symposium: Responses to Charles S. Maier; "Marking Time: the Historiography of International Relations"'.

Disarm or Die (1978) published by Taylor and Francis on behalf of the Non-Partisan Fund for World Disarmament and Development, London.

Donelan, M. (ed.) (1978) *The Reason of States*. London, Allen & Unwin.

Downs, A. (1957) *An Economic Theory of Democracy*. New York, Harper and Row.

Draper, T. (1983) *Present History: On Nuclear War, Detente and Other Controversies*. New York, Random House.

Duchene, F., Mushakoji, K., Owen, H. (1974) *The Crisis of International Cooperation*. New York, Trilateral Commission.

Dunn, D.J. (1978) 'Peace Research'. In T. Taylor (ed.) *Approaches and Theory in International Relations,* London, Longman, pp.257–79.

Earle, E.M. (1943) *Makers of Modern Strategy: Military Thought from Machiavelli to Hitler*. Princeton, N.J., Princeton University Press.

East, M., Salmore, S., Hermann, C. (1978) *Why Nations Act*. Beverly Hills, Sage.

Easton, D. (1981) 'The Political System Besieged by the State'. *Political Theory,* 9 (3), pp.303–25.

Emmerson, J.T. (1977) *The Rhineland Crisis, 7 March 1936*. London, Temple Smith in association with the London School of Economics and Political Science.

Eulau, H. (1967) 'Segments of Political Science Most Susceptible to Behaviouristic Treatment'. In J.C. Charlesworth (ed.) *Contemporary Political Analysis,* New York, Free Press.

Falk, R.A. (1971) *This Endangered Planet: Prospects and Proposals for Human Survival*. New York, Random House.

Falk, R.A. (1975a) *A Study of Future Worlds*. New York, Free Press.

Falk, R.A. (1975b) 'A New Paradigm for International Legal Studies: Prospects and Proposals'. *The Yale Law Journal,* 84 (5), pp.969–1022.

Falk, R.A. (1980) Interview with S. Gill. Lancaster University, 16 December 1980.

Falk, R.A. (1982) 'Pondering the Third Revolution'. Paper given at Virginia Commonwealth University, 27 January 1982.

Falk, R.A., Kim, S.S., Mendlovitz, S. (1982) *Studies on a Just World Order: Vol. 1, Toward a Just World Order*. Boulder, Colorado, Westview Press.

Festinger, L. (1962) *A Theory of Cognitive Dissonance*. Stanford, Stanford University Press.

Fischer, F. (1975) *World Power or Decline: The Controversy over Germany's Aims in the First World War*. London, Weidenfeld and Nicolson.

Fisher, I. (1923) *League or War?* New York, Harper and Row.

Fishlow, A., Carriere, J., Sekiguchi, S. (1981) *Trade in Manufactured Products with Developing Countries: Reinforcing North–South Partnerships*. New York, Trilateral Commission.

Fitzgerald, G., Levi, A., Kitahara, H., Sisco, J. (1981) *The Middle East and the Trilateral Countries*. New York, Trilateral Commission.

Foreign Relations of the United States (FRUS) (1946). Department of State, Washington, 1.

Foreign Relations of the United States (FRUS) (1950). Department of State, Washington, 2.

Forsyth, M. (1978) 'The Classical Theory of International Relations'. *Political Studies,* 26 (3), pp.410–16.

Forsyth, M. (1981) *Unions of States.* Leicester, Leicester University Press.

Fox, W.T. (1968) 'Growing Points in the Study of International Relations'. In his book *The American Study of International Relations,* Columbia, University of South Carolina Press, pp.97–116.

Frank, A.G. (1969) *Latin America: Underdevelopment or Revolution.* New York, Monthly Review Press.

Frankel, J. (1963) *The Making of Foreign Policy.* London, Oxford University Press.

Frankel, J. (1973) *Contemporary International Theory and the Behaviour of States.* London, Oxford University Press.

Frankel, J. (1975) *British Foreign Policy 1945–1973.* London, Oxford University Press, for the Royal Institute of International Affairs.

Frankel, J. (1981) 'Conventional and Theorising Diplomats: A Critique'. *International Affairs,* 57 (4), pp.537–48.

Freedman, L. (1981) *The Evolution of Nuclear Strategy.* London, Macmillan.

Freedman, L. (1982) 'The Development of the Think-Tank'. *Royal United Services Institute Journal,* 127 (1), pp.13–18.

Frey, B.S. (1984) 'The Public Choice View of International Political Economy'. *International Organization,* 38 (1), pp.199–223.

Gaddis, J. (1982) *Strategies of Containment: A Critical Appraisal of Postwar American National Security Policy.* New York, Oxford University Press.

Galtung, J. (1975) *Essays in Peace Research Vol. I.* Copenhagen, dk Ejler's Forlag.

Galtung, J. (1976) *Essays in Peace Research Vol. II.* Copenhagen, dk Ejler's Forlag.

Galtung, J. (1978) *Essays in Peace Research Vol. III.* Copenhagen, dk Ejler's Forlag.

Galtung, J. (1980) *The True Worlds.* New York, Free Press.

Gardner, R.N., Okita, S., Udink, B.J. (1974) *A Turning Point in North–South Economic Relations.* New York, Trilateral Commission.

Gardner, R.J., Okita, S., Udink, B.J. (1975) *OPEC, The Trilateral World and the Developing Countries: New Arrangements for Co-operation, 1976–80.* New York, Trilateral Commission.

Gareau, F.H. (1981) 'The Discipline of International Relations: a Multi-National Perspective'. *Journal of Politics,* 43 (3), pp.779–802.

Geertz, C. (1983) *Local Knowledge.* New York, Basic Books.

George, A. (1980) *Presidential Decision-Making in Foreign Policy: the Effective Use of Information and Advice.* Boulder, Colorado, Westview Press.

George, A., Craig, G. (1983) *Force and Statecraft: Diplomatic Problems of Our Time.* New York, Oxford University Press.

George, S. (1976) 'The Reconciliation of the "Classical" and "Scientific" Approaches to International Relations'. *Millennium,* 5 (1), pp.28–40.

Geyl, P. (1962) *Debates with Historians*. London, Fontana Collins.

Gill, S.R. (1980) 'The Trilateral Commission, the International Economy and Structural Policy'. *Journal of Industrial Affairs,* 7 (2), pp.38–43.

Gilpin, R. (1971) 'The Politics of Transnational Economic Relations'. In R.O. Keohane and J.S. Nye (eds) *Transnational Relations and World Politics,* Cambridge, Mass., Harvard University Press.

Gilpin, R. (1976) *US Power and the Multinational Corporation: The Political Economy of Direct Investment*. London, Macmillan.

Goldmann, K., Sjöstedt, G. (eds) (1979) *Power, Capabilities, Interdependence: Problems in the Study of International Influence*. Beverly Hills, Sage.

Goodwin, B., Taylor, K. (1982) *The Politics of Utopia: A Study in Theory and Practice*. London, Hutchinson.

Goodwin, G.L. (1957) *Britain and the United Nations*. London, Oxford University Press.

Goodwin, G.L. (1978) 'Theories of International Relations: The Normative and Policy Dimensions'. In T. Taylor (ed.) *Approaches and Theory in International Relations,* London, Longman.

Goodwin, G.L. (1979) 'Yet Another Paradigm?'. *Millennium,* 7 (3), pp.251–9.

Goold-Adams, R. (1956) *On Limiting Atomic Warfare*. London, Royal Institute of International Affairs.

Gowing, M. (1974) *Independence and Deterrence: Britain and Atomic Energy 1945–1952. Volume II Policy-Making*. London, Macmillan.

Grant, A.J., Greenwood, A., Hughes, J.D., Kerr, P.H., Urquhart, F.F. (1916) *An Introduction to the Study of International Relations*. London, Macmillan.

Gray, C. (1982) *Strategic Studies: A Critical Assessment*. London, Aldwych Press.

Guetzkow, H., Alger, C.F., Brody, R.A., Noel, R.C., Snyder, R.C. (1963) *Simulation in International Relations: Developments for Research and Teaching*. Englewood Cliffs, N.J., Prentice-Hall.

Guetzkow, H., Valadez, J.J. (eds) (1981) *Simulated International Processes: Theories and Research in Global Modelling*. Beverly Hills, Sage.

Gunnell, J.G. (1975) *Philosophy, Science and Political Inquiry*. Morristown, New Jersey, General Learning Press.

Gunnell, J.G. (1979) 'Philosophy and Political Theory'. *Government and Opposition,* 14 (2), pp.198–216.

Haas, E.B. (1964) *Beyond the Nation State*. Stanford, Stanford University Press.

Haas, E.B. (1970) 'The Study of Regional Integration: Reflections on the Joy and Anguish of Pretheorizing'. *International Organization,* 24 (4), pp.607–46.

Haas, E.B. (1976) 'Turbulent Fields and the Theory of Regional Integration'. *International Organization,* 30 (2), pp.173–212.

Haas, E.B. (1980) 'Technological Self-Reliance for Latin America: The OAS Contribution'. *International Organization,* 34 (4), pp.541–70.

Haas, E.B. (1982) 'Words Can Hurt You; or, Who Said What to Whom About Regimes'. *International Organization,* 36 (2), pp.207–43.

Hanrieder, W. (1978) 'Dissolving International Politics: Reflections on the Nation-State'. *American Political Science Review,* 72 (4), pp.1276–87.

Harary, F. (1961) 'A Structural Analysis of the Situation in the Middle East in 1956'. *Journal of Conflict Resolution,* 5 (2), pp.165–78.

Hardy, M., Hollick, A.L., Holst, J.J., Johnston, D.M., Oda, S. (1976) *A New Regime for the Oceans.* New York, Trilateral Commission.

Harré, H.R. (1972) *The Philosophies of Science.* London, Oxford University Press.

Harré, H.R., Secord, P.F. (1972) *The Explanation of Social Behaviour.* Oxford, Basil Blackwell.

Harvard Nuclear Study Group (1983) *Living With Nuclear Weapons.* Cambridge, Mass., Harvard University Press.

Hayek, F.A. (1973) *Law, Legislation and Liberty,* vol. 1. London, Routledge and Kegan Paul.

Heatley, D.P. (1919) *Diplomacy and the Study of International Relations.* Oxford, Clarendon Press.

Hempel, H.G. (1965) *Aspects of Scientific Explanation.* New York, Free Press.

Herz, J. (1951) *Political Realism and Political Idealism: A Study in Theories and Realities.* Chicago, University of Chicago Press.

Herz, J. (1959) *International Politics in the Atomic Age.* New York, Columbia University Press.

Herz, J. (1976) *The Nation-State and the Crisis of World Politics.* New York, McKay.

Hesse, M. (1980) *Revolutions and Reconstructions in the Philosophy of Science.* Brighton, Harvester.

Hicks, S.M., Couloumbis, T.A., Forgette, E.M. (1982) 'Influencing the Prince: A Role for Academicians?'. *Polity,* 15 (2), pp.279–93.

Hill, C. (1979) 'Theories of Foreign Policy-Making for the Developing Countries'. In C. Clapham (ed.) *Foreign Policy-Making in Developing States,* Farnborough, Saxon House.

Hinsley, F.H. (1963) *Power and the Pursuit of Peace.* Cambridge, Cambridge University Press.

Hinsley, F.H. (ed.) (1977) *The Foreign Policy of Sir Edward Grey.* London, Cambridge University Press.

Hirsch, F. (1976) 'Is There a New International Economic Order?'. *International Organisation,* 30 (3), pp.521–31.

Hirschman, A.O. (1945) *National Power and the Structure of Foreign Trade.* Berkeley, University of California Press.

Hirschman, A.O. (1978) 'Exit, Voice and the State'. *World Politics,* 31 (1), pp.90–107.

Hiscocks, R. (1973) *The Security Council: A Study in Adolescence.* London, Longman.

History Today, 34, (May, 1984), 'What is History? The Great Debate'.

Hodges, M. (1978) 'Integration Theory'. In T. Taylor (ed.) *Approaches and Theory in International Relations,* London, Longman.

Hoffmann, S. (1960) *Contemporary Theory in International Relations.* Englewood Cliffs, Prentice-Hall.

Hoffmann, S. (1977) 'An American Social Science: International Relations'. *Daedalus,* 106 (3), pp.41–60.

Hoffmann, S. (1978) *Primacy or World Order: American Foreign Policy Since the Cold War.* New York, McGraw-Hill.

Hollist, W.L., Rosenau, J.N. (1981a) 'World Systems Debate'. Special issue of *International Studies Quarterly,* 25 (1).

Hollist, W.L., Rosenau, J.N. (eds) (1981b) *World System Structure: Continuity and Change.* Beverly Hills, Sage.

Holsti, K.J. (1980) 'Change in the International System: Interdependence, Integration, and Fragmentation'. In O.R. Holsti, R.M. Siverson and A.L. George (eds) *Change in the International System,* Boulder, Colorado, Westview Press, pp.23–53.

Holt, R.T., Job, O., Markus, L. (1978) 'Catastrophe Theory and the Study of War'. *Journal of Conflict Resolution,* 22 (2), pp.171–208.

Hoover, H., Gibson, H. (1942) *The Problems of Lasting Peace.* New York, Doubleday.

Hopkins, T.K. (1978) 'World-System Analysis: Methodological Issues'. In B.H. Kaplan (ed.) *Social Change in the Capitalist World Economy,* Beverly Hills, Sage.

Hosoya, C., Owen, H., Shonfield, A. (1977) *Collaboration with Communist Countries in Managing Global Problems: An Examination of the Options.* New York, Trilateral Commission.

Huntington, S.P. (1973) 'Transnational Organizations in World Politics'. *World Politics,* 25 (3), pp.333–68.

Inkeles, A. (1975) 'The Emerging Social Structure of the World'. *World Politics,* 27 (4), pp.467–95.

James, A. (ed.) (1973) *The Bases of International Order: Essays in Honour of C.A.W. Manning.* London, Oxford University Press.

James, A. (1976) 'International Institutions: Independent Actors?'. In A. Shlaim (ed.) *International Organisations in World Politics Yearbook 1976,* London, Croom Helm.

James, A. (1978) 'International Society'. *British Journal of International Studies,* 4 (2), pp.91–106.

Japan Center for International Exchange (1973) *Research Institutions in Japan.* Tokyo, JCIE.

Japan Center for International Exchange (1977) *Proceedings of the Second Europe/Japan Conference, Hakone.* Tokyo, JCIE.

Jervis, R. (1976) *Perception and Misperception in International Politics.* Princeton, N.J., Princeton University Press.

Johnstone, D. (1976) 'Une Strategie Trilaterale'. *Le Monde Diplomatique,* 23 November 1976.

Joll, J. (1960) *Intellectuals in Politics*. London, Weidenfeld and Nicolson.

Joll, J. (1973) *Europe Since 1870*. London, Weidenfeld and Nicolson.

Jolly, R. (1978) *Disarmament and World Development*. London, Pergamon.

Jones, R.E. (1973) *The Changing Structure of British Foreign Policy*. London, Longman.

Jones, R.E. (1979) *Principles of Foreign Policy*. Oxford, Martin Robertson.

Jones, R.E. (1981) 'The English School of International Relations: A Case for Closure'. *Review of International Studies*, 7 (1), pp.1–14.

Josephson, H. (1975) *James T. Shotwell and the Rise of Internationalism in America*. London, Associated University Press.

Kaiser, K., Lord, W., de Montbrial, T., Watt, D. (1981) *Western Security: What has Changed? What Should be Done?* New York, Council on Foreign Relations.

Kammen, M. (ed.) (1980) *The Past Before Us: Contemporary Historical Writing in the United States*, Ithaca, Cornell University Press.

Kamura, P. (1981) *International Relations in Japan – A Policy Research and Analysis Perspective*. Tokyo, Japan Center for International Exchange/Rockefeller Foundation.

Kaplan, F. (1983) *The Wizards of Armageddon*. New York, Simon and Schuster.

Kaplan, M.A. (1957) *System and Process in International Politics*. New York, John Wiley.

Kaplan, M.A. (1961) 'Problems of Theory Building and Theory Confirmation in International Politics.' *World Politics*, 13 (1), pp.6–24.

Kaplan, M.A. (1976) *Justice, Human Nature and Political Obligation*. New York, Free Press.

Katzenstein, P. (1975) 'International Interdependence: Some Long-term Trends and Recent Changes'. *International Organization*, 29 (4), pp.1021–34.

Kaufmann, W. (ed.) (1956) *Military Policy and National Security*. Princeton, N.J., Princeton University Press.

Keat, R., Urry, J. (1975) *Social Theory as Science*. London, Routledge and Kegan Paul.

Keens-Soper, M. (1978) 'The Practice of a States-System'. In M. Donelan (ed.) *The Reason of States*, London, Allen & Unwin.

Kegley, C. (1980) *The Comparative Study of Foreign Policy: Paradigm Lost?* Columbia, South Carolina, University of South Carolina.

Kennedy, P. (1981) *The Realities Behind Diplomacy: Background Influences on British External Policy, 1865–1980*. London, Fontana.

Keohane, R.O. (1980) 'The Theory of Hegemonic Stability and Changes in International Economic Regimes, 1967–1977'. In O.R. Holsti, R.M. Siverson and A.L. George (eds) *Change in the International System*, Boulder, Colorado, Westview Press.

Keohane, R.O. (1982) 'The Demand for International Regimes'. *International Organization*, 36 (2), pp.325–55.

Keohane, R.O., Nye, J.S. (eds) (1971) *Transnational Relations and World Politics*. Cambridge, Mass., Harvard University Press.

Keohane, R.O., Nye, J.S., (1974) 'Transgovernmental Relations and International Organizations'. *World Politics,* 27 (1), pp.39–62.

Keohane, R.O., Nye, J.S. (1977) *Power and Interdependence.* Boston, Little Brown.

Kindleberger, C.P. (1970) *Power and Money: The Economics of International Politics and the Politics of International Economics.* New York, Basic Books.

Kirk, G., Sharp, W. (1944) *Contemporary International Politics.* New York, Farrar and Rinehart.

Kissinger, H. (1957) *Nuclear Weapons and Foreign Policy.* New York, Harper and Row.

Knorr, K., Read, T. (eds) (1962) *Limited Strategic War.* New York, Praeger.

Knorr, K., Rosenau, J.N. (eds) (1969) *Contending Approaches to International Politics.* Princeton, N.J., Princeton University Press.

Knorr, K., Verba, S. (eds) (1961) *The International System: Theoretical Essays.* Princeton, N.J., Princeton University Press.

Kothari, A. (1974) *Footsteps into the Future: Diagnosis of the Present World and a Design for the Future.* New York, Free Press.

Krasner, S.D. (1979) 'North–South Economic Relations'. In K.A. Oye, D. Rothchild, R.J. Lieber (eds) *Eagle Entangled: US Foreign Policy in a Complex World,* London, Longman, pp.123–46.

Krasner, S.D. (1981) 'Power Structures and Regional Development Banks'. *International Organization,* 35 (2).

Krasner, S.D. (ed.) (1982a) *International Regimes.* Special issue of *International Organization,* 36 (2).

Krasner, S.D. (1982b) 'Structural Causes and Regime Consequences: Regimes as Intervening Variables'. *International Organization,* 36 (2), pp.185–205.

Krasner, S.D. (1982c) 'Regimes and the Limits of Realism: Regimes as Autonomous Variables'. *International Organization,* 36 (2), pp.497–510.

Kuhn, T.S. (1970) *The Structure of Scientific Revolutions* (2nd edn). Chicago, University of Chicago Press.

Kuniholm, B.R. (1980) *The Origins of the Cold War in the Near East: Great Power Conflict and Diplomacy in Iran, Turkey and Greece.* Princeton, N.J., Princeton University Press.

Lagos, G., Godoy, H.H. (1977) *Revolution in Being: A Latin American View of the Future.* New York, Free Press.

Lakatos, I., Musgrave, A. (eds) (1970) *Criticism and the Growth of Knowledge.* Cambridge, Cambridge University Press.

Lasky, M.J. (1976) *Utopia and Revolution.* Chicago, University of Chicago Press.

Lasswell, H.D. (1935) *World Politics and Personal Insecurity.* New York, McGraw-Hill.

Lauren, P. (ed.) (1979) *Diplomacy: New Approaches in History, Theory, and Policy.* New York, Free Press.

Leurdijk, J.H. (1974) 'From International to Transnational Politics: A Change of Paradigms?' *International Social Science Journal,* 26 (1), pp.53–69.

Levinson, C. (1977) *Vodka-Cola*. Paris, Editions Stock.

Lewinsohn, R. (1936) *The Profits of War*. London, Routledge and Kegan Paul.

Liddell Hart, B. (1946) *The Revolution in Warfare*. London, Faber and Faber.

Lindberg, L.N. (1963) *The Political Dynamics of European Economic Integration*. Stanford, Stanford University Press.

Lindberg, L.N., Scheingold, S.A. (1970) *Europe's Would-Be Polity*. Englewood Cliffs, N.J., Prentice-Hall.

Linklater, A. (1982) *Men and Citizens in the Theory of International Relations*. London, Macmillan.

Lipgens, W. (1982) *A History of European Integration Vol II The Formation of the European Unity Movement*. Oxford, Clarendon Press.

Liska, G. (1966) 'The Heroic Decade and After: International Relations as Events, Discipline and Profession'. *SAIS Review*, 10 (4), pp.5–11.

List, F. (1928) *The National System of Political Economy*. London, Longmans Green.

Little, R. (1977) 'Three Approaches to the International System: Some Ontological and Epistemological Considerations'. *British Journal of International Studies*, 3 (3), pp.269–85.

Little, R. (1981) 'Ideology and Change'. In B. Buzan and R.J. Barry Jones, *Change and the Study of International Relations*, London, Frances Pinter.

Little, R. (1984) 'Teaching International Relations: Working with Paradigms'. *Interstate: A Journal of International Relations*, 1, pp.3–10.

Lotka, A.J. (1956) *Elements of Mathematical Biology* (1st edn, 1926). New York, Dover.

Luard, E. (1982) *A History of the United Nations*. London, Macmillan.

Luce, R.D., Raiffa, H. (1957) *Games and Decisions*. New York, John Wiley.

Lukes, S. (1974) *Power: A Radical View*. London, Macmillan.

Lyons, G.M. (1982) 'Expanding the Study of International Relations: The French Connection'. *World Politics*, 35 (1), pp.135–49.

McClelland, C.A. (1958) 'System and History in International Relations'. *General System Yearbook*, 3, pp.221–47.

McClelland, C.A. (1970) 'Conceptualization, Not theory'. In N.D. Palmer (ed.) *A Design for International Relations Research* (monograph 10), Philadelphia, The American Academy of Political and Social Science.

McGowan, P., Shapiro, H. (1973) *The Comparative Study of Foreign Policy*. Beverly Hills, Sage.

MacGwire, M. (1983) 'Arms Debate: A Crucial Disagreement'. *New York Times*, 2 November 1983.

Maclean, J. (1981) 'Political Theory, International Theory and Problems of Ideology'. *Millennium: Journal of International Studies*, 10 (2), pp.102–25.

Maier, C.S. (1975) *Recasting Bourgeois Europe: Stabilization in France, Germany and Italy in the Decade after World War I*. Princeton, N.J., Princeton University Press.

Maier, C.S. (1980) 'Marking Time: The Historiography of International Relations'. In M. Kammen, (ed.), *The Past Before Us: Contemporary Historical Writing in the United States,* Ithaca, Cornell University Press.

Makins, C. (1975) 'Is Reform an Illusion?'. *Trialogue,* 8 (fall) pp.1–4.

Makins, C. (1979) 'The Trilateral Relationship Today: Is There Life After Trilateralism?'. Mimeo.

Manning, C.A.W. (1975) *The Nature of International Society* (1st edn, 1962). London, Macmillan.

Manuel, F.E., Manuel, F.P. (1979) *Utopian Thought in the Western World.* Oxford, Basil Blackwell.

Martin, L. (1962) 'The Market for Strategic Ideas in Britain: The "Sandys Era"'. *The American Political Science Review,* 56 (1), pp.23–41.

Mason, C. (ed.) (1979) *The Effective Management of Resources: The International Politics of the North Sea.* London, Frances Pinter.

May, E. (1971) 'The Decline of Diplomatic History'. In G.A. Billias and G.N. Grob (eds) *American History: Retrospect and Prospect,* New York, Free Press.

Mayall, J. (ed.) (1982) *The Community of States.* London, Allen & Unwin.

Mazrui, A.A. (1976) *A World Federation of Cultures.* New York, Free Press.

Meadows, D.J., Meadows, D.L., Randers, J., Behrens, W.W. (1972) *The Limits to Growth,* a report to the Club of Rome. New York, Universe.

Medlicott, W.M. (1955) 'The Scope and Study of International History'. *International Affairs,* 31 (4), pp.413–26.

Mendlovitz, S. (ed.) (1975) *On the Creation of a Just World Order.* New York, Free Press.

Merritt, R.L., Russett, B.M. (eds) (1981) *From National Development to Global Community.* London, Allen & Unwin.

Mesarovic, M., Pestel, E. (1974) *Mankind at the Turning Point,* the second report to the Club of Rome. New York, Signet edn.

Michalak, S.J. (1979) 'Theoretical Perspectives for Understanding International Interdependence'. *World Politics,* 32 (1), pp.136–50.

Middlemas, K. (1972) *Diplomacy of Illusion.* London, Weidenfeld and Nicolson.

Midgly, E.B.F. (1975) *The Natural Law Tradition and the Theory of International Relations.* London, Elek.

Miller, D.H. (1928) *The Drafting of the Covenant.* New York, G.P. Putnams.

Ministry of Defence (1980) *The Future United Kingdom Strategic Nuclear Deterrent Force.* London, HMSO – Defence Open Government Document 80/23.

Ministry of Defence (1982) *The United Kingdom Trident Programme.* London, HMSO – Defence Open Government Document 82/1.

Mische, G., Mische, P. (1977) *Towards a Human World Order.* Ramsey, N.J., Paulist Press.

Mitrany, D. (1943) *A Working Peace System,* London, Royal Institute of International Affairs.

Mommsen, W.J., Kettenacker, L. (eds) (1983) *The Fascist Challenge and the Policy of Appeasement.* London, Allen & Unwin.

Moon, P. (1925) *Syllabus of International Relations.* New York, Macmillan.

Morgenthau, H.J. (1946) *Scientific Man v. Power Politics.* Chicago, Ill., University of Chicago Press.

Morgenthau, H.J. (1948) *Politics Among Nations.* New York, Knopf.

Morgenthau, H.J. (1951) *In Defense of the National Interest.* New York, Knopf.

Morgenthau, H.J. (1970) 'International Relations: Quantitative and Qualitative Approaches'. In N.D. Palmer (ed.) *A Design for International Relations Research* (monograph 10), Philadelphia, The American Academy of Political and Social Science.

Morgenthau, H.J. (1973) *Politics Among Nations* (5th edn). New York, Knopf.

Morgenthau, H.J. (1978) *Politics Among Nations* (5th edn revised). New York, Knopf.

Morgenthau, H.J., Thompson, K.W. (1956) *Principles and Problems of International Politics.* New York, Knopf.

Morse, E.L. (1970) 'The Transformation of Foreign Policies: Modernization, Interdependence and Externalization'. *World Politics,* 22 (3), pp.371–92.

Morse, E.L. (1972) 'Crisis Diplomacy, Interdependence, and the Politics of International Economic Relations'. In R. Tanter and R.H. Ullman (eds) *Theory and Policy in International Relations,* Princeton, N.J., Princeton University Press, pp.123–50.

Morse, E.L. (1976a) 'Interdependence in World Affairs'. In J.N. Rosenau, K.W. Thompson and G. Boyd (eds) *World Politics: An Introduction,* New York, Free Press.

Morse, E.L. (1976b) *Modernization and the Transformation of International Relations.* New York, Free Press.

Mumford, L. (1959) *The Story of Utopias* (1st edn, 1922). Gloucester, Mass., Smith.

Murray, G. (1929) *The Ordeal of this Generation.* New York, Harper and Row.

Newman, J.R. (ed.) (1956) *The World of Mathematics* (4 vols). New York, Simon and Schuster.

Nicholson, M.B. (1983) *The Scientific Analysis of Social Behaviour: A Defence of Empiricism in Social Science.* London, Frances Pinter.

Nicholson, P.P. (1976) 'Philosophical Idealism and International Politics: A Reply to Dr. Savigear'. *British Journal of International Studies,* 2 (1), pp.76–83.

Nicolson, H. (1933) *Peacemaking 1919.* London, Constable.

Noel-Baker, P. (1936) *The Private Manufacture of Armaments.* London, Gollancz.

Noel-Baker, P. (1958) *The Arms Race.* London, Calder.

Northedge, F.S. (1974a) 'The Nature of Foreign Policy'. In F.S. Northedge (ed.) *The Foreign Policies of the Powers* (2nd edn), London, Faber and Faber.

Northedge, F.S. (1974b) *Descent from Power: British Foreign Policy, 1945–73.* London, Faber and Faber.

Northedge, F.S. (1976a) *The International Political System.* London, Faber and Faber.

Northedge, F.S. (1976b) 'Transnationalism: The American Illusion'. *Millennium,* 5 (1), pp.21–7.

Nye, J.S. (1970) 'Comparing Common Markets: A Revised Neo-Functionalist Model'. *International Organization,* 24 (4), pp.796–835.

Nye J.S. (1972) 'Regional Institutions'. In C.E. Black, R.A. Falk (eds) *The Future of the International Legal Order, Vol IV, The Structure of the International Environment,* Princeton, N.J., Princeton University Press.

O'Neill, J. (ed.) (1973) *Models of Individualism and Collectivism.* London, Heinemann.

Ortona, E., Schaetzel, J.R., Ushiba, N. (1976) *The Problem of International Consultations.* New York, Trilateral Commission.

Osgood, R.E. (1957) *Limited War: The Challenge to American Strategy.* Chicago, University of Chicago Press.

Oye, K.A., Rothchild, D., Lieber, R.J. (eds) (1979) *Eagle Entangled: US Foreign Policy in a Complex World.* London, Longman.

Palme Commission (1982) *Common Security: A Programme for Disarmament.* London, Pan.

Parkinson, F. (1977) *The Philosophy of International Relations: A Study in the History of Thought.* London, Sage.

Pentland, C. (1973) *International Theory and European Integration.* New York, Free Press.

Pinder, J., Hosomi, T., Diebold, W. (1979) *Industrial Policy and the International Economy.* New York, Trilateral Commission.

Polanyi, K. (1944) *The Great Transformation.* Boston, Beacon Press.

Porter, B. (1972) *The Aberystwyth Papers: International Politics 1919–1969.* London, Oxford University Press.

Puchala, D.J. (1972) 'Of Blind Men, Elephants and International Integration'. *Journal of Common Market Studies,* 10 (3), pp.267–84.

Pym, F. (1982) 'British Foreign Policy: Constraints and Opportunities'. *International Affairs,* 59 (1), pp.1–6.

Ransom, H. (1968) 'International Relations'. *Journal of Politics,* 30 (2), pp.345–71.

Rapoport, A. (1957) 'Lewis F. Richardson's Mathematical Theory of War'. *Journal of Conflict Resolution,* 1 (3), pp.249–99.

Rapoport, A. (1960) *Fights, Games and Debates.* Ann Arbor, University of Michigan Press.

Rashevsky, N. (1951) *The Mathematical Biology of Social Behavior.* Chicago, Chicago University Press.

Rashevsky, N. (1968) *Looking at History Through Mathematics.* Cambridge, Mass., MIT Press.

Reinsch, P. (1900) *World Politics at the End of the Nineteenth Century*. New York, Macmillan.

Reynolds, C. (1973) *Theory and Explanation in International Politics*. London, Martin Robertson.

Reynolds, P.A. (1971) *An Introduction to International Relations*. London, Longman.

Reynolds, P.A. (1975) 'International Studies: Retrospect and Prospect'. *British Journal of International Studies*, 1 (1), pp.1–19.

Reynolds, P.A. (1979) 'Non-state Actors and International Outcomes'. *British Journal of International Studies*, 5 (2), pp.91–111.

Reynolds, P.A., McKinlay, R.D. (1979) 'The Concept of Interdependence: Its Uses and Misuses'. In K. Goldmann and G. Sjöstedt (eds) *Power, Capabilities, Interdependence*, Beverly Hills, Sage.

Richardson, L.F. (1960a) *Arms and Insecurity*. Pittsburgh and Chicago, Buxwood and Quadrangle.

Richardson, L.F. (1960b) *Statistics of Deadly Quarrels*. Pittsburgh and Chicago, Buxwood and Quadrangle.

Roberts, A. (1983) 'Britain and Non-Nuclear Defence'. In J. Baylis (ed.) *Alternative Approaches to British Defence Policy*, London, Macmillan.

Rockefeller, D. (1979) Interview with S. Gill. New York City, 20 June 1979.

Rogers, P., Dando, M., van den Gungen, P. (1981) *As Lambs to the Slaughter: The Facts about Nuclear War*. London, Arrow.

Roosa, R.V., Gutowski, A., Matsukawa, A. (1982) *East/West Trade at a Crossroads: Economic Relations with the Soviet Union and Eastern Europe*. New York, Trilateral Commission.

Rosecrance, R., Stein, A. (1973) 'Interdependence: Myth or Reality?' *World Politics*, 26 (1), pp.1–27.

Rosenau, J.N. (ed.) (1961) *International Politics and Foreign Policy*. New York, Free Press.

Rosenau, J.N. (ed.) (1969a) *International Politics and Foreign Policy* (2nd edn). New York, Free Press.

Rosenau, J.N. (ed.) (1969b) *Linkage Politics: Essays on the Convergence of National and International Systems*. New York, Free Press.

Rosenau, J.N. (ed.) (1974) *Comparing Foreign Policies*. New York, John Wiley.

Rosenau, J.N. (1975) 'Comparative Foreign Policy: One-Time Fad, Realized Fantasy and Normal Field'. In C. Kegley, G. Raymond, R. Rood and R. Skinner (eds) (1975) *International Events and the Comparative Analysis of Foreign Policy*, Columbia, South Carolina, University of South Carolina Press.

Rosenau, J.N. (1976a) 'Restlessness, Change and Foreign Policy Analysis'. In J.N. Rosenau, (ed.) *In Search of Global Patterns*, New York, Free Press.

Rosenau, J.N. (1976b) 'Puzzlement in Foreign Policy'. *Jerusalem Journal of International Relations*, 1 (1), pp.1–10.

Rosenau, J.N. (1976c) 'International Studies in a Transnational World'. *Millennium*, 5 (1), pp.1–20.

Rosenau, J.N. (1976d) 'Capabilities and Control in an Interdependent World'. *International Security*, 1 (1), pp.32–49.

Rosenau, J.N. (1979) 'Muddling, Meddling and Modelling: Alternative Approaches to the Study of World Politics in an Era of Rapid Change'. *Millennium*, 8 (2), pp.130–43.

Rosenau, J.N. (1980a) *The Scientific Study of Foreign Policy* (2nd edn). London, Frances Pinter.

Rosenau, J.N. (1980b) 'Pre-Theories and Theories of Foreign Policy'. In J.N. Rosenau, *The Scientific Study of Foreign Policy*, London, Frances Pinter.

Rosenau, J.N. (1980c) *The Study of Global Interdependence: Essays on the Transnationalization of World Affairs*. London, Frances Pinter.

Rosenau, J.N. (1981) *The Study of Political Adaptation*. London, Frances Pinter.

Rosenau, J.N., Burgess, P., Hermann, C. (1973) 'The Adaptation of Foreign Policy Research'. *International Studies Quarterly*, 17 (1), pp.119–44.

Rosenau, J.N., Holsti, O.R. (1983) 'US Leadership in a Shrinking World'. *World Politics*, 35 (3), pp.368–92.

Rostow, W.W. (1960) *The Stages of Economic Growth: A Non-Communist Manifesto*. Cambridge, Cambridge University Press.

Ruggie, J.G. (1982) 'International Regimes, Transactions and Change: Embedded Liberalism in the Postwar Economic Order'. *International Organization*, 36 (2), pp.379–415.

Rummel, R.J. (1976) 'The Roots of Faith'. In J.N. Rosenau (ed.) *In Search of Global Patterns*, New York, Free Press.

Rummel, R.J., (1981) *Understanding Conflict and War: Vol. 5 The Just Peace*. London, Sage.

Runciman, W.G. (1983) *A Treatise on Social Theory, Vol. 1 The Methodology of Social Theory*. Cambridge, Cambridge University Press.

Ruof, P., Goodwin, J. (1979a) 'The Constituencies of the Tricom'. *Ford Foundation*, file no. 790–0465, January/February 1979.

Ruof, P., Goodwin, J. (1979b) Interview with S. Gill. Ford Foundation, New York City, 15 August 1979.

Russett, B. (1969) 'The Young Science of International Politics'. *World Politics*, 22 (1), pp.87–94.

Sage International Yearbook of Foreign Policy Studies (1973; 1974; 1975; 1979; 1980; 1981; 1982; 1983). Beverly Hills, Sage.

Saturday Review, 3 September 1960.

Savigear, P. (1975) 'Philosophical Idealism and International Politics: Bosanquet, Treischke and War'. *British Journal of International Studies*, 1 (1), pp.48–59.

Scalapino, R. (ed.) (1977) *The Foreign Policy of Modern Japan*. Berkeley, University of California Press.

Schelling, T.C. (1960) *Strategy of Conflict*. Cambridge, Mass., Harvard University Press.

Schroeder, P. (1976) 'Alliances, 1815–1945: Weapons of Power and Tools of Management'. In K. Knorr (ed.) *Historical Dimensions of National Security Problems,* Lawrence, University Press of Kansas.

Schuman, F.L. (1933) *International Politics.* New York, McGraw-Hill.

Schwarzenberger, G. (1951) *Power Politics: A Study of International Society* (2nd edn). London, Stevens and Sons.

Scott, A. (1977) 'The Logic of International Interaction'. *International Studies Quarterly,* 21 (3), pp.429–60.

Shonfield, A. (1969) *Modern Capitalism: The Changing Balance of Public and Private Power.* Oxford, Oxford University Press.

Shonfield, A. (ed.) (1976) *International Economic Relations of the Western World, 1959–1971, Vol 1 'Politics and Trade'.* Oxford, Oxford University Press, for the Royal Institute of International Affairs.

Simon, H.A. (1957) *Models of Man: Social and Rational.* New York, John Wiley.

Simpson, J. (1983) *The Independent Nuclear State.* London, Macmillan.

Singer, J.D. (1961) 'The Level-of-Analysis Problem in International Relations'. *World Politics,* 14 (1), pp.72–92.

Singer, J.D. (1966) 'The Behavioural Science Approach to International Relations: Payoff and Prospects'. *SAIS Review,* 10 (4), pp.12–20.

Singer, J.D. (ed.) (1968) *Quantitative International Politics.* New York, Free Press.

Singer, J.D., Small, M. (1972) *The Wages of War 1816–1965. A Statistical Handbook.* New York, John Wiley.

Sivard, R.L. (1983) *World Social and Military Expenditures: 1983.* Washington DC, World Priorities.

Sklar, H. (ed.) (1980) *Trilateralism: The Trilateral Commission and Elite Planning for World Management.* Boston, South End Press.

Slessor, Sir John (1954) *Strategy for the West.* London, Cassell.

Smith, D. (1983) 'The Crisis of Atlanticism'. In J. Baylis (ed.) *Alternative Approaches to British Defense Policy,* London, Macmillan.

Smith, G.C., Vittorelli, P., Saeki, K. (1983) *Trilateral Security: Defense and Arms Control Policies in the 1980s.* New York, Trilateral Commission.

Smith, M.S. (1978) 'Rearmament and Deterrence in the 1930s'. *Journal of Strategic Studies,* 1 (4), pp.313–37.

Smith, S. (1980) 'Brother Can You Paradigm? A Reply to Professor Rosenau'. *Millennium,* 8 (3), pp.235–45.

Smith, S. (1981) *Foreign Policy Adaptation.* Aldershot, Gower.

Smith, S. (1982) 'Berridge on International Relations'. *Teaching Politics,* 11 (1), pp.23–9.

Smith, S. (1983) 'Foreign Policy Analysis: British and American Orientations and Methodologies'. *Political Studies,* 31 (4), pp.556–65.

Smith, S. (1985) 'Describing and Explaining Foreign Policy Behavior'. *Polity,* 17 (3), forthcoming.

Snyder, R.C., Bruck, H.W., Sapin, B. (1962) *Foreign Policy Decision-Making.* New York, Free Press.

Spegele, R.D. (1982) 'From the Incoherence of Systems Theory to a Philosophy of International Relations'. *Review of Politics,* 44 (4), pp.559–89.

Spencer, M.E. (1982) 'The Ontologies of Social Science'. *Philosophy of Social Science,* 12 (2), pp.121–41.

Spero, J. (1981) *The Politics of International Economic Relations* (2nd edn). London, Allen & Unwin.

Sprout, H., Sprout, M. (1945) *Foundations of National Power.* Princeton, N.J., Princeton University Press.

Sprout, H., Sprout, M. (1965) *The Ecological Perspective on Human Affairs.* Princeton, N.J., Princeton University Press.

Sprout, H., Sprout, M. (1971) *Towards a Politics of the Planet Earth.* New York, Von Nostrand Rheinhold.

Spykman, N. (1942) *America's Strategy in World Politics.* New York, Harcourt Brace.

Steed, H.W. (1936) *Vital Peace: A Study of Risks.* London, Constable.

Stein, H. (1978) 'International Coordination of Domestic Economic Policies'. *The AEI Economist,* Washington DC, American Enterprise Institute.

Steinbruner, J. (1974) *The Cybernetic Theory of Decision.* Princeton, N.J., Princeton University Press.

Steiner, Z. (1969) *The Foreign Office and Foreign Policy.* Cambridge, Cambridge University Press.

Steiner, Z. (ed.) (1982) *The Times Survey of Foreign Ministries of the World.* London, Times Books.

Strange, S. (1970) 'International Economics and International Relations: A Case of Mutual Neglect'. *International Affairs,* 46 (2), 304–15.

Strange, S. (1971) *Sterling and British Policy: A Political Study of an International Currency in Decline.* Oxford, Oxford University Press.

Strange, S. (1976) 'The Study of Transnational Relations'. *International Affairs,* 52 (3), pp.333–45.

Strange, S. (1982) 'Cave! Hic Dragones: A Critique of Regime Analysis'. *International Organization,* 36 (2), pp.479–96.

Suganami, H. (1978) 'The "peace through law" approach: a critical examination of its ideas'. In T. Taylor (ed.) *Approaches and Theory in International Relations,* London, Longman.

Suganami, H. (1983) 'The Structure of Institutionalism: An Anatomy of British Mainstream International Relations'. *International Relations,* 7 (5), pp.2361–81.

Taylor, A.J.P. (1954) *The Struggle for Mastery in Europe, 1848–1918.* London, Oxford University Press.

Taylor, P. (1983) *The Limits of European Integration.* London, Croom Helm.

Taylor, T. (ed.) (1978) *Approaches and Theory in International Relations.* London, Longman.

Teggart, F.J. (1977) *Theory and Processes of History* (1st edn, 1918). Berkeley, University of California Press.

Thompson, D'Arcy (1917) *Growth and Form*. Cambridge, Cambridge University Press.

Thompson, E.P., Smith, D. (eds) (1980) *Protest and Survive*. London, Penguin.

Thompson, K.W. (1955) 'Toynbee's Approach to History'. *Ethics*, 65 (4), pp.287–303.

Thompson, K.W. (1956) 'Toynbee and the Theory of International Politics'. *Political Science Quarterly*, 71 (3), pp.365–86.

Thorne, C. (1972) *The Limits of Foreign Policy: The West, the League and the Far Eastern Crisis of 1931–33*. London, Hamish Hamilton.

Thorne, C. (1978) *Allies of a Kind: The United States, Britain, and the War Against Japan, 1941–45*. London, Hamish Hamilton.

Tooze, R.I. (1978) 'Communications Theory'. In T. Taylor (ed.) *Approaches and Theory in International Relations*, London, Longman.

Tooze, R.I. (1981) 'Economics, International Political Economy and Change in the International System'. In B. Buzan and B. Jones (eds) *Change and the Study of International Relations*, London, Frances Pinter.

Toulmin, S.E. (1961) *Foresight and Understanding: An Inquiry into the Aims of Science*. London, Hutchinson.

Trilateral Commission (1973) 'Process of Organization'. Mimeo.

Trilateral Commission (1982) 'Intra-Trilateral Trade Tensions and Strengthening the Gatt System'. Tokyo, Dai Nippon Printing Co.

Trimberger, E.G. (1979) 'World Systems Analysis: The Problem of Unequal Development'. *Theory and Society*, 8 (1), pp.127–37.

Tucker, R. (1977) *The Inequality of Nations*. London, Martin Robertson.

Tucker, R. (1981) *The Purposes of American Power: An Essay on National Security*. New York, Praeger.

Tuttle, F.G. (1931) *Alternatives to War*. New York, Harper and Row.

Ullman, R.H. (1976) 'Trilateralism: "Partnership" for What?'. *Foreign Affairs*, 55 (1), pp.1–19.

Ushiba, N., Allison, G., De Montbrial, T. (1983) *Sharing International Responsibilities Among the Trilateral Countries*. New York, Trilateral Commission.

Vance, C. (1980) Speech at Harvard University, 5 June 1980. *New York Times*, 6 June 1980.

Vasquez, J.A. (1983) *The Power of Power Politics*. London, Frances Pinter.

Vernon, R. (1977) *Storm Over the Multinationals*. Cambridge, Mass., Harvard University Press.

Vernon, R. (1981) '*Sovereignty at Bay* ten years after'. *International Organization*, 35 (3), pp.517–29.

Vincent, R.J. (1974) *Nonintervention and International Order*. Princeton, N.J., Princeton University Press.

Von Neumann, Morgenstern, O. (1953) *The Theory of Games and Behavior* (3rd edn) (1st edn, 1944). Princeton, N.J., Princeton University Press.

Wallace, H. (1983) 'Negotiation, Conflict and Compromise: The Elusive Pursuit of Common Policies'. In H. Wallace, W. Wallace and C. Webb (eds) *Policy-Making in the European Community* (2nd edn), Chichester, John Wiley.

Wallace, H., Wallace, W., Webb, C. (eds) (1983) *Policy-Making in the European Community* (2nd edn), Chichester, John Wiley.

Wallace, W. (1975) *The Foreign Policy Process in Britain*. London, Royal Institute of International Affairs.

Wallace, W. (1978) 'Old States and New Circumstances: The International Predicament of Britain, France and Germany'. In W. Wallace and W.E. Paterson (eds) *Foreign Policy-Making in Western Europe: A Comparative Approach,* Farnborough, Saxon House.

Wallace, W. (ed.) (1980) *Britain in Europe*. London, Heinemann.

Wallace, W. (1983a) 'Less Than a Federation, More Than a Regime: The Community as a Political System'. In H. Wallace, W. Wallace and C. Webb (eds) *Policy-Making in the European Community* (2nd edn), Chichester, John Wiley.

Wallace, W. (1983b) 'Political Cooperation: Integration through Intergovernmentalism'. In H. Wallace, W. Wallace and C. Webb (eds) *Policy-Making in the European Community* (2nd edn), Chichester, John Wiley.

Wallace, W., Paterson, W. (eds) (1978) *Foreign Policy-Making in Western Europe*. Farnborough, Saxon House.

Wallerstein, I. (1974) *The Modern World System: Capitalist Agriculture and the Origins of the European World-Economy in the Sixteenth Century*. New York, Academic Press.

Wallerstein, I. (1979a) *The Capitalist World Economy*. Cambridge, Cambridge University Press.

Wallerstein, I. (1979b) 'Some Reflections on History, The Social Sciences and Politics'. In his *The Capitalist World-Economy,* Cambridge, Cambridge University Press.

Wallerstein, I. (1980) *The Modern World System II*. New York, Academic Press.

Waltz, K. (1959) *Man, the State and War*. New York, Columbia University Press.

Waltz, K. (1979) *Theory of International Politics*. Reading, Mass., Addison-Wesley.

Ward, B. (1979) *Progress for a Small Planet*. London, Penguin.

Ward, B., Dubos, R. (1972) *Only One Earth*. London, Penguin.

Watanabe, T., Lesbourne, J., McNamara, R.S. (1983) *Facilitating Development in a Changing Third World: Finance, Trade, Aid*. New York, Trilateral Commission.

Watt, D.C., (1965) *Personalities and Policies*. London, Longman.

Watt, D.C. (1975) *Too Serious a Business: European Armed Forces and the Approach to the Second World War*. London, Temple Smith.

Watt, D.C. (1977) 'A Return to Americanism? The Foreign Policy of President Carter'. *Political Quarterly,* 48 (4), pp.429–39.

Watt, D.C. (1983) 'What about the People? Abstraction and Reality in History and the Social Sciences'. Inaugural lecture, published by the London School of Economics.

Watt, D.C., Bourne, K. (eds) (1967) *Studies in International History: Essays Presented to W. Norton Medlicott.* London, Longman.

Webb, C. (1983) 'Theoretical Perspectives and Problems'. In H. Wallace, W. Wallace and C. Webb (eds) *Policy-Making in the European Community* (2nd edn), Chichester, John Wiley.

Webster, C.K. (1923) *The Study of International Politics.* Cardiff, University of Wales Press.

Weiler, L.D., Simons, A.P. (1967); *The United States and the United Nations.* New York, Manhattan Publishing Co.

Wells, H.G. (1918) *In the Fourth Year: Anticipations of a World Peace.* London, Chatto and Windus.

Weltman, J.F. (1973) *Systems Theory in International Relations: A Study in Metaphoric Hypertrophy.* Lexington, Heath.

Weltman, J.F. (1982) 'On the Interpretation of International Thought'. *Review of Politics,* 44 (1), pp 27-41.

Wieseltici, L. (1983) *Nuclear War, Nuclear Peace.* New York, Holt, Rinehart and Winston.

Wight, M. (1966) 'Why is there no International Theory?'. In H. Butterfield and M. Wight (eds) *Diplomatic Investigations,* London, Allen & Unwin.

Wight, M. (1977) *Systems of States.* Leicester, Leicester University Press.

Wight, M. (1978) *Power Politics.* Leicester, Leicester University Press.

Wilkenfeld, J., Hopple, G., Rossa, P., Andriole, S. (1980) *Foreign Policy Behavior.* Beverly Hills, Sage.

Williams, P. (1976) *Crisis Management.* Oxford, Martin Robertson.

Williams, S.W. (1981) 'Realism, Marxism and Human Geography'. *Antipode,* 13, pp.31–8.

Winch, P. (1958) *The Idea of a Social Science and its Relation to Philosophy.* London, Routledge and Kegan Paul.

Wohlstetter, A. (1959) 'The Delicate Balance of Terror'. *Foreign Affairs,* 37 (2), pp.211–34.

Wolfe, A. (1977) *The Limits of Legitimacy: Political Contradictions of Contemporary Capitalism.* New York, Free Press.

Wrong, D. (1979) *Power, Its Forms, Bases and Use.* Oxford, Basil Blackwell.

Wright, Q. (1942) *A Study of War* (2 vols), Chicago, Chicago University Press.

Wright, Q. (1955) *The Study of International Relations.* New York, Appleton Century Crofts Inc.

Wright, Q. (1969–70) *On Predicting International Relations: The Year 2000.* Denver, The Social Science Foundation and Graduate School of International Studies, Monograph Series no. 1.

Yalem, R.J. (1978) 'Transnational Politics Versus International Politics' *Yearbook of World Affairs.* London, Stevens.

Yergin, D. (1978) *The Shattered Peace: The Origins of the Cold War and the National Security State.* London, Deutsch.

Yost, D.S. (1979) 'New Perspectives on Historical States-Systems'. *World Politics,* 32 (1), pp.151–68.

Young, O. (1969) 'Professor Russett: Industrious Tailor to a Naked Emperor'. *World Politics,* 21 (3), pp.486–512.

Young, O. (1972) 'The Actors in World Politics'. In J.N. Rosenau, V. Davis and M.A. East (eds) *The Analysis of International Politics,* New York, Free Press.

Young, O. (1980) 'International Regimes: Problems of Concept Formation'. *World Politics,* 32 (3), pp.331–56.

Zilliacus, K. (1944) *The Mirror of the Past.* London, Gollancz.

Zimmern, A. (1936) *The League of Nations and the Rule of Law, 1918–1935.* London, Macmillan.

Zinnes, D. (1980) 'Prerequisites for the Study of System Transformation'. In O. Holsti, R. Siverson and A. George (eds) *Change in the International System,* Boulder, Colorado, Westview Press.

Zuckerman, S. (1962) 'Judgement and Control in Modern Warfare'. *Foreign Affairs,* 40 (2), pp.196–212.

Zuckerman, S. (1982) *Nuclear Illusion and Reality.* London, Collins.

Index